I0811086

Advance praise for

Reckoning: Kalamazoo College Uncovers Its Racial and Colonial Past

"Kalamazoo College has been a center of social justice teaching and leadership training for decades. Anne Dueweke's excellent new book reminds us of that practice, but she also reveals that few long-standing institutions, including K College, are untouched by the legacies of racism and colonialism. An important case study of the political and ethical issues facing college campuses in the 21st century."

—Barbara Ransby, John D. MacArthur Chair and Professor at University of Illinois at Chicago, and author of the award-winning biography, Ella Baker and the Black Freedom Movement

"*Reckoning* is the fascinating story of the nearly two centuries history of Kalamazoo College, viewed through the powerful lens of White privilege. It is the story of trying to reconcile lofty ideals with the stark realities of racism. And it is an unfinished story because we don't know whether Kalamazoo College will ultimately succeed in achieving its social justice goals. *Reckoning* shows us the importance of taking time to reflect on what has gone before so that we can contemplate what is yet to come. It should be required reading for all who profess a renewed commitment to dismantling structural racism."

—David J. Asai, Senior Director, Science Education Howard Hughes Medical Institute

"Dueweke traces the history of Kalamazoo College's origins in settler colonialism and its evolution to the cusp of America's current racial reckoning. Without fanfare or oversentimentality, this historical case study uncovers contradictions between progress and backlash, between courageous institutional leadership and resistance to change, between grassroots activism and institutional repression. Recounting Indigenous, Black, Asian students' experiences brings era-specific socio-political contexts to life as national politics played out within Kalamazoo. Revealing this troubled past—restores and clarifies what higher education, and particularly, the liberal arts has been—leading us to wonder what it might still become. . ."

—Toni King, Associate Professor of Black Studies and Women's & Gender Studies, Charles and Nancy Brickman Distinguished Leadership Chair, Denison University

"Carefully researched and passionately written, Dueweke's history illuminates both the longstanding progressive commitments of Kalamazoo College and its enduring entanglements with colonialism, enslavement, and institutional racism. This book is a model for the kind of reckoning required of all American educational institutions if we are to truly live up to our social justice commitments."

—*Laura Barraclough, Professor of American Studies, Yale University*

"Anne Dueweke reminds us that the time for reckoning is always at hand. As she traces the history of one liberal arts college, she outlines the limits of American humility and the power of visionary leadership. From the shadow of the Indian Removal Act, cast to clear the physical and social landscape, to recent efforts to listen attentively to diverse students and respond to their needs, this is a re-counting of facts that tells the full story. It does not romanticize racism, nor does it make excuses for ethnic exclusion. *Reckoning: Kalamazoo College Uncovers Its Racial and Colonial Past* is an act of reconciliation and redirection. By moving beyond theory to assess practices, this is a book centered on the education and evolution of humanity. It is the record of one institution finding its soul."

—*Margaret Ann Noodin, Professor of English and American Indian Studies and Associate Dean of Humanities, University of Wisconsin–Milwaukee*

RECKONING

RECKONING

Kalamazoo College Uncovers Its Racial and Colonial Past

BY ANNE DUEWEKE

Myers Education Press

GORHAM, MAINE

Myers Education Press

Copyright © 2022 | Myers Education Press, LLC

Published by Myers Education Press, LLC
P.O. Box 424, Gorham, ME 04038

All rights reserved. No part of this book may be reprinted or reproduced in any form or by any electronic, mechanical, or other means, now known or hereafter invented, including photocopying, recording, and information storage and retrieval, without permission in writing from the publisher.

Myers Education Press is an academic publisher specializing in books, e-books, and digital content in the field of education. All of our books are subjected to a rigorous peer review process and produced in compliance with the standards of the Council on Library and Information Resources.

13-digit ISBN 978-1-9755-0506-6 (paperback)
13-digit ISBN 978-1-9755-0507-3 (library networkable e-edition)
13-digit ISBN 978-1-9755-0508-0 (consumer e-edition)

Printed in the United States of America.

All first editions printed on acid-free paper that meets the American National Standards Institute Z39-48 standard.

Books published by Myers Education Press may be purchased at special quantity discount rates for groups, workshops, training organizations, and classroom usage. Please call our customer service department at 1-800-232-0223 for details.

Cover design by Morgan Birtwell Design

Cover photo taken by Chris McGuire

Visit us on the web at **www.myersedpress.com** to browse our complete list of titles.

"Kalamazoo"

Derived from a Potawatomi word possibly meaning

"The mirage of reflecting river,"
"Mist rising from the river,"
or
"Bubbling or boiling water"

This book is dedicated to the students of Kalamazoo College, past, present, and future.

Contents

Acknowledgments

Looking back, I realize that I had no idea what I was getting into when I began this project. I don't know what I imagined the finished product to be, but it wasn't a book. The amount of material I found surprised me and drew me in, and so the scope of work kept expanding. It also took a long time to find my way of telling this story. The first chapter in particular went through multiple drafts. And I struggled for a while to find my voice. If not for a host of people supporting, encouraging, and guiding me, this book would never have been written.

First and foremost, I am deeply grateful to Lisa Brock, former academic director of the Arcus Center for Social Justice Leadership, and Mia Henry, former executive director of Arcus. They were the first people I talked to about writing a racial and colonial history of Kalamazoo College, and they supported me immediately and completely. The Arcus Center provided significant financial support over six years in the form of a fellowship, which allowed me to hire student researchers, buy books, and travel to visit archives and interview alumni of color. Mia and Lisa served as sounding boards, offered guidance, and created venues for me to present what I was learning along the way. Lisa also read drafts of chapters and offered her feedback as a historian. Their faith in me helped me to have faith in myself.

Well before I started this project, Reid Gómez, Kalamazoo College's first professor of critical ethnic studies, challenged my thinking on race, which had left out the colonization of Indigenous people. She opened my mind through many conversations and reading recommendations. I will always be grateful for her patience, brilliance, and gentleness. Reid's teachings and my involvement in the Arcus Center both played a critical role in preparing me to take on a project like this one.

Additional financial support came from my friends and Kalamazoo College alumni Chris Gawart '83, Will Oberholtzer '83, and Amy (Carr) Oberholtzer '84. Their generous donation funded a student research assistant, Allia Howard '17. Allia helped with archival research, provided invaluable assistance in inviting alumni of color to participate in oral history interviews, and conducted several of the interviews.

Donna Odom '67, and Bruce Mills, professor of English, shared their expertise in oral history, and Donna also helped reach out to alumni of color. I am very grateful to the alumni who agreed to tell their stories and to Dr. Romeo Phillips, professor emeritus, who shared his story as well. Jaakan Page-Wood's technical assistance with recording the interviews was also key to the oral history portion of the project.

I was ably assisted with research in the Kalamazoo College archives by a few other students in addition to Allia Howard. Shelby Long '17, provided an annotated roadmap for Chapter Three, Samantha Weaver '17, located documents that were crucial to understanding the College's attitudes towards the minstrel shows in the 1950s, and Tamara Morrison '20, helped to uncover the John Dobbs collection, which shed light on the push for multiculturalism in the 1990s. The project was greatly enriched by the contributions of Allia, Shelby, Samantha, and Tamara.

Lisa Murphy '98, Kalamazoo College's archivist, also worked with my student researchers and provided me with a tremendous amount of help in locating sources and tracking down information. I greatly appreciate her deep knowledge of the archival holdings, facility with online search tools, and ability to provide historical context for interpreting archival materials.

I am indebted to many other friends and colleagues who believed in me and in this project and contributed in various ways. Natalia Carvalho-Pinto and Jax Gardner offered wisdom and support. Reid Gómez made insightful comments on Chapter One and, as a fellow writer, encouraged me through difficult stretches in the writing and publication process. Bruce Mills provided background and context for James Baldwin's visit and gave feedback on that portion of the manuscript. Josie Csete '83, allowed me to use her lovely cottage on the Straits of Mackinac as a writer's retreat over successive summers. Gail Griffin, Binney Girdler, and Paul Sotherland all read chapters and made helpful suggestions for improvement. I am particularly grateful to Gail, my friend and former English professor, who offered substantial feedback, often on multiple drafts. And Binney, perhaps more than anyone, listened as I processed all that I was learning and worked through how to tell this story.

I am also grateful to my friend and former colleague Terri Raich, a citizen of the Pokagon Band of Potawatomi, for inviting me on a historical bus tour led by the Pokagon Band's director of language and culture; to Ben Secunda, also a citizen of the Pokagon Band, for sharing his dissertation on the Pokagon Band during the years of Indian Removal; to Eduard Avis '89, for his consultation and feedback on Chapter Five and recollections of his interview with Chokwe Lumumba '69; to Elizabeth Harris, great-great-granddaughter of James and Lucinda Stone, for sharing her manuscript on the life of Lucinda Stone and pointing me to key resources on Rufus Perry; to my son Zack Dueweke for visiting the Burton Historical Collection in the Detroit Public Library on my behalf and sending scanned copies of Rufus Perry's letters published in the *Michigan Christian Herald*; and to Dan Boudreau at the American Antiquarian Society for locating and sending me two issues of Rufus Perry's *National Monitor*. Permission to use quotes from Leonard Slater's letters to the Baptist Board of Foreign Missions and from a Consolidated American Educational Association pamphlet published while Rufus Perry was serving as corresponding secretary was provided courtesy of the American Baptist Historical Society, Atlanta, GA.

Finally, I would like to thank the leadership of Kalamazoo College for their support of this project. Former Provost Mickey McDonald encouraged my involvement in equity and inclusion efforts and allowed me to work on the book during regular working hours in the summer when my workload was lighter. Former Vice President for Advancement Al DeSimone invited my research student Allia Howard to present a poster on her contributions to the project during the inauguration of President Jorge G. Gonzalez. Jax Gardner and Lisa Brock of the Arcus Center and Renee Boelcke in Human Resources found a way to continue my fellowship after I left Kalamazoo College in 2019. Last but not least, I am grateful to President Gonzalez and Provost Danette Ifert Johnson for having the courage to embrace a critical history of Kalamazoo College and providing financial assistance for the publication of this book.

Notes on Language

I have capitalized the words "Black," "Brown," and "White" when referring to groups of people who have been racialized as such in the United States. Likewise, I have capitalized "Indigenous" and "Native" when referring to Native Americans.

Indigenous people in Michigan include the Ojibwe, Odawa, and Bodéwadmik. Their Anglicized names are the Chippewa, Ottawa, and Potawatomi. These tribes are, and have historically been, closely allied with strong kinship ties. They are known collectively as the Council of the Three Fires, the Three Fires Confederacy, or the People of the Three Fires. The People of the Three Fires are part of the Anishinaabe, a group of culturally related peoples indigenous to the Great Lakes region in the United States and Canada. "Anishinaabe" means "original people."

There are twelve federally recognized tribes in Michigan. Some use Anglicized names, others use Native names, while others use both depending on the circumstances. Because most Michigan tribes use Anglicized names, I have used Anglicized names as well.

Some of the quoted material in the book contains racial slurs and other offensive language. The purpose of including these quotes is to demonstrate the racial climate and attitudes that prevailed at various times in Kalamazoo College's history. How to handle the N-word and similar terms on the printed page is the subject of much debate, and no agreed-upon conventions currently exist. Because of the N-word's potency and violence, I do not show it spelled out. When the word is part of a direct quote, I have replaced it with "N-word" in brackets ([N-word]). When referring to the word, but not quoting, I use "N-word" without brackets. Similarly, I do not spell out racial slurs that refer to people of Japanese descent and American Indians, and instead show only the first and last letters. For the sake of clarity, these words will appear here and only here to explain how they will be represented in the quoted material. "Jap" will be shown as [J-p], "squaw" as [s---w], and "redskin" as [r-----n].

Introduction

Higher education was already struggling with issues of race as changing demographics were bringing more and more students of color to historically White campuses. Then 2020 happened. White resentment stoked by Donald Trump, widespread racial disparities laid bare by the COVID-19 pandemic, and the particularly brutal police killing of George Floyd all converged to form a tipping point on which American society now teeters. While some are doubling down on White supremacy, many others—individuals, organizations, institutions, and corporations—are facing racial reckonings.

In higher education such reckonings have been largely confined to America's oldest institutions, many of which participated in the Atlantic slave trade as described in Craig Steven Wilder's 2013 book *Ebony and Ivy: Race, Slavery, and the Troubled History of America's Universities.* Several institutions, notably Georgetown and Brown, have undertaken serious study of how their legacies are entwined with slavery, and Southern universities, such as the University of Richmond and the University of Virginia, have been grappling with what to do with Confederate statues on their campuses and buildings named in honor of slaveholders.

In those cases, the racist history is obvious. But if we have learned anything from the pandemic, it is that structural racism permeates every corner of American society, and Kalamazoo College, my alma mater and place of employment for over twenty years, is no exception.

Kalamazoo College is a four-year liberal arts institution with about 1,500 students located in the city of Kalamazoo, Michigan, a college town that is also home to Western Michigan University and Kalamazoo Valley Community College. I began this book project in 2015 as an attempt to understand why Kalamazoo College, an institution considered open and progressive, and an institution that I loved, could be such a hostile and bewildering place for students of color. I had been serving as director of faculty grants and institutional research and had become involved in diversity and inclusion initiatives after leading a focus group project about students' experiences with the racial climate in 2013.

Though issues of race usually remained just beneath the friendly Midwestern veneer of Kalamazoo's predominantly White campus, they would surface now and then, as they did in the fall of 2012. By then the College had achieved some success in attracting more students of color and was closing in on long-held diversity goals. But despite greater diversity, many students of color did not feel welcome on campus. That September, at the end of a provocative performance by the Chicano artist and activist Guillermo Gómez-Peña, students belonging to the Movimiento Estudiantil Chicano de Aztlán (MEChA) took to the stage and issued a set of demands to the College's senior administrators, many of whom were in the audience.

The students wanted a Chicano studies major, more Latinx professors, and more support from the administration. As Aldo Macias, founder of Kalamazoo College's MEChA chapter, later explained, Chicano studies is "not just about Chicanos; this history is also American. If students would engage in this kind of education it would bring so much understanding about the way the world functions." The action had come after months of asking for greater support including the creation of a student intercultural center, an idea the College's leadership had rejected. According to Macias, the administration was "really resistant about it" and worried that it would "segregate the school."[1]

That action by MEChA kicked off three years of student activism known as the Intercultural Movement, which grew to include students of all races and backgrounds. By 2015, tensions were running high among students and between the student activists and the administration. During that time, I was serving on yet another committee to examine the College's racial climate and was growing disillusioned with committee work as a means of addressing systemic racial issues. In fact, more and more, it felt like a way to forestall rather than enact change.

That January I took part in an anti-racism workshop sponsored by Kalamazoo College's Arcus Center for Social Justice Leadership, known on campus simply as "Arcus" or "the Arcus Center." The facilitator began the workshop by telling the history of the United States through the lens of colonization and race. As she spoke, walking us through the origins and permutations of race and racism in America, she noted major events on a timeline laid out on portable whiteboards that spanned the room. After recounting the devastating history, she invited participants to add sticky notes with events we recalled from our own lives and other notable incidents from the past that we thought should be included.

As I sat in the workshop thinking about how racism manifested at my institution, one event on the timeline especially stood out to me—the passage of the Indian Removal Act in 1830, right around the time that Kalamazoo College was coming into being. It made me wonder what was happening in this part of Michigan then, how the College's founders had interacted, or not, with the region's Indigenous people, and what they had thought about the idea of removing all the tribes whose homelands lay east of the Mississippi River to a new Indian territory in the West to make way for White settlers, people such as themselves. I also wondered how other events in the College's past tracked with the history of race in the United States. I had read several College histories and knew that the early leaders had been abolitionists, but beyond that, I had little idea of how racial attitudes and events had shaped the institution.

So, when I approached the timeline and placed a sticky note bearing the words "Kalamazoo College founded 1833" right next to "Indian Removal Act 1830," a seed was planted in my mind. What if instead of committee work, I devoted my energies to researching and writing a history of Kalamazoo College with attention to issues of colonization and race? Perhaps knowing the College's colonial and racial history would shed light on the current campus climate and help us chart a more productive way forward.

Not long afterward, I applied for and was granted a staff fellowship from the Arcus Center to support the project. I naively imagined that I could complete the work in three years, but three years quickly grew to six as I delved into archives at Kalamazoo College and elsewhere, interviewed alumni of color, and read multiple histories of the region and the country to place events at the College in a larger context. Fortunately, Arcus continued to support the work as I repeatedly requested extensions.

Given the focus of the project, what follows is necessarily a critical history of Kalamazoo College. As David Silverman, author of an account of Thanksgiving that centers the Wampanoag, wrote, "serious, critical history tends to be hard on the living." "Because critical history challenges assumptions and authority," he went on, "it often leaves us feeling uncomfortable. Yet it also has the capacity to help us become more humble and humane."[2] I would add that critical history can also explain and contextualize complex and highly charged issues, which of course did not spring from nowhere. I hope it will be clear to readers that my intent is not to disparage but rather to provide a clear-eyed account of racial attitudes and actions at Kalamazoo College over time as well as to highlight the experiences of some of the students of color who have attended the institution since as far back as before the Civil War.

Though I would like to believe that I would have felt and behaved differently than the majority of White people in the past with regard to race and colonization, the reality is that I would have been socialized in the same environment they were and more than likely would have shared their views. In our own time, I must constantly monitor my unconscious tendencies when it comes to race because I, like all of us in this country, continue to be shaped by what the writer Isabel Wilkerson has compellingly described as a racial caste system.[3] As a White person in America, I have internalized ideas of White superiority and normalcy that influence my thinking and behavior in countless ways no matter how much my conscious mind abhors the idea of racial hierarchies. Therefore, I do not place myself above the White people who appear in this history, which in itself is humbling.

I embarked upon this work because I believe in Kalamazoo College. It is a remarkable institution with an accomplished and dedicated faculty, students who are eager to learn, and a combination of academic and experiential programs that offers a transformative education. It also has the raw material necessary to become a truly intercultural and anti-racist institution, including a critical mass of faculty and staff across disciplines and departments who are working in that direction. Yet, for a multitude of reasons, students, faculty, and staff continue to have disparate experiences based on race.

Racist legacies are easy to see in institutions with endowments enriched by investments in the slave trade and buildings named for slaveholders. Owing to its geographical location and time of its founding, the history of race at Kalamazoo College manifests differently, and yet there is a robust story to tell. Though the details are unique to Kalamazoo, other Midwestern institutions that look at their pasts in this way will find similar historical trajectories, for in the end our institutional histories reflect the history of the United States.

As students of color attend college in greater numbers than ever before, they are making it known that our institutions need to change. Academic leaders have been mostly reactive in the face of student protests, which have raised objections to a range of issues, from Eurocentric curricula to a lack of diversity among the faculty, to having to contend with racism from White peers. Every time a racist incident occurs, mortified presidents and deans issue statements denouncing the act. Their words bear a striking similarity: "This is not who we are. These acts violate our values." But do they? Racist acts may fly in the face of an institution's stated mission and values, but what about the mission as it is lived out in day-to-day operations and the values implicit in interpersonal interactions and the many choices, large and small, made in designing curricula, policies, and programs?

James Baldwin said that White people "are trapped in a history which they do not understand; and until they understand it, they cannot be released from it."[4] This lack of historical understanding also hinders institutions of higher education from proactively addressing issues of race that continually rise up on campuses. The vast majority of America's colleges and universities were founded by White people for the implicit purpose of educating White people, and they have honed this craft over decades, sometimes centuries. Representational diversity alone will not change an institution's ethos, which is why so many students of color feel marginalized even at progressive colleges and universities where diversity and inclusion are prevalent in mission and values statements. To make our institutions work well for all of our students, we need to begin to understand how American racial and colonial ideas have permeated and shaped many aspects of higher education. To understand how these ideas have shaped Kalamazoo College, I invite you now to take a journey into its racial and colonial past.

Endnotes

1 Jennifer Wendel, "MECHA STUDENTS MAKE DEMANDS OF SCHOOL," *Index*, September 26, 2012, 1.

2 David Silverman, *This Land Is Their Land: The Wampanoag Indians, Plymouth Colony, and the Troubled History of Thanksgiving* (New York: Bloomsbury, 2019), 1.

3 Isabel Wilkerson, *Caste: The Origins of Our Discontents* (New York: Random House, 2020).

4 James Baldwin, "Letter to My Nephew on the One Hundredth Anniversary of the Emancipation," in *The Fire Next Time* (New York: The Dial Press, 1963), 22.

Chapter One

Ascendancy

In November of 1832, a young Baptist minister rode north on horseback through the still forests of late Michigan autumn. He was Thomas Ward Merrill, and he had been summoned by fellow Baptist Leonard Slater, a missionary to a group of Ottawa living at the Thomas Mission near the rapids of the Grand River. Isaac McCoy, another Baptist missionary, had established the mission several years earlier at the request of Noonday and Blackskin, Grand River Ottawa chiefs who were trying to help their people adapt to life amidst a growing White population. The chiefs sought resources "to build houses, make fence, plow, and the like" and for their children "to be instructed like the whites." "Then, when we shall have dealings with the whites," Noonday explained to McCoy, "our children can stand by and transact our business for us." The chiefs were wary, however, about handing over too much control. They were particularly emphatic about keeping their children nearby. As Noonday relayed, perhaps reflecting past experience, "many of our children are afraid that if they give up their children to you to be educated, they will be taken entirely away from them." Echoing Noonday's concern, Blackskin added, "If you will keep them here, and educate them in our own country, they will be willing to send them. I have a daughter, and some other near relations in Montreal. Their absence has been a grief to me, and I now wish I could get them hither to live with you."[1]

While Noonday and Blackskin were intent on helping their people survive colonization, the Baptists were preoccupied with saving their immortal souls and believed that "civilization" was a necessary precondition to religious conversion. Their goal of civilizing Native people dovetailed with the federal government's desire for a settled frontier. "Civilized Indians" required less land and were less threatening to White people, thus facilitating westward expansion. It is no surprise then that the Thomas Mission was sponsored by both the Baptist Board of Foreign Missions and the U.S. government.[2]

The motives of the Ottawa, Baptist missionaries, and federal government—at times converging, at others competing—drove life at the Thomas Mission, but it was the Baptists' evangelical aims that had occasioned Merrill's visit that November. Leonard Slater, who had taken charge of the Thomas Mission in 1827, earnestly desired to bring salvation to the Ottawa, but he had met with little success. Recently, however, there had been a revival during which several Ottawa converted, including Noonday. Because Slater had not yet been ordained, he asked Merrill to visit the mission to baptize Noonday and the other converts.[3]

Like Leonard Slater, Thomas Merrill had a missionary appointment. While the Baptist Board of Foreign Missions had charged Slater with Christianizing the Grand River Ottawa, the newly founded American Baptist Home Mission Society had given its first commission to Thomas Merrill to establish an educational institution in the Michigan Territory. These parallel projects served a common purpose: to promote the expansion of the United States by bringing "civilization" to the Western frontier. Years later, feeling demoralized and isolated in his work with the Ottawa, Slater would shift his energies to the Baptist institution that would become Kalamazoo College and join Merrill on the board of trustees.

In April of 1833, five months after baptizing Noonday, Merrill and his cofounder Caleb Eldred secured a charter for their institution from the Michigan Territorial Legislature. The next step was to identify a location. Among those making suggestions was Leonard Slater, who "wrote on July 10th to urge that the new school be established at Grand Rapids and that it take over the existing mission and absorb and continue the work with the Indians."[4] The idea was not novel. As a young man, Eldred had attended the Hamilton-Oneida Academy in New York (later Hamilton College)[5] whose mission was to educate Oneida children alongside those of the White settlers,[6] and when nearby Albion College was founded in 1835, it opened with an Indian Preparatory Department. But although

Indigenous leaders like Noonday and Blackskin sought educational opportunities for their children, including Native people in the new institution seems not to have been what the founders had in mind, and in 1835 they selected Kalamazoo as the location for the future Kalamazoo College after the townspeople pledged $2,500 to support it.[7]

"Hardly Enough Left to Cover the Bones"

The time of Kalamazoo College's founding, while full of excitement and adventure for White settlers, was one of unimaginable loss for the Anishinaabe[8] of Michigan and a source of economic, social, and psychological stress. That Noonday and Blackskin sought out a missionary speaks to the critical nature of their situation. Native people did not generally associate with missions unless they wanted to convert or were in need of resources or protection,[9] and conversion was not what had drawn the chiefs. Blackskin never converted and later had a falling out with Slater,[10] and Noonday converted only after being associated with the mission for several years. It is more likely that they were running out of options as they tried to adapt to radically changing circumstances.

As a young man in the late 1700s, Noonday had joined an alliance of warriors from throughout the Great Lakes region who fought against the United States in a series of conflicts known as the Northwest Indian War. Their aim was to stem the flow of White settlers into the Ohio Valley—land that had not been ceded—and to fend off further encroachment west. During the War of 1812, Noonday and Sagamaw, a Potawatomi chief living just south of present-day Kalamazoo, fought alongside the British under the leadership of the famed Shawnee warrior Tecumseh. When Tecumseh was killed in the 1813 Battle of the Thames, Noonday "seized him at once, and, with the assistance of [Sagamaw[11]], bore him from the field." As Noonday later recalled, "when he fell the Indians stopped fighting and the battle ended. We laid him down on a blanket in a wigwam, and we all wept, we loved him so much."[12] With the loss of their leader, the defeat of their British allies, and reeling from decades of war, Native people of the Great Lakes region no longer had the resources to resist American colonization.

The U.S. government stepped up its efforts to acquire land in Michigan soon after the War of 1812 ended. Beginning in the eastern portion of the territory and moving west, the United States started claiming large chunks of Michigan in treaty after treaty. The 1821 Treaty of Chicago resulted in the cession of land in Western Michigan south of the Grand River with small tracts reserved at the sites of prominent Potawatomi villages. These included a three-mile square area comprising a settlement headed by Match-e-be-nash-she-wish at the bend in the Ke-kalamazoo River in what now comprises most of the city of Kalamazoo,[13] and another three-mile square tract at Prairie Ronde near present-day Schoolcraft, the site of Sagamaw's village.

The 1821 Treaty was highly unpopular with the Potawatomi and Ottawa. The Potawatomi chief Metea spoke for many when he said, "our land has been wasting away ever since the white people became our neighbors, and we have now hardly enough left to cover the bones of our tribe."[14] Ke-way-goosh-cum, the chief who signed on behalf of the Grand River Ottawa, lost standing among his people as a result and was succeeded by Noonday. Sagamaw avoided the treaty negotiations, but his friend Match-e-be-nash-she-wish signed the treaty. According to William Church, historian for the Match-e-be-nash-she-wish Band of Pottawatomi Indians, Match-e-be-nash-she-wish may have made sure that the area around Prairie Ronde was reserved for Sagamaw. Nevertheless, Match-e-be-nash-she-wish lost stature among his people as well, and thereafter Sagamaw "became commonly known as the Chief of Kalamazoo County Pottawatomi likely because of exercising his right to withhold his signature from the treaty."[15]

Just six years later, with the 1827 Treaty of St. Joseph, the federal government claimed four of these five reserves in an attempt to consolidate the Potawatomi "at a point removed from the road leading from Detroit to Chicago, and as far as practicable from the settlements of the Whites."[16] Among the reserves ceded were those at Ke-kalamazoo and Prairie Ronde, and the remaining Nottawaseppi reserve was enlarged with the idea of accommodating the displaced Potawatomi.[17] American negotiators saw this consolidation as a precursor to removing the tribes to territories west of the Mississippi River, a new and dire threat that would be realized during the founding years of Kalamazoo College.[18]

Despite ceding the Match-e-be-nash-she-wish reserve, however, the Potawatomi living in and around Ke-kalamazoo remained in their villages. Helen Tanner's 1830 atlas shows no fewer than nine Potawatomi villages in the area, the oldest and largest being that of Match-e-be-nash-she-wish.[19]

Records also show "that 'Ke kan a ma zoo village' with 94 heads of families and 208 individuals was paid its annuity at Chicago, September 30, 1833."[20] Though the Anishinaabe of Southwest Michigan had become legally untethered from their land, that abstract notion codified in deeply resented treaties meant little when it came to day-to-day life. The threat of White encroachment loomed more ominously than ever, but as the history of the Ohio Valley had shown, White settlers would come whether the United States held treaty rights to the land or not. So, life continued as before. There was no reason to leave. Indeed, relocating was unfathomable.

"To Take Ascendancy by Right of Priority"

It is no accident that this was the historical moment in which the College's founders, Thomas Merrill and Caleb Eldred, arrived in the Michigan Territory. The region had been readied for White settlement through military conquest and subsequent land cessions. By the late 1820s several other developments were bringing many more White people into Michigan. Completed in 1825, the Erie Canal greatly facilitated travel from the East and brought a steady stream of White settlers from the eastern states. As a New York state legislator, Caleb Eldred played a pivotal role in bringing about the canal's construction, and among his most prized possessions was a letter from the governor expressing appreciation for his efforts.[21]

Another factor was the Second Great Awakening, a period of intense religious revival that swept the country in the early to mid-nineteenth century. Missionaries moved ever further west to Christianize Indigenous people and unchurched frontiersmen, helping to smooth the way for settlement. By this time, Leonard Slater and several other missionaries were engaged in "civilizing" and evangelizing the Anishinaabe of Michigan, which had the effect of containing their seasonally migratory lifestyle and making them appear less "savage" to White people.

Talk of "Indian removal" was also in the air. The idea of removing Native people to lands west of the Mississippi, first proposed by Thomas Jefferson in 1803, was gaining momentum with the election of President Andrew Jackson. At Jackson's urging, Congress passed the controversial Indian Removal Act in 1830. Its radical intent was to make way for White settlement by removing all Native people east of the Mississippi River and resettling them in a new territory in the West. The policy was often justified on moral and religious grounds, with many proponents arguing that because Native people "perished" when coming into contact with White people, removal was a way of saving them from extinction.

This was the context in which Thomas Merrill came of age. In the late 1820s, he was a young, idealistic New Englander just completing his studies at the Newton Theological Seminary. These were heady times for young Americans, with the United States emerging from its tenuous beginnings and seeming to offer limitless opportunity and adventure. While many sought material wealth, pious young men like Merrill were caught up in the missionary zeal to Christianize the American frontier. His father had founded Waterville College (later Colby College) in Maine, and Merrill became intent on establishing a Baptist institute of his own in what he saw as the wilds of Michigan to provide Christian education to the sons and daughters of White settlers.

Eager to ensure that Baptist religious and cultural values were brought to bear upon growing White settlements in Southwest Michigan, Merrill wrote in 1832 to the American Baptist Home Mission Society seeking support:

> The western or St. Joseph section of the Territory in which I propose to labor, is emphatically missionary ground. The first emigrants in this section located on government land about four years since, and coming from different States, attached to dissimilar views, tenets and customs, and most of them devoted supremely to gain, compose a disorganized and irreligious population . . . I wish to be able to secure one or two eighty-acre lots of land for a public institution, to be located in the Territory, combining manual and mental exercise. The importance of early laying the foundation of an institution to rise with the increase of population and to take the ascendency by right of priority must be obvious.[22]

If Merrill reflected the missionary zeal of the age, his cofounder, Caleb Eldred, embodied the entrepreneurial spirit of the frontiersman. Like Merrill, Eldred had a strong Baptist faith, but he did not shrink from material gain and engaged in a wide range of business ventures over the course of his life. More than twenty years Merrill's senior, Eldred was well into middle age by the early 1830s and had already established a comfortable life for himself and his large family in Otsego County, New York. He had been a successful farmer, but in the 1820s health issues forced him to abandon farming for less physically demanding pursuits. He became a dealer in livestock and was the first person to drive a herd of cattle from central New York to market in Philadelphia.[23] Together with his brother Mumford, he opened a meat market and grocery store. As a result of these and other ventures, Eldred became well-to-do.

Eldred was forty-nine years old in 1830 when he and his son Daniel made their first journey to scout out the Michigan Territory. Having been an early settler in New York, perhaps he could not resist the opportunity for another adventure as the American frontier moved west. But it could also have been that he was looking for a fresh start. He had lost his wealth "indorsing notes for others" and had resorted to working on shares of the farm he had been forced to sell.[24] His health improved after coming to Michigan and he again took up farming, eventually settling on a prairie in what is now Climax.[25] Once established with his family in Kalamazoo County, he quickly became a community leader, serving as the first postmaster of both Comstock and Climax and elected to the Michigan Territorial Legislature in 1835 and 1836.[26]

When Eldred and Merrill met in 1831 they found they shared a common interest in exerting a Baptist influence on the Michigan frontier and joined forces to establish a Baptist school.[27] In June of 1833, a few months after the Territorial Legislature granted the charter for the Michigan and Huron Institute (the future Kalamazoo College), Eldred penned a letter to the American Baptist Home Mission Society describing "the most destitute condition of the whole of Western Michigan . . . with settlements forming in every county, with emigrants from the different States of the Republic and from Europe, bringing with them their different views of religion; a countless train constantly following, with but here and there an individual who careth for his Master's work." He continued, seeking reinforcements, "I pray you, as you regard the Baptist cause in this growing region, send us able ministers, who will combat the enemy, expose error, and command by their faithfulness and zeal an influence in this cause, give character to our denomination and successfully (under the blessing of heaven) enlarge the borders of Zion."[28]

Both Merrill and Eldred were concerned about settlers arriving from various states and European countries and holding "different views of religion." These concerns were consistent with romantic nationalism, an intellectual tradition that took hold in the early nineteenth century in which people believed "that nations should be composed of people who had fundamental qualities, inherent qualities, in common: they thought the same way; they believed the same things; they spoke the same language; they looked the same."[29] While this way of thinking hardened beliefs about racial differences, progressive Baptists such as Merrill and Eldred, who were also staunch abolitionists, believed that Christianity, not race, was the path to national belonging. As the United States expanded west and grew in population with steady immigration from Europe, Kalamazoo College's founders were anxious to ensure that their country remained a Christian nation. They were sure of the righteousness of their cause and saw Christianity, specifically the Baptist version, as the glue that would bind the highly diverse population together.

"Not Counting Indians"

That the Michigan Territory had a resident Indigenous population was an inconvenience White settlers sought to minimize. The tendency to discount the presence of Native people is apparent in this description of the settlement that would become Kalamazoo: "In the spring of 1833 there were about 15 families in the place, and probably about 100 people,—men, women, and children (not counting Indians, who were quite numerous in the vicinity)."[30]

The settlers told themselves they were entering a pristine wilderness unaltered by human beings. The features of the landscape they most prized—the oak openings and parklike forests—they failed to recognize as the result of Indigenous labor. Far from being natural parts of an untouched wilderness, however, many of these openings, prairies, and parklike forests had been intentionally created and maintained by the Potawatomi and Ottawa using controlled burns. The openings and prairies provided fertile areas in which to grow crops, aided in wildlife management for easier hunting, and increased the variety and yield of seeds and berries, including raspberries, strawberries, and huckleberries.[31] The Anishinaabe had also blazed trails throughout Michigan, no fewer than sixteen of which intersected in Kalamazoo,[32] and they knew how to navigate the complex web of lakes and rivers. Whether the White settlers acknowledged it or not, they benefited greatly from all of this infrastructure and knowledge.

Settlers also saw Native people's seasonally migratory lifestyle as ungrounded, referring to them as "wandering," and concluded that they were "not using" the land. On the contrary, the Anishinaabeg scholar Leanne Simpson notes that the relationship of the Anishinaabe to the land was (and is) intimately place-based, characterized by "deep, reciprocal, consensual *attachment*."[33] Their way of living "generate[d] life—not just human life but the life of all living things."[34]

Because of this deep attachment to the land, one that was generative rather than extractive, Southwest Michigan was by all accounts an arrestingly beautiful place. The Kalamazoo River flowed free and clear, undammed and unpolluted, and teemed with fish and wildlife. Beech-maple and oak forests covered large portions of the region, interspersed here and there with oak openings, prairies, and wetlands where the Potawatomi harvested wild rice. The region supported ample game, edible and medicinal plants grew in abundance, and the openings provided rich soil in which Potawatomi women grew squash, corn, and beans, among other crops. It is difficult to describe the Michigan landscape of the 1830s without romanticizing it, but as Simpson remarks, "it sounds idyllic, because compared to now it was idyllic."[35]

There were many birch trees in Michigan, and the Anishinaabe put the bark to a multitude of uses. As the Potawatomi chief Simon Pokagon later wrote:

> Out of the bark of this wonderful tree were made hats, caps and dishes for domestic use, while our maidens tied with it the knot that sealed their marriage vow; wigwams were made of it, as well as large canoes that outrode the violent storms on lake and sea; it was also used for light and fuel at our war councils and spirit dances. Originally the shores of our northern lakes and streams were fringed with it and evergreen, and the white charmingly contrasted with the green mirrored from the water was indeed beautiful.[36]

According to an early settler in Kalamazoo County:

> The woods and hillsides and openings . . . were fairly red with the largest and most delicious of strawberries, while the wild plum grew

> along the streams, the huckleberry and cranberry on the marshes, and the aromatic sassafras was found throughout the woods. The annual fires burnt up the underwood . . . and debris in the oak openings, leaving them clear of obstructions. You could see through the trees . . . for miles around you; and you could walk, ride on horseback, or drive a wagon wherever you pleased in these woods, as freely as you could in a neat and beautiful park.[37]

Though they were loath to admit it, White settlers in the Michigan Territory were displacing people who had long lived there and quickly taking over the attractive and tillable openings and prairies. They "utilized oak openings for growing crops, pasturing livestock, and harvesting timber for fuel and building supplies."[38] Many of Michigan's towns, colleges, parks, and cemeteries were established on oak openings and prairies created by the Potawatomi and other Native people.[39] Indeed, one of the early buildings comprising the institution that would become Kalamazoo College was built on an oak opening in what is now Bronson Park.[40]

"Swap and Dicker"

As Thomas Merrill, Caleb Eldred, and other White settlers began making themselves at home, the Potawatomi and Ottawa had little choice but to accommodate these newcomers. Mindful of the threat of removal, they sought to establish friendly relations with the settlers, engage them as trading partners, and demonstrate that their coexistence could be mutually beneficial. They helped new arrivals learn their way around, brought gifts of food, and helped with barn raisings, including a forty-by-eighty-foot structure belonging to Caleb Eldred.[41] As Eldred's daughter, Mrs. L. W. Lovell, later recalled, "we could not have done without the Indians. They were our marketmen and women. They brought us venison, huckleberries, maple sugar and many other things that we in a new settlement needed."[42] Another settler described familial relationships with the Potawatomi, noting that "the Indians were friends and very kind neighbors to the early settlers. They treated us so much like kith and kin, that we called them our 'country cousins.' And although extremely backwoodish in habit and mode of living, yet we could not wish for kinder and more accommodating neighbors."[43] This neighborly approach was consistent with Potawatomi ideas of reciprocity. According to Ben Secunda of the Pokagon Band, "the Potawatomi, like other Great Lakes Native peoples, believed that power and prestige were garnered through reciprocity, the sharing of one's resources."[44]

Merrill and Eldred were part of a burgeoning White population in Kalamazoo County that led to a land boom in 1835 and 1836. During that time, the U.S. Land Office in Kalamazoo was the busiest in the nation.[45] Where in 1833 there had been about 100 White people, by 1840 there were 1,500. "When it became settled there in Kalamazoo, the Indian didn't want to be bothered with the white men, with the hunting and all that, he had his way," Selkirk Sprague, leader of the Match-e-be-nash-she-wish Band of Pottawatomi, explained during a meeting of the Allegan County Historical Society in 1957. "They moved to Plainwell. They didn't stay there very long, maybe 2 or 3 years, and the white men, they come and settled in Plainwell. They moved a little bit further north to Martin."[46] It was not long before the Potawatomi were driven out of Martin as well, including a small band who had been living on land purchased by Caleb Eldred's brother Mumford. These Potawatomi left shortly after Mumford Eldred threatened to fell a large tree on their wigwams[47] and resettled near Sagamaw's band, which had also moved north to Gun Lake.[48]

By the late 1830s a severe economic downturn known as the Panic of 1837 was postponing implementation of U.S. Indian Removal policy and buying the Anishinaabe time to adapt to life among White settlers. For new settlers who had been counting on rapid economic growth, the recession meant no developing infrastructure to get their goods to market and a serious lack of cash. The situation was so dire that settlers were caught in a sustained period of reliance on a barter system, a system to which Native people were integral.[49] About the only people with cash were the Potawatomi and Ottawa, who were paid their annuities in specie.[50] The circulation of their coin through trade was a lifeline to the settlers in an otherwise cashless economy. Venison, berries, maple syrup, and other Anishinaabe trade goods were also in demand.

Writing about her early days in Kalamazoo, Lucinda Hinsdale Stone, who would become head of Kalamazoo College's Female Department, recalled, "we had much to tell our eastern friends of this strange new country in stories of which figured many Indians and accounts as I recollect of their strange ways of trade or barter with the whites, they measuring out a cup full of berries, which were one of their chief staples of trade, and receiving in return (measured it must be in the same cup) a cup full of flour. They would not trust a count of five or even two measures, only upon an immediate and direct 'swap'."[51] Another settler also expressed bewilderment about the Potawatomi's approach to trade. "I never knew an Indian to sell to white people any part of the carcass of a deer except the ham," he recalled. "The price for a ham of venison was always two shillings, no more, no less, no matter how small or large it was. Whenever we sold a [s---w] any goods that had to be made up into any of their garments a needle and a thread for each garment must be given; only goods for one garment could be bought or swapped at a time."[52]

While the settlers acted on the assumption of a market economy, the Potawatomi followed their practice of taking only what they needed and attempting to foster kinship ties with the settlers through a mutually beneficial exchange of goods.[53] While the settlers relied on trade with the Potawatomi and benefitted from their kindness, developing kinship ties with Native people was not foremost in their minds, and the fact that they saw themselves as superior prevented them from practicing true reciprocity.

The sense of superiority felt by the settlers pervades many of the reminiscences in the Michigan Pioneer and Historical Collections. Such is the case when Caleb Eldred's daughter, Mrs. L. W. Lovell, describes a White man named Johnson who had been raised by the Potawatomi. "He was now more Indian than white man," she recalled, and "at times in his talk with the settlers seemed to feel the full sense of his lost manhood, that he was now, as compared with the whites, an inferior person—an underling."[54] Mrs. Lovell goes on to say, "Johnson's daughter, being half white, seemed to have more energy and thrift than the other [s---ws]."[55]

Even Leonard Slater's eldest daughter, who had been cared for by an Ottawa nurse[56] and grown up alongside the Ottawa children at the mission, expressed disdain toward the Native people she had known, remarking that "their moral code partook of the crude simplicity of their minds" and that their medicine dances "consisted in making as much and as horrible a noise as they could with dry gourd shells with a few pebbles in them."[57] Such views were pervasive and would have hindered Native people's attempts to establish familial and reciprocal relationships with the settlers on which they could depend for the long term.

After several years, economic recovery finally brought an end to the "unhallowed 'dicker' traffic," as the editor of the *Kalamazoo Gazette* termed it in 1851. He continued, "there is not one evil which can afflict a community in a business point of view more calamitously than the 'swap and dicker' operations which have reigned among us for the last twelve years."[58] As trade with the Potawatomi waned, items they intended as goods in an ongoing, reciprocal relationship became for the settlers relics of what they believed to be a vanishing people. Recalling the *mococks*, birch-bark baskets the Potawatomi used to package maple sugar, Lucinda Hinsdale Stone wrote, "these later were special mementoes of the 'wild west,' sent 'home,' and the children kept them among their treasures as curios, as we bring home scarals [*sic*] and beads and little images from the tombs in Egypt. I have found these mococks carefully put away when I have gone back to the old home, years after they had been sent, and after the Indian sugar in them had become like rock."[59]

"For the Instruction of Young Ladies and Gentlemen"

While the Potawatomi and Ottawa accommodated, relocated, and adapted to an endless stream of immigrants, Thomas Merrill and Caleb Eldred were making progress with their educational endeavor. With the charter secured, a location chosen, and $2,500 dollars in hand, the founders set about raising additional funds, constructing a building, and finding a suitable teacher for the school they called the Michigan and Huron Institute. They purchased 115 acres of land in what is now downtown Kalamazoo, running south from Cedar Street between Park and Westnedge on a beautiful burr-oak plain.[60] A two-story frame building set near the current corner of Walnut and Westnedge was completed in 1836, and the Michigan and Huron Institute opened for classes that fall.[61]

The early board of trustees comprised an illustrious lot, reflecting the investment of community leaders in the success of the Institute and the important role they anticipated it would play in the growing village of Kalamazoo. As recounted in the Michigan Pioneer and Historical Collections, "among these thirty-three trustees were Hon. Epaphroditus Ransom, first governor at Lansing; Ezekiel Ransom, the governor's father, the only Revolutionary soldier whose remains lie buried in 'Mountain Home Cemetery'; Horace H. Comstock, for whom Comstock is named, whose wife was the niece of J. Fennimore Cooper, author of 'Oak Openings'—the plot being laid in the surrounding area; Col. Anthony Cooley, who painted 'View of Kalamazoo in 1832,' . . . ; Col. F. W. Curtenius; Hon. Caleb Eldred, president; Rev. Thomas W. Merrill, (one of the pioneers if not the pioneer in the work) secretary."[62]

The developing Institute went through many changes in the early years. In 1837, the charter was amended to change the name to the Kalamazoo Literary Institute, which according to Marlene Crandell Francis, alumna and trustee emerita, "honored the support of local citizens in raising the initial funds, appealed to local ambition and pride, and invited the community to identify with the school and to continue providing it with funds and local leaders."[63] That same amendment also clarified the nondenominational character of the Institute, stating "said Institute and Departments shall be open to all Christian denominations, and the profession of any religious faith shall not be required of those who become students."[64] "It should be remembered, however," writes Francis, "that in practice Baptists controlled the board of trustees, most of the early teachers were Baptist clergymen, and practically every college in the country during this time expected students to attend prayers and chapel daily. Most also welcomed students from all denominations, to assure as broad an appeal and as large an enrollment as possible."[65]

The trustees succeeded in attracting well-qualified principals who offered instruction in a wide variety of subjects, but there was frequent turnover in the early years. Between 1836 and 1843, five different men served as principal of the Institute. All came from the East and most had been educated at Baptist institutions, notably Hamilton College and Brown University.

The Kalamazoo Literary Institute advertised "instruction of young Ladies and Gentlemen in the ordinary branches of a thorough academic education."[66] The ambitiously broad curriculum included "reading, orthography, English grammar, arithmetic, ancient and modern geography, elements of history, natural philosophy, rhetoric, composition and declamation," all for four dollars per quarter. For a dollar more, students could receive instruction in "Greek, Latin and French languages, intellectual and moral philosophy, chemistry, botany, political economy, logic, bookkeeping, natural theology, evidences of Christianity and the higher branches of Mathematics."[67] This curriculum, while "on a high plane of . . . scholarship,"[68] was considered preparatory rather than college-level, and the institution would not gain the right to grant degrees until 1855. Still, lofty academic standards seemed to have been in place from the first. After the University of Michigan in Ann Arbor opened its doors to students in 1841, it was not unusual for Kalamazoo students to enter the University at the sophomore or junior level, suggesting that "the forbear of Kalamazoo College offered instruction of a collegiate grade before the University opened."[69]

"We Have Not a Mind to Remove to a Distant Land"

While the Kalamazoo Literary Institute was setting down roots, calls to uproot Native peoples from their homelands were growing louder. When Congress passed the Indian Removal Act in 1830, it gave the federal government the right to negotiate land cessions with tribes in exchange for land west of the Mississippi River. While the legislation did not stipulate forced removal, the attitude of the Jackson administration was such that removal was going to happen whether the tribes wanted to go or not. The idea was controversial and had been hotly debated in Congress. New Jersey Senator Theodore Frelinghuysen was among those who vehemently opposed removal, arguing that, "such a process will disgrace us in the estimation of the whole civilized world. It will degrade us in our own eyes, and blot the page of our history with indelible dishonor."[70]

The Baptist General Convention and the Board of Missions, on the other hand, had gone on record supporting the removal of the northern tribes. As explained in the *American Baptist Magazine*:

> These Indians [of the Great Lakes] are uncivilized, and subsist chiefly by hunting. They have no regular forms of government, nor permanent homes. The missionary cannot obtain access to the adults, unless he follow them in their hunting expeditions, or visit their huts during the winter. He cannot collect the children into schools, except those whom the parents may be induced to relinquish to his care . . . These are the Indians among whom Mr. M'Coy has labored; and the experience of ten years has convinced him that they must perish, or be removed to some position where they can be placed together, on lands appropriated to their use.[71]

Mr. M'Coy was Isaac McCoy, the missionary who had established the Thomas Mission for Noonday and Blackskin in 1826, which Leonard Slater then took over. McCoy was an avid proponent of Indian removal and persuaded many in power that it was for Native peoples' own good.

Three years after Congress passed the Indian Removal Act and five months after Thomas Merrill and Caleb Eldred secured their charter for the future Kalamazoo College, U.S. officials called for a sweeping removal treaty targeting the northern tribes, particularly the Potawatomi. Negotiations were to take place in Chicago in late September of 1833.[72] "Michigan Pottawatomi remember this treaty in the same way that Americans remember December 7, 1941," writes William Church of the Gun Lake Tribe. "It was also a day to go down in southwest Michigan Indian community history as 'a day of infamy'."[73]

The Potawatomi were vehemently opposed to removal and to selling their few remaining reserves. Leopold Pokagon, leader of a band of Potawatomi with large villages and farms in the Niles area, was unequivocal on this point and threatened to kill anyone who agreed to land cessions. Despite the determination of Pokagon and other Potawatomi leaders, however, many ultimately had little choice but to sign the 1833 treaty. Lathrup M. Taylor, a fur trader who knew Pokagon and witnessed the treaty negotiations, sheds light on what transpired. Among other dubious tactics, individuals were taken aside and offered bribes if they would sign, causing some Potawatomi to break ranks. According to Taylor, "this and similar transactions made such changes that... Pokagon was compelled to sign the treaty."[74]

Taylor advised the anguished Pokagon that, "the Government was powerful, and was bound to have his reserves, and that he better dispose of them when he could make the best terms."[75] Many of the chiefs believed their bands would be able to avoid removal by going north, while some of the more southern bands in Illinois and Indiana had resigned themselves to moving west. "Still others," Church writes, "who had yet to receive annuities from earlier treaties saw the treaty as a means to survival even if it meant being uprooted."[76]

Describing the agony many Potawatomi leaders must have felt, Pokagon recounted all that his people had done to satisfy the United States while remaining in their territory. He spoke of "the great amount of land his people had ceded to the Government; the confidence he had entertained that the Government would deal justly with them; the attachment to their reserves, and the advantages of religion, education, and subsistence they had enjoyed on the hunting-grounds of their people," and yet the federal government still wanted more. Pokagon reportedly concluded, "'if I could save the reserves for my children, I would gladly die in defense of their rights before I would sign the treaty ceding the lands of [my] children and people away;' and he cried like a child when he signed the treaty."[77]

Yet in the midst of defeat, Pokagon managed to negotiate a reprieve. Though he was forced to cede his reserves, language was added to the treaty saying that the Pokagon Band was exempt from removal on account of religious creed. The Band had ties with Catholic missionaries and many had converted to Catholicism. All other Michigan Potawatomi were to depart for lands west of the Mississippi after three years. Neither Match-e-be-nash-she-wish nor his son Penassee signed the treaty. Sagamaw agreed to sign believing that he and his people could avoid removal by going north, and shortly thereafter he and his band moved north to Gun Lake.[78]

The Grand River Ottawa at Leonard Slater's Thomas Mission were just far enough north to escape the land cessions of earlier treaties, but in 1836, the same year the Michigan and Huron Institute opened for classes, the federal government sought to extinguish the title of the Ottawa and Chippewa to their land north of the Grand River,[79] including the land on which the Thomas Mission stood. The treaty would result in massive land cessions—more than 14 million acres comprising the northwest portion of Michigan's lower peninsula and the eastern half of the upper peninsula—which would pave the way for statehood. It also assumed the eventual removal of the northern tribes, stating that "when the Indians wish it, the United States will remove them, at their expence, provide them a year's subsistence in the country to which they go, and furnish the same articles and equipments to each person as are stipulated to be given to the Pottowatomies in the final treaty of cession concluded at Chicago."[80]

The Grand River Ottawa had no interest in attending the treaty negotiations and had sent a petition to President Jackson stating, "you know we obtained our land from the Great Spirit. He made it for us who are Indians. When we die, we expect to rest on this land . . . We have not a mind to remove to a distant land."[81]

Ultimately, however, the Grand River Ottawa decided to attend the negotiations in hopes of reserving a ten-mile square area encompassing the Thomas Mission. Leonard Slater and a group of younger chiefs set out for Washington with a written statement dictated by Noonday outlining their position.[82] After arriving, however, they found they had little agency in the negotiations. Andrew Jackson had directed Henry Schoolcraft, lead negotiator, not to allow reservations of any kind. During the negotiations, Slater frequently wrote to the Board of Missions seeking advice. He was deeply disturbed by how events were unfolding, writing, "I never was so much grieved and mortified in seeing the transactions of man as at this treaty."[83]

At one point, Schoolcraft offered Slater $6,400 as compensation for the land at the Thomas Mission. Whether this was intended as a bribe is not clear. Certainly, Slater could have pocketed the money. Instead, he and the Ottawa decided to use the funds to purchase land elsewhere in Michigan, and several months after returning from Washington, Slater and the Grand River Ottawa purchased a large tract in Prairieville, Barry County, about twelve miles northeast of Kalamazoo.[84] As Slater wrote to the Baptist Board, "after much painful anxiety and suspense in regard to finding a home for the native brethren and others, I succeeded in closing a contract . . . for 800 acres of land situated 3 miles from Gull Prairie."[85] The land, surrounded by lakes and made up of oak openings, was easy to plow and offered "sufficient timber for fencing, buildings, and firewood."[86] It was also near "plenty of the sugar tree which could be purchased at 2 or 3 dollars per acre."[87] Slater and the Grand River Ottawa seemed pleased with the purchase.

While the Grand River Ottawa had been able to navigate the treacherous proceedings of the Treaty of Washington, it had meant leaving their village at the rapids of the Grand River where they had long lived and had invested both financial and sweat equity in establishing farms and a school. After they left, White settlers quickly took over their farms and buildings. Though they were supposed to pay the Ottawa rent, Slater lamented in his letters to the Baptist Board that the rent monies had not been received.[88]

Surviving in this new landscape required endless trade-offs. Noonday's conversion to Christianity in 1832 had facilitated Slater's attempts to suppress the Ottawa's religious practices. After his conversion, Noonday, who had been "the head man in their Medicine dances," said he would "talk no more about the earth."[89] In 1833, Slater reported what he saw as further progress:

> At this season not a pole was erected, nor a word said to resume their former practice of the Medicine Dance, the most sacred rite practiced by them for ages past and on which they relied to secure to themselves . . . health and prosperity, and . . . to heal all diseases both of body and mind. This practice they have wholly relinquished . . . The Conjurers and head men of their feasts were dismayed. They found no employment. When we consider how deeply rooted in the heart these satanical practices had become and now wholly to relinquish them constrained us to exclaim, What hath the Lord wrought.[90]

What Slater saw as a victory for Christ was for the Ottawa yet another assault on their culture and way of life. Most of the Ottawa did not convert to Christianity. And although there continued to be conversions here and there, nothing like the revival of 1832 ever happened again and most Ottawa seemed not to appreciate attempts to convert them. As Joseph Eliot, a young Ottawa man who had converted, said, "I visited ... [one of the upper villages] I told the Inds. what God said in the bible I had with me. They would not listen. They hated the sight of my bible."[91]

Noonday's conversion almost certainly involved personal trade-offs as well. Though Slater was in charge of the mission, Noonday remained the undisputed leader of the Ottawa and played an important role in maintaining the social integrity of the mission community. Slater conducted mission affairs in close collaboration with Noonday and learned the Ottawa language under Noonday's tutelage. When preparing to preach in Ottawa, Slater would first deliver the sermon to Noonday and make corrections based on his feedback.[92] Given that many Christian concepts had no clear equivalent in Ottawa language and culture, as teacher and translator Noonday would have had tremendous control over Slater's message.

Noonday's conversion may well have been sincere, but it could also have been a means of not ceding to Slater his role as spiritual leader of his people, though he knew it would mean alienating many Ottawa who rejected Christianity.[93] He had to walk an extremely fine line. After his conversion, Noonday held daily prayer meetings at his home. He would also preach during Slater's absences and when the Ottawa were at their maple sugar camps. Slater consulted him in all matters and seemed to respect his wishes. When Noonday welcomed a Catholic priest into their village, Slater, who saw the priest as a rival as well as an infidel, questioned Noonday's decision but acquiesced.[94] Later when Slater invited an Episcopal bishop and several clergy to visit the Ottawa Colony, Noonday insisted on holding the prayer meeting in his home. After a large group had assembled and the bishop had made a brief address, Noonday said, "he would be glad to have the bishop pray with them, but as they could not understand him, and a prayer to be interpreted would not have a good effect, he himself would pray."[95]

Although Slater was often frustrated in his attempts at conversion, life at the mission went more smoothly where his goals and those of the Ottawa better aligned. This was the case when it came to farming and education, which Slater referred to as "temporal things." Writing in 1830, he reported, "their prospect of harvest exceeds any year previous. The chief will probably have one hundred bushels of corn and a considerable quantity of Potatoes."[96] In 1844, a farmer assigned by the government to help the Ottawa at the mission informed the Superintendent of Indian Affairs that his services were not needed. "The Indians wish me to work on their houses, make cupboards, trunks, etc.," he wrote. "They did not wish me to work on their land, as they say they could drive team, hold plough, plant, and sow wheat, as well as any white man."[97]

The Ottawa were engaging in what Ben Secunda calls "adaptive resistance."[98] They integrated farming and education into long-standing seasonal activities and participated in a trade economy with the settlers. Slater often mentioned needing to suspend the school because the Ottawa were away at their sugar camp, as they were every spring, or on hunting expeditions during the winter. Writing in 1841, Slater complained, "the call for furs the present season has operated to the disadvantage of the Indians; many of them, instead of farming . . . have employed their time hunting abroad." "Another circumstance operating to their disadvantage," he went on, "has been a ready sale for berries among the white population. Much time has been spent, and every domestic avocation must stop or suffer, for the whole family must leave to collect berries."[99] As the scholar Susan Gray remarked, "the Ottawa . . . were far less interested in becoming like white men than in learning to live as Indians in the midst of white settlement. For them, the missions were less cradles of civilization than bases from which to pursue a seasonally migratory economy."[100]

As the federal government turned its attention to enforcing the 1833 Treaty of Chicago in the late 1830s, President Martin Van Buren authorized several Christian denominations to establish missions to gather together as many Potawatomi and Ottawa as possible to facilitate removal. These denominations included the Baptists, with Leonard Slater designated as subagent. Thus, Slater's mission was now being seen as a vehicle for removal.

James Selkirk, subagent for the Episcopalians, began recruiting Native people to a new mission he was planning. Among those with whom he met was Sagamaw at Gun Lake. Although Sagamaw gave Selkirk a chilly reception at first, he eventually agreed to join the mission. Sagamaw suggested a piece of land near Bradley, and Selkirk established the Griswold Mission there. Sagamaw's band moved to the mission soon afterward, and the Match-e-be-nash-she-wish Pottawatomi joined the Griswold Mission as well.

By 1839 then, the Potawatomi bands led by Match-e-be-nash-she-wish and Sagamaw, and Noonday's Grand River Ottawa, were living in close proximity on two missions—the Griswold mission in Bradley near Gun Lake and Slater's mission near Richland. There were close ties among the people associated with the two missions and they made frequent visits back and forth.

As removal pressures increased, the Potawatomi remained steadfast in their refusal to leave. In August of 1839, Anishinaabe chiefs from throughout Michigan held a two-day summit thirty miles south of Kalamazoo. There they made their views clear to Agent Ketchum, who was overseeing removal. As a chief named Muckmote stated during the gathering on the Nottawaseppi Prairie, "we have held our consultation with the three nations, and what you said to us yesterday does not please us at all. You told us that we must go West of the Mississippi. In our formal councils we always said we would not go, and our minds have not changed yet. At the council at Niles the same question was put to us and we said we would not go. You also wished to know when we would be ready to go. We say again, we will not go. We wish to die where our forefathers died."[101]

Despite intense protests of Michigan's tribes, by 1840 the removal process in Michigan was underway. General Hugh Brady started rounding up

Potawatomi in the southern region of the state with a man named H. M. Rice assisting.[102] Rice may have earlier been a student at the Kalamazoo Literary Institute, because his biography notes that he attended an academy in Kalamazoo.[103]

In their attempts to avoid forced relocation, the Potawatomi sought various escape routes. According to the Huron Band, "many avoided removal by going to Canada, but others were intercepted by American troops on the way."[104] Some people managed to escape during the trek west, and a few even found ways to return after being relocated in Kansas. As it turned out, the Potawatomi and Ottawa at the Slater and Griswold Missions were spared removal. Because they were not perceived as threatening by their White neighbors, the federal government chose to ignore the fact that they remained. Many Nottawaseppi Potawatomi, living south of Kalamazoo in the fertile area near Athens, sought refuge at the Slater and Griswold missions during the roundup of 1840 and returned later after removal pressures had subsided.[105]

The area just north of Kalamazoo's train station served as a gathering point for the Potawatomi who had been rounded up. As they awaited the journey west, "they were visited by many of the inhabitants [of Kalamazoo], who went to have a last look at the former owners of the soil," according to the writers of a history of Kalamazoo County. "At Kalamazoo they were joined by other parties of Indians from the north and west . . . Their tents and household goods were loaded on the backs of their ponies . . . while the able-bodied men, women, and children, accompanied by their dogs, followed on foot. The sick and aged were carried on the ponies, and the 'pappooses' on the backs of the [s---ws]. There was great reluctance among them to [be] leaving the homes of their ancestors."[106]

It is hard to know for sure how many Anishinaabe were ultimately forced to leave Michigan. Sources vary in their estimates, ranging from 650 to 3,000,[107] but in the end the removal policy resulted in what we would now refer to as ethnic cleansing. The Potawatomi, who lived in the southern portion of the state, which was better suited to farming, were more targeted for removal than the Ottawa and Chippewa who lived further north. What we now see as a cruel and reprehensible course of action was largely accepted without remonstrance by the White population. The people of Kalamazoo "went to have a last look" at the Potawatomi but seemed not to grasp the scope of the tragedy in their midst. Those who witnessed the event spoke of it with "a tinge of sadness" and recognized that "the ties which bound [the Potawatomi] to this beautiful region were deeply rooted."[108] But so powerful was the colonial narrative of "civilization" and "progress" that most White people saw it as natural that Native people should "pass away,"[109] believing "the Indian was at the sunset of his existence; night was about to swallow a race fated to vanish 'as the snow melts before the sunbeam,' or 'like the morning dew, insensibly and mysteriously to disappear, before the lights of civilization and christianity.'"[110]

In the Michigan Pioneer and Historical Collections, there is a story about an encounter between Caleb Eldred and a local Potawatomi woman:

> Pe-ne-moo had a patch of land on Major Lovell's farm that he for many seasons cultivated . . . [His wife] was a member of the M. E. church, and a few years ago communed with its members at Climax. At the time of the removal of the Indians westward . . . most of the Pottawattomie band known here went to Canada. Says Judge [Caleb] Eldred: "while I was at the 'corners' a few years ago, a [s---w] came up to me, apparently much pleased, as she held out her hand and exclaimed, 'How do you do, Judge Eldred, don't you know me? Me Pe-ne-moo's [s---w]!" The Judge was very happy, he said, to meet this good Indian woman. She and her husband had returned from Canada.[111]

This Potawatomi woman and her husband Pe-ne-moo had for many years maintained a plot of land on the farm of Major Willard Lovell. Major Lovell was the father-in-law of Caleb Eldred's daughter Catharine, and Caleb Eldred and Major Lovell both lived on the Climax Prairie.[112] The Potawatomi woman clearly knew Caleb Eldred, yet, though he was "very happy to meet this good Indian woman," he seemed not to remember her and appeared to be unaware that she had fled to Canada to avoid removal.

The Potawatomi, Ottawa, and other Native people did not "vanish" except in the minds of the settlers. Many Native people remained in Michigan, and their descendants have maintained their band identities and cultural integrity to this day. Noonday's Grand River Ottawa eventually joined the Sagamaw and Match-e-be-nash-she-wish bands of Potawatomi in Bradley, forming an enduring community now known as the sovereign nation of the Gun Lake Tribe: Match-e-be-nash-she-wish Band of Pottawatomi Indians. Throughout Kalamazoo College's history, the Pokagon, Gun Lake, and Huron Bands have always been within a thirty- to fifty-mile radius. Potawatomi communities would of course be even closer had they not been driven out of Kalamazoo by White settlement. According to members of the Gun Lake Tribe, Match-e-be-nash-she-wish was never compensated for his Kalamazoo reserve that was ceded in 1827, meaning that Kalamazoo College and the city of Kalamazoo are built on contested land.[113]

"An Academic Grove Worthy of Plato and His Pupils"

Though a time of infamy for the Potawatomi of southwest Michigan, 1840 turned out to be a propitious year for Merrill and Eldred's young institution. The Kalamazoo Literary Institute had been in operation only a few years when a competing educational institution was established in 1838. The University of Michigan system was coming into being, and towns throughout Michigan vied to have branches of the university established in their communities. A group of citizens in Kalamazoo offered a location and funds to erect a school building, and the Kalamazoo Branch of the University of Michigan soon opened in what is now the northeast corner of Bronson Park.

Despite Kalamazoo not being large enough to support two educational institutions, some citizens were uncomfortable with the Baptist control of the Kalamazoo Literary Institute.[114] Church affiliation drove much of the social life at this time, and "narrow prejudice of one sect against another" was common. Lucinda Hinsdale Stone recalled being a target of such prejudice when she came to Kalamazoo. "Bringing a letter of introduction to a minister, and his wife, whose brother had been from my childhood my beloved pastor," she wrote, "I took an early opportunity to deliver the letter. Weeks and months passed and I did not receive a call in return. I learned afterward that the minister's wife did not call upon me because she did not wish to make acquaintances outside her own church."[115]

Despite such sectarian feelings, the Kalamazoo Literary Institute continued to enjoy robust support, and the Institute's enrollments were larger than those of the Branch. Operating two separate institutions soon became untenable, and in 1840, the Kalamazoo Literary Institute merged with the Kalamazoo Branch of the University of Michigan.[116] Instruction moved to the two-story frame structure where the Branch had operated sporadically since 1838. The school building was nestled in a shady burr-oak opening near an Indian mound, an area inhabited by the Match-e-be-nash-she-wish Potawatomi several years before. One hundred years later, this site would feature the Fountain of the Pioneers depicting a westward-facing settler with raised sword subjugating an Indian figure "in a posture of noble resistance, yet being absorbed as the white man advances."[117]

The merged institution received some financial support from the University regents, but the board of the Kalamazoo Literary Institute retained the right to name the principal, effectively ensuring Baptist control. The board soon hired William Dutton, a recent graduate of Brown University, and under Dutton's leadership enrollment in the institution, commonly referred to as "the Branch," increased from twenty-one in 1840 to sixty-five in 1843.[118] Though the institution continued to struggle with finances, it enjoyed strong support from the local community and Michigan Baptists, and by the early 1840s had become a stable fixture in the growing village of Kalamazoo.

"The Kalamazoo Branch had attracted and drawn together within its walls a large number of students from various parts of this state and from other states," recalled A. D. P. Van Buren, a student in the early days. "The young men and young ladies whose names were enrolled as its students in the spring of 1843 would have done honor by their intellectual endowments to any academy in the land."[119]

Leonard Slater had close ties to the Kalamazoo Branch and at least three of his children were among its early students, but there is no indication that any of the Ottawa youth with whom his children had grown up enrolled at the institution.[120] This is surprising, given the importance of education to Noonday and the Ottawa, Slater's involvement with the Branch, and his earlier vision of merging the Institute and the Ottawa mission. There are accounts of Native youth from Slater's mission attending Albion's Indian Preparatory Department and institutions in the East, but there is no record of any of the Ottawa or Potawatomi youth from the Baptist mission attending the Baptist institution just twelve miles away.

It is possible that some Native youth did attend and there is no record of it. If they had taken Christian names, as many who converted did, the fact that they were Potawatomi or Ottawa would not have been evident in the school's records. And, because many records from the early years were lost, enrollment information is incomplete. Still, it seems that mention would have been made of a Potawatomi or Ottawa youth attending the Branch in Slater's many letters to the Baptist Board of Foreign Missions or in the Michigan Pioneer and Historical Collections, which gathered accounts of early settlers.

Kalamazoo College seems to have begun its history with little thought to the Potawatomi and Ottawa. A student in the early years described the institution's setting in the burr-oak opening in the following way:

> The old branch building . . . stood among the burr-oaks of the northeast corner of the park,—truly an academic grove worthy of Plato and his pupils. A spirit of old classical mythology seemed to pervade the place; one thought of a *genius loci* and nymphs and dryads hiding among these oaks, that half-embowered this seat of learning and half-hid the entire village with their beautiful foliage.[121]

This description overlays the Potawatomi oak opening with classical images from ancient Greece and Rome, transplanting a very different history. In the same way, students at the Kalamazoo Branch learned Greek and Latin and studied the histories and cultures of distant lands while remaining ignorant of the people whom they had displaced and all that had transpired on the soil beneath their feet.

Endnotes

1 *The American Baptist Magazine* 7, no. 4 (April 1827): 105–106, Google Books.

2 Leonard Slater's letters to the Baptist Board of Foreign Missions, Leonard Slater (1802–1866), 1826–1856, International Ministries—Missionary Correspondence, Group 1-Series 1, on microfilm, Reel FM-101, American Baptist Historical Society, Atlanta, Georgia. Courtesy of the American Baptist Historical Society, Atlanta, GA. [All of Slater's letters archived by the American Baptist Historical Society are on the same microfilm reel and are hereafter cited as "Slater, letter to ____, date, ABHS"]; Leonard Slater's letters to the Michigan Superintendency of the Bureau of Indian Affairs, http://digital.library.wisc.edu/1711.dl/History.AnnRep4045.

3 *Michigan Historical Collections* 10 (Lansing [etc.] Michigan Historical Commission, 1886), 158–159, https://hdl.handle.net/2027/mdp.39015071219474?urlappend=%3Bseq=176. "Deacon M______ remembers that in November

of 1832 Elder Merrill came on horseback to his log cabin inquiring the way to Grand Rapids, whither he was going to organize a Baptist church, and to baptize Noonday and the converted Indians. The elder on his return told Deacon M______ that he had to sleep in the woods one night both going to and coming from Grand Rapids."

4 Charles True Goodsell and Willis Frederick Dunbar, *Centennial History of Kalamazoo College* (Kalamazoo, MI: Kalamazoo College, 1933), 20.

5 Goodsell and Dunbar say that Eldred attended Hamilton College. This was probably the Hamilton-Oneida Academy (founded 1793), which later became Hamilton College (chartered 1812). There was also the Hamilton Theological and Literary Institution, which later became Colgate University, but the Hamilton Theological and Literary Institution was not chartered until 1819 when Eldred was 38 years old.

6 "College History," Hamilton College. https://www.hamilton.edu/about/history/full.

7 Goodsell and Dunbar, *Centennial History*, 32.

8 Indigenous people of the Great Lakes region are known as the Anishinaabe, or original people. The Potawatomi, Ottawa, and Chippewa—also known as the Bodéwadmik, Odawa, and Ojibwe—belong to the Anishinaabe linguistic and cultural group.

9 Carol L. Higham, "Christian Missions to the Indians," *Oxford Research Encyclopedias*, May 9, 2016. https://doi.org/10.1093/acrefore/9780199329175.013.323.

10 Slater, letter to Lucius Bolles, Baptist Board of Foreign Missions, October 7, 1833, ABHS.

11 William L. Church, Petition for Federal Acknowledgment of the Match-E-Be-Nash-She-Wish Band of Pottawatomi Indians of Michigan, May 16, 1994, 37 (n. pag., numbers correspond to the page numbers of the pdf). https://www.bia.gov/sites/bia.gov/files/assets/as-ia/ofa/admindocs/SampleNarrative.pdf. Church explains that Saginaw came to be known as Sagamaw.

12 D. B. Cook, "Letter to the Editor," *The Century Magazine*, v. 30 (May–Oct. 1885). https://babel.hathitrust.org/cgi/pt?id=mdp.39015024249263&view=1up&seq=346. From an interview between D. B. Cook, Editor of the *Niles Mirror*, and Noonday that took place in 1838. Cook transcribed the interview in his journal and later published excerpts from it in a letter to the editor of the *Century Magazine* in June 1885. Leonard Slater served as interpreter during the interview.

13 "App Shows Historic Boundary of Native American Land in Kalamazoo," MLive, http://www.mlive.com/news/kalamazoo/index.ssf/2017/07/app_shows_historic_boundary_of.html, July 17, 2017; updated Jan. 19, 2019.

14 "Treaty of Chicago," Wikipedia. https://en.wikipedia.org/wiki/Treaty_of_Chicago.

15 Church, Petition for Federal Acknowledgment, 42–43.

16 "Treaty with the Potawatomi," Potawatomi Web. http://www.kansasheritage.org/PBP/books/treaties/t_1827.html.

17 Church, Petition for Federal Acknowledgment, 46.

18 Church, Petition for Federal Acknowledgment, 47. "By 1815 a policy of removal had been clearly outlined by the U.S. and by 1824 was being implemented by key figures in U.S. policy making. These included Lewis Cass, Andrew Jackson, and John C. Calhoun. The treaty process after 1821 suggests an internment phase supporting outright removal later was contemplated by the U.S. Government where Indians were concentrated away from points of settlement to await removal."

19 Helen Hornbeck Tanner and Miklos Pinther, *Atlas of Great Lakes Indian History* (Norman: University of Oklahoma Press for the Newberry Library, 1987), 135.

20 Summary under the Criteria and Evidence for Proposed Finding Match-e-be-nash-she-wish Band of Pottawatomi Indians of Michigan, prepared in response to a petition submitted to the Secretary of the Interior for Federal Acknowledgment that this group exists as an Indian tribe, approved June 23, 1997, United States Department of the Interior, Office of Federal Acknowledgement, MBP-V001-D004, 107.

21 "Judge Caleb Eldred and His Descendants." Compiled by Stephen Claude Eldred with Supplemental Data by Lisle Richardson Lovell and Helena Eldred Dusenbury. Kalamazoo College Archives, Biographical Files collection, Record Group 74, Box 21, Folder: Eldred, Caleb.

22 Mary Elizabeth Day Trowbridge, *History of Baptists in Michigan* (Michigan Baptist State Convention, 1909), 36, a letter to the Board of the American Baptist Home Mission Society dated March 27, 1832. [Goodsell and Dunbar, *Centennial History*, give the letter's date as May 3, 1832, see p. 17.]

23 Samuel W. Durant, *History of Kalamazoo County, Michigan, Its Prominent Men and Pioneers* (Philadelphia: Everts & Abbott, 1880), 345.

24 Durant, *History of Kalamazoo County*, 347 (under the sketch of Thomas Eldred).

25 Durant, *History of Kalamazoo County*, 345–346.

26 Durant, *History of Kalamazoo County*, 346–347.

27 Goodsell and Dunbar, *Centennial History*, 15.

28 Trowbridge, *History of Baptists in Michigan,* 37, excerpt from a letter from Caleb Eldred dated June 21, 1833.

29 California Newsreel (producer), *Race: The Power of an Illusion* (PBS, 2003). Background Reading, Interview with Theda Perdue. https://www.pbs.org/race/ 000_About/002_04-background-02-07.htm.

30 Durant, *History of Kalamazoo County,* 216.

31 Gerald W. Williams, "Introduction to Aboriginal Fire Use in North America," *Fire Management Today* 60, no. 3, (Summer 2000): 11.

32 Durant, *History of Kalamazoo County,* 77.

33 Leanne Betasamosake Simpson, *As We Have Always Done: Indigenous Freedom Through Radical Resistance* (Minneapolis: University of Minnesota Press, 2017), 43.

34 Simpson, *As We Have Always Done,* 3.

35 Simpson, *As We Have Always Done,* 3.

36 Simon Pokagon, *The Red Man's Rebuke* (Hartford, MI: C. H. Engle,1893), Author's Note.

37 Durant, *History of Kalamazoo County,* 91.

38 Oak Openings, Michigan State Natural Features Inventory, https://mnfi.anr.msu.edu/communities/community.cfm?id=10691.

39 Oak Openings.

40 Willis Dunbar, *Kalamazoo and How It Grew* (Kalamazoo, MI: Western Michigan University), 80; Durant, *History of Kalamazoo County,* 66. Bronson Park was an oak opening: "A branch of the University of Michigan began classes in a building on Academy Square [in what is now Bronson Park] in 1838. It later became a Baptist academy and finally the first site of Kalamazoo College, before being removed in 1857" (http://www.kpl.gov/local-history/parks/bronson.aspx). Also see *Michigan Historical Collections* 38 (Lansing [etc.] Michigan Historical Commission, 1912), 528 for a description of the burr-oak plain where K College was first situated.

41 Durant, *History of Kalamazoo County,* 327.

42 Quoted in Susan E. Gray, "Limits and Possibilities: White-Indian Relations in Western Michigan in the Era of Removal," *Michigan Historical Review* 20, no. 2, American Indians (Fall 1994): 88–89, https://www.jstor.org/stable/20173461?seq=1&cid=pdf-reference.

43 *Michigan Historical Collections* 10, 157.

44 W. Benjamin Secunda, "In the Shadow of the Eagle's Wings: The Effects of Removal on the Unremoved Potawatomi" (PhD diss., University of Notre Dame, 2008), 484–485.

45 Marlene Crandell Francis, *A Fellowship in Learning: Kalamazoo College, 1833–2008* (Kalamazoo, MI: Kalamazoo College, 2008), 16.

46 Response to the MBPI Petition for Federal Acknowledgment, United States Department of the Interior, Office of Federal Acknowledgement, MBP-V001-D004, 123.

47 Crisfield Johnson, *History of Allegan and Barry Counties, Michigan* (Philadelphia: D. W. Ensign & Co., 1880), 270–271.

48 Church, Petition for Federal Acknowledgment, 53.

49 Gray, "Limits and Possibilities," 80–81.

50 Gray, "Limits and Possibilities," 84.

51 Lucinda Hinsdale Stone, "In Bygone Days," *Kalamazoo Daily News*, 1894, Kalamazoo Public Library.

52 Durant, *History of Kalamazoo County*, 79.

53 Gray, "Limits and Possibilities," 89.

54 *Michigan Historical Collections* 10, 156.

55 *Michigan Historical Collections* 10, 156.

56 *Michigan Historical Collections* 35, 147–148.

57 *Michigan Historical Collections* 10, 169.

58 *Kalamazoo Gazette*, January 3, 1851, 2, quoted in Gray, "Limits and Possibilities," 90.

59 Lucinda Hinsdale Stone, "In Former Days," *Kalamazoo Daily*, July 22, 1894, Kalamazoo Public Library.

60 *Michigan Historical Collections* 38, 528.

61 Goodsell and Dunbar, *Centennial History*, 22–24.

62 *Michigan Historical Collections* 38, 528.

63 Francis, *A Fellowship in Learning*, 23.

64 Goodsell and Dunbar, *Centennial History*, 24.

65 Francis, *A Fellowship in Learning*, 24.

66 Goodsell and Dunbar, *Centennial History*, 25.

67 Goodsell and Dunbar, *Centennial History*, 26.

68 Goodsell and Dunbar, *Centennial History*, 27.

69 Goodsell and Dunbar, *Centennial History*, 35.

70 Theodore Frelinghuysen, *Speeches on the Passage of the Bill for the Removal of the Indians, Delivered in the Congress of the United States, April and May 1830*, ed. Jeremiah Evarts (Boston: Perkins and Marvin, 1830), 5.

71 Roger Williams, "Removal of the Indians," *The American Baptist Magazine* 10 (1830): 362–364.

72 Secunda, "In the Shadow of the Eagle's Wings," 525.

73 Church, Petition for Federal Acknowledgment, 50.

74 Indians Residing in Michigan and Indians, Supplementary Memorial of Certain Indians Residing in Michigan and Indiana, House of Representatives, 42D Congress, 2d Session, Mis. Doc, No. 137, March 19, 1872, p. 13.

75 Indians Residing in Michigan.

76 Church, Petition for Federal Acknowledgment, 51.

77 House Supplementary Memorial, p. 13.

78 Church, Petition for Federal Acknowledgment, 53.

79 Isaac McCoy, *History of Baptist Indian Missions* (Washington, DC: William M. Morrison, 1840), 494.

80 "At Washington, District of Columbia Treaty with the Ottawa, etc., 1836." Central Michigan University, Clarke Historical Library, https://www.cmich.edu/library/clarke/ResearchResources/Native_American_Material/Treaty_Rights/Text_of_Michigan_Related_Treaties/Pages/Washington,-1836.aspx.

81 Elizabeth Neumeyer, "Michigan Indians Battle Against Removal," *Michigan History* 4 (1971): 279, n. 14. https://turtletalk.files.wordpress.com/2008/01/neumeyer-michigan-indians-battle-against-removal.pdf.

82 Slater, letter to Lucius Bolles, March 1, 1836, ABHS.

83 Slater, letter to Lucius Bolles, March 26, 1836, ABHS.

84 *Michigan Historical Collections* 10, 158, and *Michigan Historical Collections* 35, 151 (which says two and a half miles north of Richland).

85 Slater, letter to Lucius Bolles, November 13, 1836, ABHS.

86 Slater, to the Commissioner of Indians Affairs, September 2, 1842, http://digital.library.wisc.edu/1711.dl/History.AnnRep4045.

87 Slater, letter to Lucius Bolles, December 24, 1836, ABHS.

88 Slater, letter to Lucius Bolles, July 17, 1838, ABHS.

89 Slater, letter to Lucius Bolles, January 24, 1832, ABHS.

90 Slater, letter to Lucius Bolles, February 20, 1833, ABHS.

91 Slater, letter to Lucius Bolles, January 25, 1832, ABHS.

92 *Michigan Historical Collections* 10, 159.

93 Slater, letter to Lucius Bolles, March 23, 1832, ABHS.

94 Slater, letter to Lucius Bolles, October 7, 1833, ABHS.

95 *The Baptist Missionary Magazine* 19, no. 9 (September 1839): 227, https://archive.org/details/sim_baptist-missionary-magazine_1839-09_19_9/page/226/mode/2up

96 Slater, letter to Lucius Bolles, September 29, 1830, ABHS.

97 Letter from Stephen Fairbanks to Robert Stuart, September 30, 1844. United States Office of Indian Affairs, *Annual Report of the Commissioner of Indian Affairs, for the years 1840–1845*, 190, http://digicoll.library.wisc.edu/cgi-bin/History/History-idx?type=browse&scope=HISTORY.COMMREP.

98 Secunda, "In the Shadow of the Eagle's Wings," 5.

99 Leonard Slater, letter to the Commissioner of Indian Affairs, August 18, 1841, United States Office of Indian Affairs, *Annual Report of the Commissioner of Indian Affairs, for the years 1840–1845*, 286, http://digicoll.library.wisc.edu/cgi-bin/History/History-idx?type=browse&scope=HISTORY.COMMREP.

100 Gray, "Limits and Possibilities," 83.

101 Muckmote to Isaac Ketchum, Nottawaseppi Prairie, 1839, in *Michigan Historical Collections* 10, 171–172.

102 Durant, *History of Kalamazoo County*, 77.

103 "Rice, Henry Mower, 1816–1894," Biographical Directory of the United States Congress, http://bioguide.congress.gov/scripts/biodisplay.pl?index=R000198.

104 Huron Band of Potawatomi, Petition for Federal Recognition, Historical Report, 1995, 277–278, https://www.bia.gov/sites/bia.gov/files/assets/as-ia/ofa/petition/009_hurpot_MI/009_pf.pdf.

105 Church, Petition for Federal Acknowledgment, 77.

106 Durant, *History of Kalamazoo County*, 77.

107 Elizabeth Neumeyer, "Michigan Indians Battle Against Removal," 278, says 651 Potawatomi were removed. The plaque by the train station says 3,000 Potawatomi and Ottawa were removed.

108 Durant, *History of Kalamazoo County*, 78.

109 Durant, *History of Kalamazoo County*, 78.

110 Brian Dippie, *The Vanishing American: White Attitudes and U.S. Indian Policy* (Lawrence: University Press of Kansas, 1982), 13, quoting essayists from the early 1800s.

111 *Michigan Historical Collections* 10, 156.

112 *Michigan Historical Collections* 5, (Lansing: W. S. George & Co., 1884), 367; Ellery Bicknell Crane, *The Rawson Family* (Worcester: Published by the family, 1875), 71.

113 Church, Petition for Federal Acknowledgement, 47; "Claim Big Chunk of Kalamazoo: Potawatomis Search Old Records for Proof," *Kalamazoo Gazette*, December 14, 1954.

114 Goodsell and Dunbar, *Centennial History*, 31.

115 Belle McArthur Perry, *Lucinda Hinsdale Stone, Her Life Story and Reminiscences* (Detroit, MI: The Blinn Publishing Company, 1902), 180.

116 Goodsell and Dunbar, *Centennial History*, 33–34.

117 Alfonso Iannelli, the sculptor who designed the fountain, describing its meaning. https://www.kpl.gov/local-history/kalamazoo-history/parks/fountain-of-the-pioneers/.

118 Goodsell and Dunbar, *Centennial History*, 197.

119 *Michigan Historical Collections* 10, 26.

120 Kalamazoo College Archives, enrollment ledgers, 1838–1852. Records from those years are incomplete, but Sarah Emily, George, and Brainerd Slater are among the students listed.

121 Durant, *History of Kalamazoo County*, 142.

Chapter Two

Dissenters and Heretics

In the years leading up to the Civil War, Kalamazoo College became a nexus of antislavery sentiment, progressive thought on women's issues, and openness with regard to religious beliefs. President James Andrus Blinn Stone and his wife Lucinda Hinsdale Stone, principal of the Female Department, were turning Kalamazoo College into a remarkable institution, shaking off its provincialism and engaging with people, issues, and ideas on a national level. Their broadminded ambition would be both their greatest legacy and their downfall, as more conservative elements of Kalamazoo College and the local community grew increasingly uneasy with their liberal approach to education and college administration. During this time of national and institutional fervor, there enrolled a young man who would go on to become perhaps the most accomplished of all the Stones' students. He was Rufus Lewis Perry, and he was a fugitive slave. His presence at the College reflected the Stones' deeply held antislavery beliefs but almost certainly added to growing consternation among their critics. James Stone, Lucinda Stone, and Rufus Perry all shared a deep commitment to social justice, and Lucinda Stone and Rufus Perry in particular would go on to gain national recognition, Stone for her work on behalf of women and Perry for his work on behalf of Black people.

From Slavery to a Black Mecca

Rufus Perry, the first African American student known to enroll at Kalamazoo College, was born into slavery in Tennessee in 1834. His parents, Maria and Lewis Perry, were owned by Archibald Waller Overton, a lawyer and planter in White County. Lewis Perry was a Baptist preacher as well as a talented cabinetmaker and mechanic.[1] With these skills he was able to hire himself out, allowing his family to live in Nashville, although his earnings were sent back to Overton. In Nashville, young Rufus was considered emancipated and he attended a clandestine school for Black children, run by a Mrs. Sally Porter,[2] where he learned to read and write, crucial skills that would later allow him to flourish as a student under James Stone in the Kalamazoo Theological Seminary and go on to a career as a well-known and highly regarded minister, scholar, writer, and newspaper editor.

Fortunately for young Rufus, Tennessee at that time had a number of schools for Black children, and "Nashville may well have been the center of schooling activities in the state."[3] But that by no means meant that access to education was easy. If Thomas Merrill and Caleb Eldred found starting a school on the frontier challenging, their hardships were nowhere near as daunting as those faced by people trying to provide educational opportunities for Black children. Alfonso Sumner, a Black barber, had opened a school for Black children in Nashville in 1833, but it closed three years later after White vigilantes beat Sumner nearly to death for writing letters on behalf of enslaved people who had escaped their bondage. According to Daniel Wadkins, a teacher at Sumner's school, "this occurrence occasioned so much feeling against colored schools that the free colored people, then numbering about two hundred, being intimidated, thought it best to wait until the storm blew over."[4]

Two years later, "a petition by an energetic group of free blacks secured permission to open a school for free black children, on the condition they were taught by a white man."[5] This condition was strategic, the petitioners believing that a White teacher would be more palatable to the White people of Nashville. Soon afterward, John Yandle, a White man, began teaching "reading, writing, arithmetic, and geography to about thirty scholars." Yandle hired Wadkins and Sally Porter, a free, educated Black woman, to teach in the school as well.[6] This would have been young Rufus's first opportunity to attend school, being four years old at the time.

According to Wadkins, Yandle was "a Christian hearted gentleman, and though threatened with violence more than once, he trusted in God, and was not further troubled." After Yandle left the school for "other business that paid better,"[7] Sally Porter quietly opened a school in her home, which Rufus Perry reportedly attended. His time in Porter's school was brief, however. In 1841 his father fled to Canada, and seven-year-old Rufus and his family were compelled to return to Overton's plantation, ending his formal schooling and forcing him into life as a slave.

Little is known about Perry's years on the plantation, but he must have found ways to continue his education away from the watchful eye of Archibald Overton, later described by Perry as an "old, frosty headed 'secesher'" (secessionist) who was "harsh and void of pity."[8] By the time he was eighteen years old, Rufus Perry was considered "dangerous" due to his level of learning, so Overton sold him to a trader who planned to take him further south. After a few weeks in the trader's custody, Perry, like his father before him, managed to escape and fled north through Michigan's Underground Railroad to Canada.[9]

This was just a few years after the passage of the 1850 Fugitive Slave Act, and many Black people, both free and enslaved, were seeking safety in Canada. While in Canada, Perry enrolled in school and also took a job teaching others who had escaped slavery.[10] He likely settled in Chatham,[11] which in the 1850s became a haven for fugitive slaves and free Blacks alike. Later referred to as a "black Mecca," Chatham was "one of the first Canadian destinations of abolitionists looking for ways to network" and a place for fugitive slaves "to ponder available future possibilities."[12] Among well-known abolitionists who passed through or lived in Chatham were Mary Ann Shadd, John Brown,[13] and Martin Delany. Delany, known as the father of Black nationalism, lived in Chatham from 1856 until the start of the Civil War,[14] and while there wrote his novel *Blake* (1859) in response to Harriet Beecher Stowe's portrayal of Black people as docile and intellectually inferior in *Uncle Tom's Cabin* (1852). During that time, Delany was also making plans to emigrate to Africa. Rufus Perry, who by 1858 had become interested in emigrating to Africa as well[15] and later worked with Delany under the auspices of the African Civilization Society, probably first met Delany in the late 1850s in Chatham, which "was dubbed by many the 'capital of the African emigrationist community.'"[16] Indeed, Delany may well have been the one to inspire Perry's Africa ambitions.

After the 1857 Dred Scott Supreme Court decision ruling that Black people were not and could never be citizens, the idea of emigrating to Africa gained broader appeal among free Black people, and Henry Highland Garnet founded the African Civilization Society for the "civilization and christianization of Africa, and of the descendants of African ancestors in any portion of the earth, wherever dispersed. Also, the destruction of the African Slave-trade . . . and generally, the elevation of the condition of the colored population of our own country, and of other lands."[17] A central goal of the Society was to establish cotton production in Africa to create competition for Southern planters as a way to end slavery.

The African Civilization Society (AfCS) made some people—notably Frederick Douglass—uncomfortable because of its similarity in aims to the American Colonization Society (ACS), with both promoting Black emigration. However, the AfCS was based on a completely distinct paradigm. Whereas the ACS, founded in 1816 by mostly White men, cast Black emigration as a charitable gesture while intending to, as Henry Clay said, "rid our country of a useless and pernicious, if not dangerous portion of its population,"[18] the AfCS was founded by Black men to offer an alternative to remaining in a country in which Black people "had no rights which the white man was bound to respect"[19] and emphasized pan-African empowerment and self-determination. To address the tendency of people to conflate the two societies, in 1861 Martin Delany helped draw up a supplement to the AfCS constitution clarifying that it did not encourage general emigration to Africa but only "carefully selected and well recommended individuals," and that "ulterior objects in encouraging emigration, shall be—Self-Reliance and Self-Government, on the principle of an African Nationality, the African race being the ruling element of the nation, controlling and directing their own affairs."[20]

In May of 1859, Martin Delany embarked on a journey to "make explorations in certain portions of Africa."[21] While there, he signed a treaty "with the king and chiefs of Abbeokuta, in view of advancing the future prosperity of his fatherland." Abeokuta, meaning "refugees under a rock," was settled in 1830 by the Egba people, who were fleeing intertribal warfare, some of which had to do with slave trading.[22] The village was nestled under a large rock on the east bank of the Ogun river in present-day Southwest Nigeria.[23] The treaty signed by Delaney and the Abeokuta chiefs in December of 1859 stipulated that select Black

American emigrants could settle "in common with the Egda *[sic]* people, on any part of the territory belonging to Abbeokuta not otherwise occupied" and that "settlers shall bring with them, as an equivalent for the privileges above accorded, intelligence, education, a knowledge of the arts and sciences, agriculture and other mechanical and industrial occupations." The treaty also stated that "the laws of the Egba people shall be strictly respected by the settlers."[24]

Perry probably knew of the newly established African Civilization Society and may even have been corresponding with the Reverend Henry M. Wilson, an early member of the organization.[25] He was almost certainly apprised of Delany's expedition to Central Africa, which departed a few months before Perry began his studies in Kalamazoo. Perry's desire to go to Africa drew the patronage of the Reverend John Booth, a longtime agent for Kalamazoo College, and others interested in sending a Baptist missionary to Africa.[26] So when Rufus Perry came to Kalamazoo College in 1859, he arrived with a clearly defined purpose: to prepare himself to emigrate to Africa and serve as a missionary there. Although Kalamazoo was hardly the "black Mecca" he knew in Chatham, Perry would have encountered an institution sympathetic to him and his aspirations.

Of Segregationists, Assimilationists, and Anti-Racists

The College's founders and early leaders, while accepting of the colonization and dispossession of Native people, believed the enslavement of Black people was morally reprehensible. Both Thomas Merrill and Caleb Eldred were avowed abolitionists, and Merrill in particular was active in the cause. Antislavery sentiments were even more pronounced in the views, writings, and activism of James and Lucinda Stone, who led the institution from 1843–1863 and were at the height of their influence when Rufus Perry enrolled in 1859. The Stones proved to be a nineteenth century power couple dedicated to turning the Kalamazoo Branch into a progressive coeducational college characterized by close relationships between faculty and students, equal opportunities for women, and the highest academic standards. They brought an enthusiasm for learning, devotion to teaching, and deep investment in their students' personal, moral, and intellectual growth, expecting much while providing constant support and encouragement. In this stimulating and caring atmosphere, enrollments soared[27] and students thrived. By the time Perry enrolled in 1859, the Stones had achieved their long-held goals of amending the charter to grant college degrees and establishing a theological seminary. They had overseen the expansion of the campus to its present site, Upper Hall being erected in 1848 where Hoben Hall now sits partway up a wooded slope. And, the new Lower College Building, constructed to house Lucinda Stone's Female Department, had just opened on the corner of South Street and Michigan Avenue on the plain below.[28]

The son of a Baptist preacher, Rufus Perry would have been drawn to Kalamazoo College by its Baptist affiliation and theological seminary, but also by the open and accepting atmosphere created by the Stones. Their broadmindedness shaped the institution's character, making it a place welcoming of progressive thought on important issues of the day, and in the 1850s there was no more salient issue than slavery. "There was a great drift toward and through Kalamazoo in the decade of '40 to '50 and up to the time of the Civil War," Lucinda Stone recalled. "It was on the directest route of western travel, and we were visited by the most noted lecturers in the United States in those days . . . We were openly anti-slavery in thought and acknowledged woman suffragists, as were the majority of those who filled the lecture platform."[29]

Through their hospitality the Stones developed friendships with the great thinkers of the time, bringing a cosmopolitanism to the College and the village of Kalamazoo. Among the luminaries they hosted at their "private hotel on the hill," as Lucinda Stone referred to their home during those years, were Wendell Phillips, William Lloyd Garrison, Ralph Waldo Emerson, and Frederick Douglass. According to Gail Griffin, biographer of Lucinda Stone, she "was a deep admirer of Douglass, who, in addition to his remarkable life as an abolitionist after having been born in slavery, had been the lone voice in support of [Elizabeth Cady] Stanton's resolution at Seneca Falls calling for the female franchise." Lucinda Stone corresponded with Douglass's second wife Helen later in her life. She also became close to Sojourner Truth, visiting her frequently during Truth's later years in Battle Creek, Michigan.[30]

James Stone had openly espoused antislavery sentiments since his time as a student at the Andover Theological Seminary in Massachusetts, where he enrolled in 1836. Andover was then "a stronghold of orthodox congregationalism"[31] that had been founded to "counteract the liberal tendencies of Harvard."[32] It therefore did not endear Stone to his professors or fellow students when he converted to the Baptist faith and joined the abolitionist cause. It was characteristic of Stone to follow his principles even when they made him unpopular: "'Is it true?' 'Is it right?' were questions always first in his mind."[33] Later, when asked for his opinion on women's suffrage, he said, "This is right; it is the natural, and must be the inevitable, evolution of the Declaration of Independence."[34] While at Andover, Stone would often travel to Boston to hear Wendell Phillips and William Lloyd Garrison speak out against slavery "in the days when Garrison was led through the streets of Boston, hooted and stoned by the mob, with a tarred rope around his neck."[35] As James Stone insisted, "no man can believe in the fatherhood of God, the brotherhood of man, accept Christ's teachings in the Sermon on the Mount, and believe in the righteousness of slavery at the same time. This new truth is God's truth, and it is sure to prevail."[36]

Soon after his arrival in Kalamazoo in 1843, James Stone joined the Kalamazoo River Baptist Association, which, in addition to furthering the Baptist cause in the region, took a strong, public antislavery stance. In 1843, the Association's annual letter focused on "the great sin of American slavery" and lamented the fact "that the Baptist denomination has one hundred thousand slaves in the relation of church members."[37] Two years later, Northern and Southern Baptists would split over the issue of slavery, forming separate conventions. The annual letter was reprinted in full that fall in the *Signal of Liberty*, the newspaper of the Liberty Party of Michigan and the Michigan Anti-Slavery Society.[38] Stone was a member of both organizations, as was Thomas Merrill, and in 1847 Stone was named to the Executive Committee of the Kalamazoo County chapter of the Michigan Anti-Slavery Society.[39]

In 1854, seeking a political party that would take an antislavery stance, James Stone participated in the formation of the Republican Party. Leading up to a pivotal July gathering "under the oaks" in Jackson, Michigan, which many credit with the party's founding, there had been a convention in Kalamazoo in June, "followed by a private conference of some of the leaders at the house of Dr. J. A. B. Stone, a veteran Free Soiler, and then President of Kalamazoo College."[40] According to Elizabeth Harris, the Stones' great-great-granddaughter and an independent scholar, under James Stone's influence, "the college was becoming an antislavery institution, and Kalamazoo an antislavery village. His outspoken abolitionist politics contributed to unprecedented postelection animosity in November 1854, then again two years later when the new Republican party overturned the Democrats at the polls, making a clean sweep in Michigan."[41]

In the wake of the contentious 1856 election, a group of Kalamazoo College students enraged Kalamazoo Democrats by gathering outside the home of Democratic Senator Charles Stuart and giving him "three horrid groans"[42] to protest his passive stance on slavery. The *Kalamazoo Gazette* described the incident as the "most disgraceful act ever perpetrated in this quiet village."[43] The editor went on to blame the students' behavior on "the Baptist Educational Institutions of this place," referring to Kalamazoo College and the Kalamazoo Theological Seminary. He lamented James Stone's "violent and unnecessary political demonstrations during the past few months" and asked "are such institutions, and such students, calculated to exercise the most beneficial influence on young and developing minds that may come within their sphere?" The article also insinuated that Stone's actions had offended at least some within the College, noting that "certain gentlemen connected with the Institution referred to, are themselves, deeply conscious of the fatal error which has been committed by Dr. Stone."[44] Clearly, Stone's outspoken opposition to slavery was beginning to alienate people both within and outside of the College.

Lucinda Hinsdale Stone's liberal views can be traced back to her childhood in Hinesburg, Vermont. Her father, who died when she was young, had eschewed religious dogma. "The doctrine of eternal punishment was horrible to him," she later wrote, "and he could not go to hear it preached. He was therefore thought to be a very wicked man."[45] As a child Lucinda Hinsdale was told many times by people in her village that her father "had gone to hell," and she recounts it as "one of the agonies" of her childhood.[46] For this reason, she grew to be tolerant, accepting, and slow to judge. She "was absolutely free from bigotry,"[47] according to a friend and former student. At the same time, she could be scathing in her criticism of people she considered sanctimonious and narrow-minded and did not shrink from calling out "religious cant and long-faced Pharisaical religion or its pretence."[48]

Another major force shaping her life was the discrimination she faced in pursuing her passion for learning. She had begun attending school at the age of three, and by twelve she had enrolled in the newly opened

Hinesburg Academy. At fifteen she began teaching summer school, and when she enrolled in the prestigious Middlebury Female Seminary, "ranked among the first of ladies' seminaries in that state," she was asked to teach French and geometry in addition to taking her own classes.[49]

Lucinda Hinsdale found the female seminary academically inferior to the academy in Hinesburg, and she bristled at "the petty rules of the place." "We were as closely secluded from all society of gentlemen as we would have been in a convent," [50] she later wrote, and she felt that such "proscription and convention" kept students from doing their best work and hindered personal development. This experience caused her to be "in favor of co-education, and awakened an irrepressible desire for the higher, more thorough, college education for women."[51]

She soon returned to the Hinesburg Academy at the behest of her minister, who advised her to "go right into the class with the young men fitting for college and pursue the same studies as they do." "Greek and Latin are as good for you as they are for them," he told her.[52] Her pursuit of Greek led her "through a cruel martyrdom of jokes" as the male students, repeating what their mothers said at home, referred to her as one of those girls "who wanted to be men."[53] In an unguarded moment, Hinsdale expressed her desire to attend college with her male peers. "But I had gone a step too far," she recalled. "My remark was repeated and ridiculed." The postmaster gossiped about it with the townspeople, sarcastically suggesting "that the people of Hinesburg send in a petition to the Vermont legislature to have Miss Hinsdale admitted to the university by special privilege." Though she felt humiliated, the memory of this incident "was a strong incentive in working to make Kalamazoo College co-educational, and in seeking to pry open the doors of the University of Michigan to women students."[54]

In keeping with her progressive outlook, Lucinda Hinsdale had natural abolitionist leanings, but as she later wrote, "although I had heard of slavery, I had no idea of it."[55] It would not be long, however, before she would have an opportunity to witness the "peculiar institution" up close. She had met James Stone in her last years at the Hinesburg Academy when, as a young man newly graduated from Middlebury College, he took a position as principal there. The charismatic young principal and the brilliant female scholar caught each other's eye, and it was not lost on the other students "that Mr. Stone was much attracted toward Miss

Hinsdale."[56] In 1836 James Stone and Lucinda Hinsdale parted ways for a while as he left to further his studies at the Andover Theological Seminary in Massachusetts and she accepted a teaching post at the Burlington Academy in Vermont.

While James Stone's abolitionist sentiments deepened at Andover, Lucinda Hinsdale received an invitation from a wealthy plantation owner in Natchez, Mississippi, to serve as a governess for his children. Before the Civil War, Natchez was home to the greatest number of millionaires in the United States,[57] luxuriating in an economy fueled by the unpaid labor of enslaved people during a time when cotton production was soaring to meet demand from booming textile industries in the northern states and Great Britain.[58] Because there were so few schools in the countryside surrounding Natchez, elite families often hired governesses and tutors from the North. The exceptionally well-educated Miss Hinsdale would have been much sought-after for such a post.

Hinsdale likely found the invitation to teach the children of a rich Southern family intriguing given that it would afford her a chance to learn more about slavery. She accepted the invitation and soon found herself living in the stately Beverly mansion about fourteen miles south of Natchez and six miles east of the Mississippi River. The plantation was home to John Newton Helm, his wife Helen Marie (née Timberlake), five children, and several hundred enslaved people. Hinsdale would spend the next three years of her life living among the country's wealthiest slave-holding families.

On the way to take up her position, Hinsdale passed through a slave market. At this time, Natchez and New Orleans served as major hubs in the domestic slave trade, bringing enslaved people from the eastern states, where tobacco production was declining, and selling them to cotton planters in the Southwest. Of the several slave markets in Natchez, the largest was "the Forks of the Road," located at a well-travelled intersection just east of downtown.[59] This is likely the market Hinsdale witnessed. The intersection linked the Natchez Trace, a main interstate road from the north, to the ironically named Liberty Road, which led south to Second Creek, a lush agricultural region made up of large cotton plantations, among them the expansive Beverly estate encompassing over 1,400 acres.

As Hinsdale rode from Natchez to Second Creek, probably in the Helms' "pleasure carriage" operated by their driver Edmund, she was shocked to see a girl on the block with the auctioneer "showing off her good points, making her open her mouth to show her teeth, use her limbs in various antics (as he would show off a young colt) to test her agility, while he chuckled, wheedled, scolded, and threatened, by turns, to make her do her very best."[60] As she wrote later, "I am not the same person or being now as then, else I could not have borne it. In looking back to that time, it seems to me that I must have been benumbed, or had not the same senses that I now possess."[61]

Hinsdale was appalled by the violence and depravity of slavery, which she observed on a daily basis while in Natchez and wrote about toward the end of her life. Yet she also became close to the Helm family and later gave her third son the middle name "Helm," perhaps after her Natchez employer. As she recalled:

> I found myself in a cultivated, Christian family . . . My pupils were four girls and one boy, the oldest one being fourteen years of age. They were as bright, sweet children as I ever saw, and were very kind and considerate to their servants. Few slaves have fallen into the hands of such kind masters, but one could not shut out the sights and sounds of the institution. Stories of the unimagined cruelties of slavery would come out in tales told carelessly by the children and by the servants, and one was obliged to be a daily witness of its horrible characteristics.[62]

She must have been tempted to write to James Stone to share her experiences, and perhaps she did. But it would have been dangerous to put anything critical about slavery in writing. It was related to her by Edmund, the driver who accompanied her and the children on morning horseback rides and drove them to visit friends at neighboring plantations, that her predecessor, a tutor from the North, had narrowly escaped being lynched after the discovery of a letter he had written expressing abolitionist sentiments. The idea of abolition was so taboo in the South that Edmund claimed never to have heard the word before this incident and appeared not to know its meaning, though he had been given to believe it was something terrible.[63] Although it did not cross Hinsdale's mind, Edmund may well have been feigning ignorance and relating this story either as a warning to Hinsdale or as a way to ascertain her views on slavery.

Among the frequent visitors of the Helm children was Varina Howell, the future wife of the Confederate president Jefferson Davis.[64] During the young Varina's longer visits, which sometimes lasted weeks, she became Hinsdale's pupil as well.[65] The Helms were also friendly with the Conner family, who lived on the nearby Berkley plantation. Unlike the Helms, whom Hinsdale considered "kind masters," Mr. Conner was known for meting out brutal punishments. One day "a servant from a neighboring plantation was found almost senseless . . . on the banks of a stream not far from the house," Lucinda Stone later wrote. "Her flesh was literally hanging in shreds. Mr. and Mrs. H. remarked that they knew very well whose servant she was, because of the inhuman punishment to which she had been subjected. I learned that it was not an uncommon thing for Mr. C.'s servants to die from the effects of punishment; yet this was a place where I was accustomed to visit. Their children were friends of my pupils, and they were very polite and kind to me, treating me as an equal."[66]

Although John Helm was critical of his neighbor, he himself was not above inflicting harsh beatings. There was a period of a few weeks during which Edmund was absent from the morning horseback rides. When he finally rejoined Hinsdale and the children, he was "so lame, gashed, and sore that he could hardly sit in his saddle, from the effects of the most severe punishment . . . ever administered on that plantation." "And for what?" Lucinda Stone wrote, still outraged many years later. She went on:

> His master had given a great dinner party. Ed was the table waiter, a service which he performed to the pride and satisfaction of his master. Not one of the gentlemanly guests arose from that table as sober as this colored youth; but in removing the champagne glasses, he had been tempted to drain some of them, in which a little wine had been left, so that his master noticed that his hand was a little unsteady. That was a crime which could not be passed over, so the following night Ed was called to account for it, and suffered what was considered an orthodox punishment, which an uncommonly good master and a gentleman thought such a crime in a slave was worthy of. Real drunkenness, however, in a free man and a gentleman was all right.

> Ed was taken to an outhouse, in the same building where my schoolroom was located, 'strung up,' as was the phrase, and the slave driver called to inflict the punishment. From my room I could see the place perfectly, and hear the boy's screams and pleadings for pardon, at first distinctly, but finally the voice became almost inaudible.[67]

The "orthodox punishment" she refers to was a whipping of thirty-nine lashes "so as not to exceed the strict limit of forty" as prescribed in the Bible, although it was common for enslaved people to receive many more.[68] Lucinda Stone probably never knew it, but Edmund was later among a group of enslaved men in Second Creek who were implicated in planning a rebellion soon after the start of the Civil War. Given that the whip was a defining symbol of enslaved people's suffering and bondage, it is not surprising that the word "whipping" featured prominently in the testimony of the men interrogated by the "Examination Committee," an assembly of wealthy planters and other "prominent and most staid citizens,"[69] many of whom "had cowhides in their hands."[70]

Having heard that war between the North and South had broken out, several enslaved men began preparing for a revolt to start "when Northerners whip South," as transcribed by Lemuel Conner, a Second Creek planter on the Examination Committee whom Lucinda Stone likely knew as a boy.[71] A primary motivation for the rebellion was that "whipping colored people would stop."[72] Edmund himself was quoted as saying, "if the black folks were turned loose with hoes and axes they would whip the country."[73] Tragically, Edmund was among forty or so enslaved men involved in the planned uprising who died in a series of mass hangings in the autumn of 1861, several months before the fall of New Orleans and a little over a year before the Emancipation Proclamation.[74]

Though occurring twenty years after Lucinda Stone left Mississippi, the thwarted rebellion and its aftermath speak to the terrible suffering of the people enslaved at Second Creek and reveal the system of violence and terror the planters used to maintain control. During her time in Mississippi, the White elite worked hard to mask the ugliness with a veneer of gentility and consoled themselves with the self-deluding myth of affectionate relationships with their "servants." In Lucinda Stone's reflections one senses the grinding gears of profound cognitive dissonance. On the one hand, the Helms were "a cultivated Christian family," "kind masters" with whom she was close. On the other hand, they owned people and did not shrink from inflicting brutal beatings to assert their authority. Though the scenes she witnessed in Natchez turned her into a devout abolitionist, she grappled with the bizarre contradictions inherent in slavery for the rest of her life.

In the years leading up to the Civil War, Lucinda Stone "gloried in being called an Abolitionist in any sense of the word,"[75] and "came to see abolitionism and feminism as inevitable movements of the human soul,"[76] but she, like many abolitionists, William Lloyd Garrison included, tended to take a paternalistic stance toward Black people. In a newspaper article penned by Lucinda Stone in 1898 titled "The New South," she describes meeting a Southern woman in Battle Creek, Michigan. In the course of relaying their conversation, Stone articulated how she understood equality as it pertained to Black people. "We discussed for a long time the difference of their being equal in the rights of opportunity, and equal in talents, and the obligation we are under to help them, to that opportunity that was their right—'to life, liberty, and the pursuit of happiness,' as I understood it," she explained. "That was a God-inspired idea, and that was the equality for which I contended."[77]

During her travels later in life, Lucinda Stone crossed paths with the wife of Jefferson Davis, her former pupil Varina Howell, at a hotel in Montreal. "I presume she would have received me courteously," Stone wrote, "but I did not seek the privilege of seeing her. She was not in a position to see the thing clearly, nor was I. I had not gotten far enough from the monster to see it with any degree of clearness." "You must come out of wrong before you can really see it,"[78] she wrote insightfully. Though the Emancipation Proclamation had slayed the monster of slavery, the monster of racism birthed to justify it had spread its tentacles into every aspect of American life. Few White abolitionists truly understood racism's insidious effects, either on themselves or on the people whose life, liberty, and pursuit of happiness it continued to suffocate.

Lucinda Stone's beliefs about slavery and race, though progressive for her time, reflected prevailing notions bolstered by nineteenth century ethnology about racial hierarchies and the inferiority of people of African descent. In *Stamped from the Beginning*, Ibram X. Kendi traces the history of racism in the United States, organizing ideas about race into three categories—"segregationist," "assimilationist," and "anti-racist." Segregationists believed that Black people were inherently and permanently inferior and subscribed to the theory of "polygenesis," or distinct ancestors of the various races. Assimilationists subscribed to the theory of "monogenesis," or a common ancestor for all races. They tended to attribute perceived inferiority of Black people to the "imbruting" effects of slavery and expected Black people to become more like White people in order to achieve equality. Many abolitionists, both Black and White, were assimilationist thinkers, and Lucinda Stone fell into that category as well. Rare in the nineteenth century were "anti-racists," people who believed in complete and immediate equality among the races, and that, as Kendi puts it, "the only thing wrong with Black people is that we think something is wrong with Black people" and "the only thing extraordinary about White people is that they think something is extraordinary about White people."[79] Even anti-racist thinkers could, and often did, hold assimilationist views. Among those espousing anti-racist positions in the nineteenth century were Frederick Douglass, Wendell Phillips, Martin Delany, and most certainly, Ida B. Wells. While Lucinda Stone remained stuck in an assimilationist framework her whole life and struggled to reconcile the participation of "good people," as she considered the Helms, in something as debased and morally repugnant as slavery, Rufus Perry's thinking on the subject was much less muddled and often anti-racist.

"I Want to Be Off for Africa"

Rufus Perry graduated from the Kalamazoo Theological Seminary on June 19, 1861. During the commencement exercises, each of the five graduates gave an address, and Perry's was entitled "Africa and the Gospel." As described in the *Michigan Christian Herald,* a weekly Baptist newspaper, the addresses "were, without exception, well written and well delivered," and "indicated maturity of thought, sound culture and manliness of expression." In reporting the graduates' future plans, the *Herald* stated that "Mr. Perry, a colored brother, has preached for some time to a church in Toledo."[80] While there are indications that Perry had spent time in Toledo, several weeks before his commencement he had accepted the pastorate at the Second Baptist Church in Ann Arbor, Michigan, and was ordained in that city on October 9, 1861.[81] Perry wrote a letter to the *Herald,* perhaps to correct the misleading statement about his goals and pursuits, and took the opportunity to remind the *Herald's* editors and readers that "it is well known in this State that Central Africa is my chosen field of labor, and the one to which my attention has been called for some time." He goes on to say that "as soon as the way is fully open I want to be off for Africa."[82]

Perry was soon named the African Civilization Society's general agent in the West,[83] and in March 1862, he published a letter in the *Michigan Christian Herald* announcing that he would begin raising funds among Michigan Baptists to cover the cost of his passage to Africa. He mentioned having had "several long interviews" with Martin Delany and related that "the Board of Directors of the African Civilization Society have received me as their missionary to Central Africa, and propose to send me out next summer, at the head of a select colony." He went on to say that "M.R. Delany, M.D. . . . and Prof. Campbell, explorers, have made a favorable treaty of settlement with the king and chiefs of Abbeokuta and Yoruba in Western Central Africa," referencing the treaty Delany had signed in December of 1859. He then explained the aims of the African Civilization Society including the goal of making Central Africa "the world's cotton mart." "Now if a cotton competition be established in West Central Africa that shall deprive Southern gentlemen of their boasted monopoly, their peculiar institution would be too ruinous to be kept running," Perry wrote.[84]

Being selected to lead the planned colony was an honor and demonstrates the high esteem in which members of the African Civilization Society held Rufus Perry, especially given Delany's insistence that only "carefully selected and well recommended individuals" would be chosen to emigrate.[85] That May at the Society's annual meeting in New York, Perry was asked to deliver the annual address. The other speakers were Martin Delany and Henry Highland Garnet.[86] Less than a year after his graduation from the Kalamazoo Theological Seminary, then, Rufus Perry had joined the ranks of the most forward-thinking and unapologetically pro-Black members of America's Black elite. The Society's emphasis on a brotherhood of all people of African descent and insistence on Black people "controlling and directing their own affairs"[87] would characterize Perry's activism for the remainder of his life.

Despite Rufus Perry's palpable enthusiasm for the Africa emigration plan, raising the required funds proved challenging. As he reported in the *Herald* that October, he had "travelled 3,430 miles, collected $313,00, and obtained subscriptions (yet unpaid,) to the amount of $150,00." "The $1000 is not, and will not I fear, be raised," he wrote. "This failure will check the going of my company. 'This delay,' says the Sec. of the Society, 'will be till after the war, unless we can get aid from the Government.'" Nevertheless, Perry had resolved to go with the funds in hand and urged his contributors to make good on their unpaid pledges as soon as possible. "Were I to postpone going until the war is over, as hundreds of my friends would persuade me to do, I might have a mother, a sister, and two or three brothers to accompany me—I pause and thank God for the probability, when ever I think of it," he wrote, referring to his family members still in bondage. "The inducement is strong, almost irresistible," he admitted, "but duty calls me and I will try to obey."[88]

Rufus Perry may well have made it to Africa had Michigan Baptists been a little more generous and had national events not intervened. But before he was able to raise the funds necessary to send himself and his wife Charlotte (he was married by October 1862), President Abraham Lincoln issued the Emancipation Proclamation on January 1, 1863. That pivotal event changed everything, and the African Civilization Society soon abandoned its emigration plans in favor of working "with freed people in the South, as well as with people of color in Africa, Central and South America, and the British West Indies."[89] Duty now called Rufus Perry in a different direction, and by 1865 he was serving as superintendent of the African Civilization Society's Freedmen's school in Washington, D.C.[90]

"The Narrow Spirit of Sectarianism and Bigotry"

Meanwhile, as the Civil War raged, Kalamazoo College was beset by sectionalism of its own as a rift opened up between those loyal to the Stones and those who opposed them. By late 1863, in the midst of national disunion, the College was splitting apart as well, leading to the Stones' sudden resignations and a crisis that would rend the institution, the First Baptist Church, and the village of Kalamazoo in two.

The trouble probably began as far back as 1852, when the Reverend Samuel Haskell was appointed minister of the First Baptist Church.[91] Haskell was much more conservative than the Stones and, according to Lucinda, wanted the presidency of Kalamazoo College for himself.[92] "Whether or not he is the monster of hypocrisy and mendacity of Mrs. Stone's account of the debacle," Gail Griffin writes, "he was most certainly a man of infinitely narrower spirit and creed than James Stone, and probably represented a move on the part of the church toward a more distinctly denominational institution."[93] Indeed, Lucinda Stone later reflected that "much of the trouble which caused [Dr. Stone's] resignation from the presidency of Kalamazoo College arose out of his insisting upon an open, rather than a purely Baptist corporation, for the college. He wanted Kalamazoo College to be an educational institution, not merely a Baptist College."[94]

"If charges of too great liberalism were made against Dr. Stone," write Charles Goodsell and Willis Dunbar, authors of the *Centennial History of Kalamazoo College*, "they were directed even more decidedly against Mrs. Stone as Principal of the Female Department."[95] Criticism of Lucinda Stone began to increase in the late 1850s after a confluence of events led her to temporarily move the Female Department to rooms in the First Baptist Church. One night soon after James Stone's students had groaned and hissed outside the residence of Senator Charles Stuart, a group of men, perhaps motivated by anger at the students' raucous antislavery behavior, removed the old Branch building, then serving as Lucinda Stone's Female Department, from the village square and set it down unceremoniously in the middle of Academy Street. This defiant act left Lucinda Stone with no place to teach her students.[96] Needing a quick solution, she rented rooms in the basement of the First Baptist Church—the domain of Samuel Haskell—and he seized the opportunity to exercise greater oversight of Stone and her Female Department during the three years she remained there.[97]

Haskell and others found much to criticize. Among her transgressions were reading the *Atlantic Monthly*, teaching novels such as *Ivanhoe*, and having her students memorize poetry by the "infidel" Lord Byron. She was accused of being a "realist" because she read German philosophy and a bad moral influence because of her taste for French authors.[98] The Stones' commitment to coeducation, by 1859 expensively manifested in a new building to house the Female Department, also rankled many. The closer the Stones came to realizing their vision of a progressive, open, coeducational institution, the more they ran up against what Lucinda later described as "the narrow spirit of sectarianism and bigotry that stood in the way of every noble endeavor for the interests of the College."[99]

Exacerbating the growing disapproval of the Stones was a worsening financial crisis. Though enrollment had increased dramatically under the Stones' leadership, more than quadrupling from 1843 to 1857, the numbers suddenly began to decline from a high of 407 to just 194 by 1862.[100] One cause for the drop was certainly the Civil War, as many of the male students left to enlist in the Union army, but enrollment had already begun to fall noticeably as early as 1858. Part of the cause may have been an economic depression, stricter admission requirements, and the Stones' outspoken opposition to slavery, but "the increasingly unpopular liberalism of, in particular, Mrs. Stone" was also keeping more and more students away.[101] As Samuel Haskell exerted his influence, the students and parishioners pulled into his orbit may have become distrustful of James and Lucinda Stone. Rumors about the Stones' liberalism certainly seemed to be spreading. In 1860, a report by a visitor from the Department of Public Instruction stated, "of the moral condition of the Institution, you will undoubtedly hear much from other sources. But we take pleasure in saying, that, so far as our knowledge extends, the deportment of the pupils . . . indicates . . . the maintenance of a wholesome degree of discipline."[102]

In addition to declining enrollments, Goodsell and Dunbar note that "whatever his other virtues, Dr. Stone appears to have been a very poor financier. He went on, expanding the scope of the work, without adequate means to support it. While giving of his own funds liberally he never seems to have been able to inspire very liberal contributions from others."[103] The Stones were literally giving all they had—intellectually, emotionally, and financially. According to Lucinda Stone, in their efforts to realize their vision for Kalamazoo College, "property, that would have placed us above the necessity of teaching, had been consumed."[104] Unfortunately, the money they invested was not enough to keep the College solvent, nor were they accurately assessing the depth of the animosity building against them.

At what point the Stones began to sense the danger of the gathering storm is unclear. They were used to headwinds and had come to expect them, so it may have taken a while to realize that the resistance had turned sinister. During a June 1863 trustee meeting someone ominously raised the question of whether the head of the Female Department should be a man. Then came the breaking point that November when, during a trustee meeting, J. A. Clark called for new leadership to head an ambitious fundraising effort among Michigan Baptists recently approved by the trustees.[105] The Stones jointly submitted their resignations the next day, thus opening what Goodsell and Dunbar call "one of the darkest periods in the history of the institution."[106]

While many board members and some of the faculty may have seen the resignations coming, for the students and townspeople it was "as a bolt from a clear sky." In the aftermath, "most of the Faculty resigned, many of the Trustees did likewise, and about 125 of the students left the institution."[107] For the Stones, the break from the College must have seemed like the end of their life's work. Lucinda Stone later wrote, "I felt as though it were death creeping over me, and more than half believed it was."[108] James Stone too spoke in terms of death, referring to those "who have felt that it was better that I should die, than that their own cherished plans and purposes should fail."[109] But little did the Stones know their troubles were just beginning.

Shortly after she resigned, Lucinda Stone opened a school for young women in her home as a way to make ends meet. It seems that those who wanted the Stones gone had underestimated the loyalty of their students, so the mass student exodus and subsequent enrollment of many of the female students in Lucinda Stone's home school caught the College leadership off guard. It was not long before some of the same men who had pushed for the Stones' resignations, among them Professor Edward Anderson, who had been named acting president, were trying to entice Lucinda Stone back to the College. But she steadfastly refused unless James Stone was also reinstated as president. It was then, according to Lucinda, that Anderson threatened that if she did not return to the College, "batteries would be opened upon Dr. Stone, such as we never dreamed of."[110]

True to their word, Edward Anderson, Samuel Haskell, and others soon unleashed "batteries" consisting of allegations that James Stone had embezzled College funds, was supporting an illegitimate child in Canada, and had "engaged in criminal intercourse" with a former student.[111] Rumors flew throughout the College, the First Baptist Church, and the village of Kalamazoo, further splitting these communities apart as people took sides, each bitterly opposing the other.

Lucinda Stone provides the most complete account of the scandal in a 171-page letter addressed to President John Milton Gregory, James Stone's successor. The letter, not surprisingly and certainly understandably, is full of righteous indignation as she documents all that led up to their resignations, describes the ensuing allegations against her husband, asserts an unflinching defense of James Stone, and expresses utter contempt for Samuel Haskell and his supporters. James Stone provided his own defense in a protest he delivered before the congregation of the First Baptist Church on April 1, 1864, after a hearing led by Haskell to decide whether to excommunicate him.[112] A vote was then taken to determine the fate of James Stone. By a show of hands it seemed that he had been exonerated, but Samuel Haskell tallied the votes in favor of excommunication. When the congregation reacted with surprise, Haskell explained that he had not counted the votes of the female parishioners.

The ultimate result was the breaking apart of the First Baptist Church as the Stones and their allies withdrew in protest. Griffin writes, "the tight harmony of church, College, and town which the Stones had managed to create a mere ten years earlier had vanished utterly, replaced by partisanship, slander, secrecy, and doubt. The church was riven, the college was still floundering, and the community would feel the aftershock for years."[113]

Whether there was any truth to the allegations against James Stone will never be known for sure. Samuel Haskell, who led the charge against Stone, failed to produce convincing evidence, his "proof" consisting of allegations attributed to a dead woman and a letter that appeared to be forged. Goodsell and Dunbar conjecture that Haskell may have worried that the First Baptist Church might ask Stone to serve as minister now that he was no longer with the College, and so sought to malign him. James Stone, a consummate people person, does seem to have been much more well liked than Samuel Haskell. As Lucinda Stone wrote with some bitterness, "alas, that Dr. Stone was so often called upon to marry his old pupils, to the exclusion of Mr. Haskell! It has been one of the deposits of that virus of envy that has wrought all this terrible evil, rent a church and drawn men . . . into a net of falsehood."[114] Another possible motive for Haskell's actions was that he and others were hoping to "discredit [Lucinda] Stone's school, vindicate the College authorities in their criticism of the Stones and regain for the institution public patronage." "Both these reasons seem and are unspeakably base," write Goodsell and Dunbar. "Yet, it is difficult to see what other motives there could have been."[115]

Perhaps the greater lesson is that the Stones passionately pursued a progressive agenda for the College, and in doing so they ran headlong into the proverbial brick wall protecting what was considered acceptable and tolerable in that time and place. In other words, the Stones had transgressed beyond what the institutional culture would bear by promoting coeducation, pushing for an open rather than a denominational institution, and taking a vocal stand against slavery, one of the most contentious issues of their day. For all this they are now revered, but at the time they were punished severely for it.

Heretics

To what extent Rufus Perry and his presence at the College added to the simmering disapproval of the Stones in the late 1850s and early 1860s is hard to know. The institutional record is mostly silent on Perry, beyond noting his scholarship funds in financial records and listing him in the catalogues, and even there his presence is ambiguous.[116] Many at the College were abolitionists, but that did not necessarily translate into favoring equality for Black people, and there inevitably would have been those who disapproved of a Black man enrolling at the institution. A letter published in an October 1862 issue of the *Michigan Christian Herald* questioning Rufus Perry's stewardship of donated funds suggests some rancor on the part of a former classmate. The letter's author wrote anonymously under the pseudonym of "A Pastor," but Perry recognized him as a fellow student from the Kalamazoo Theological Seminary and called him out as such in his response printed in the *Herald* a few weeks later. While "A Pastor" states that "no injury is intended to Mr. Perry or the so-called A.C.S. [African Civilization Society] by these questions," his insinuating tone would indicate otherwise:

> There is traveling among our churches one Perry—a colored man—representing the interests of the so-called A.C.S. The people make him liberal collections on the Sabbath—and many in a private way bestow on him their cash, supposing that it *all* goes to the object he pleads for . . . . Mr. Perry was to send us *regularly*, the A.C.S. "documents," in which we expected to find a *showing* for every dollar he collected as its agent . . . Mr. Perry will need to show *our* people proof that he has not devoted the funds we gave him a year ago to his *own use* without sanction of his A.C.S., before he gets any more in this community.[117]

For some reason, "A Pastor" saw fit to send his inquiry to the *Herald* rather than directly to Rufus Perry, who seemed to be blindsided by it. In the same issue there appeared a letter from Perry, clearly written with no knowledge of "A Pastor's" concerns, sending his final report on the status of his Africa missionary plans.[118]

In a subsequent issue of the *Herald*, Perry directly addressed "A Pastor" in a letter that did not mince words. In fact, the editors included a note saying that they had considered "omitting the more 'spicy' parts; but upon considering the matter more fully, we have concluded to insert it entire, notwithstanding our columns are much crowded this week."[119] In the letter, Perry responds point by point to "A Pastor" in a withering rebuttal, as seen in the following excerpts. He begins:

> I beseech you to excuse me, and grant 'space' for another communication which I am forced to write by the Article published in the HERALD of the 1st. Oct . . . The Article referred to places me in rather unfavorable light—*unfavorable!* nay, more—it even virtually characterizes me as "a colored" Floyd.

Perry then recounts some of what "A Pastor" had written, with interjections of his own:

> "There is traveling among our churches one Perry—a colored man—" (not a *white* man, else he is 'all right') "representing the interests of the so-called A.C.S. . . . Mr. Perry will need to show *our* people proof that he has not devoted the funds we gave him a year ago to his *own use* without sanction of his A.C.S., before he gets any more in this community."

Perry goes on:

> "*Our* people" is, of course, the "*Community*" under the leadership of "A Pastor." So, then, listen, ye "*our* people," and I *will* give ye "proof." I called upon you twice—once for the 2nd Baptist Church of Ann Arbor, of which I was then pastor, and again, on the invitation

> of 'A Pastor' when he expected to be absent, for the 'A.C.S.' Now write T. B. Freeman, church clerk, and ask for a copy of my reports, (or take a ride down, as you do not live a great way off) and you will get all necessary "proof" that "one Perry—a colored man"—did not "devote" that $5, you "gave him to his *own use* . . . ." Now write the Sec. of the "A.C.S." Rev. H. M. Wilson . . . and you will find sufficient "proof" that the $2 which "*our* people" donated, was fully reported. Excuse me, —it was a fraction over $2—(quite "*liberal!*") which by vote of "*our* people" went to constitute "A Pastor" an annual member of the "A.C.S."

In answer to "A Pastor" questioning why Perry had not yet departed for Africa, he writes:

> I have not raised the $1,000; who can, or would, then expect me to go and take my wife? As to the question whether I *will* or *would* go, every body acquainted with me knows that for the last four years I have been laboring for this special work . . . . Would I go? Prove me. If you would give me a passport and an outfit, I would not remain here 24 hours.
>
> Now will you give just one third the means absolutely necessary, then abuse and say hard things about us if we do not do what we promise to do with the $1,000? God forbid. "*Our* people" hardly gave enough to pay my fare to and from their place, but they demand that I shall go to Central Africa! . . . If I be a servant of another than God, prove it to me, else spare my character.

Perry later concludes:

> I hope I have said enough to satisfy "A Pastor" and "*our* people," who I cannot believe wished to harm me. "A Pastor" has been long acquainted with me, and long had the honor of sitting beside me in the Theological Class Rooms, and he will bear me witness that I did not "pick his pocket." . . . I now wish to, and do remain, truly yours, and a friend, a christian brother, and a class-mate of "A Pastor."[120]

Perhaps because of the support Perry had received from John Booth and other Baptists for his education, he had initially been optimistic about raising the funds necessary to travel to Africa from among the White Baptists of Michigan, even going so far as to assure members of the African Civilization Society "that the State of Mich. is good for it."[121] Therefore this public othering and questioning of his motives by none other than a former classmate must have been particularly galling. In his "spicy" rebuttal, Perry unmasks "A Pastor," calling out the disingenuousness of his accusations by revealing that he and "A Pastor" were well acquainted with each other. He turns "A Pastor's" rhetorical devices against him with his repeated use of "our people," at one point calling out his classmate's racism directly when he translates "one Perry—a colored man" into "not a *white* man, else he is 'all right.'"

This would not be the last time that Rufus Perry's writing would be characterized as "spicy." Twenty-five years later, one of his biographers, William J. Simmons, described the *National Monitor*, edited and published by Perry, as "a spicy paper, full of matter of interest to his denomination, and such general literature as is elevating in its tone." Simmons goes on to say that Perry "finds ample scope for his rare, splendid talents in assailing enemies as well as aggressively attacking maligners of the race. He has a sword sometimes apparently dipped in wrath, and with giant force driven in the vitals of those who dared assail him and his cause; but he did it not for self but for the cause."[122] It is hard to imagine that with such a passionate nature, a rock-solid sense of self, and no stomach for racial prejudice that Rufus Perry did not make waves at Kalamazoo College.

In many ways Lucinda Stone and Rufus Perry were a lot alike. As a little girl, Lucinda would read in secret to avoid the ridicule of her older siblings, while young Rufus would have risked far worse to covertly continue his education on the Overton plantation. They both rebelled against the limits society imposed on them, driven by experiences of discrimination and oppression to realize the best versions of themselves and to fight for the rights of others, she striving for equality for women and he tireless in combatting racism and working to expand opportunities for Black people. They seemed never to doubt their own abilities and inherent worth. Perhaps that is why they flashed with indignation and verbally skewered those who disparaged them based on gender or race.

James Stone, while achieving notable accomplishments on behalf of Kalamazoo College and in the fight against slavery, did not seem to burn quite as brightly. He went on to serve for several years as editor of the *Kalamazoo Daily* and the *Kalamazoo Telegraph* and was appointed postmaster under President Ulysses S. Grant, but the best days of his career were behind him.[123] As Griffin writes, "one does sense that Lucinda was perhaps the more intense half of the team, driven in a way that James was not . . . . With her she brought incomparable energy, awesome self-discipline, a ravenous intellect . . . and something more, something more dangerous: 'I am by inheritance for the people, a democrat—not a party Democrat, but a real one—and a heretic.'"[124] Rufus Perry was a heretic as well, refusing to conform to racist expectations, vocal in his dissent, and unfettered in his iconoclasm.

Lucinda Stone would go on to make noteworthy gains on behalf of women, achieving some national renown in the process. She became known as the "Mother of Clubs" for her work in establishing literary clubs for women.[125] Stone continued teaching students in her home until it was consumed by fire in 1866. With the help of friends she finished out the school year, but discontinued her school the following summer. She instead decided "to take a class of young ladies to Europe to continue, by travel, studies which they had pursued under my instruction."[126] This was the start of many such study tours abroad to Europe and Egypt, a highly innovative practice for the time. In the late 1860s, James and Lucinda Stone committed, along with others, to convincing the University of Michigan to open its doors to women. Their test case was Madelon Stockwell, a former pupil of Lucinda's, who in 1870 became the first woman to enroll at the University. According to Griffin, "the passage of Madelon Stockwell through the doors of the most respected state university in America sent virtual shock waves through academe and was an important milestone in the subsequent history of women's education."[127] Lucinda Stone remained active late into her life, traveling around the state to give lectures to women's groups on a wide range of topics, which she then published in a regular newspaper column called "Club Talks" in Kalamazoo, Port Huron, and Detroit newspapers.[128] On the occasion of Lucinda Stone's eightieth birthday, Susan B. Anthony wrote, "please tender to Mrs. Stone my loving and honoring appreciation of her great work for women; not only Michigan women, but the women of the nation and the world owe her very much for her persistent efforts to secure the perfect equalities of educational opportunities for girls."[129]

"A Live Man, in Every Sense of the Term"

While most White abolitionists considered their work done with the Emancipation Proclamation, for Rufus Perry and other Black activists it was just beginning. In the late 1860s, after serving as superintendent for the Freedmen's school in Washington, D.C., Rufus Perry moved to the Weeksville neighborhood in Brooklyn, New York, where the African Civilization Society was headquartered. Weeksville was another Black Mecca of sorts, founded in the 1830s as a Black community that drew residents from all over the United States as well as from the Caribbean, Western Europe, and Africa. By the late 1850s it was "was one of the two largest independent free black communities in the United States," and as Judith Wellman writes in *Brooklyn's Promised Land*, "national leaders such as Henry Highland Garnet, Rufus L. Perry, and Martin Delany consciously attempted to make Weeksville part of what Wilson Jeremiah Moses called the 'golden age' of black nationalism."[130]

Working with the African Civilization Society, Rufus Perry edited the *People's Journal*, one of the Society's two newspapers, and served as the Society's general agent, superintendent of its schools, and chairman of the building committee.[131] The African Civilization Society was located on Dean Street near Troy Avenue, the center of activity in Weeksville.[132] Later, in 1887, Perry founded the Messiah Baptist Church on the same block, which by 1895 boasted one of the largest Black congregations in the city.[133] The motto of the African Civilization Society in the years after the Civil War was "help us to help ourselves."[134]

Many Black leaders were critical of the Freedmen's Bureau for being White-dominated and not hiring more Black agents, and the AfCS promoted itself as the only organization working with freed Black people in the South that was run by Black men. Although they depended on monetary support from the Freedmen's Bureau, as did similar White-run organizations, they ran their programs independently and played a significant role in Reconstruction. The AfCS sent Black leaders and teachers to set up schools in Washington, D.C., Maryland, Virginia, North Carolina, Georgia, Mississippi, and Louisiana, reaching over 8,000 children and adults.[135] After Southern Democrats succeeded in drastically cutting the

Freedmen's Bureau's budget, the AfCS and other organizations working in the South no longer had sufficient funds to continue, and the AfCS closed its doors in 1869.[136]

Rufus Perry and other Black activists, however, had no intention of abandoning freed people as the promise of Reconstruction began to fade. Perry's vehicle for continuing the work became the Consolidated American Baptist Missionary Convention (CABMC), a national organization comprising many Black Baptist associations from all over the United States. Perry served as corresponding secretary for the CABMC from 1867 to 1877, and in 1869 he also took on the role of corresponding secretary for the Consolidated American Educational Association, a subsidiary of the CABMC which seemed to pick up where the African Civilization Society left off by "opening schools on a self-sustaining basis among ourselves, and giving employment to carefully-selected and approved colored teachers, believing that no body or society can educate us as well, permanently, and cheap as we can educate ourselves."[137] Later, Perry was active in the New England Baptist Missionary Convention, a regional reconstitution of the CABMC, serving as the organization's president from 1891 to 1892.

During his years as corresponding secretary for the CABMC, Rufus Perry often locked horns with the leadership of the White-run American Baptist Home Mission Society (ABHMS), the organization that had given its first missionary appointment to Thomas Merrill. Perry was considered "the most radical black Baptist of this period," and as corresponding secretary he held the most important office in the CABMC.[138] He and his colleagues bristled at what they referred to as "proscription" against Black Baptists within the Baptist denominational power structure and the ABHMS's financial policies.[139] Perry and the other CABMC leaders, "while condemning tokenism and cultural imperialism within the ABHMS, also repeatedly challenged its right to administer the funds given to it for Southern education and evangelization without being accountable to black Baptist leaders."[140] In 1869, Perry argued that the CABMC was a better steward of funds intended for freed people, writing:

> At the close of the war, societies sprung up all over the country for the help of the freedmen; and hundreds of thousands of dollars

> were subscribed, *but the freedmen never got it.* What has become of it? Where did it all go? Our convention has sent out a number of colored men as preachers, and they have done a good and great work. Ten thousand souls were brought into the church, and only $2,000 of money raised. The Home Mission's expenditures in this field were about 50,000, and they only received one-tenth as many as we did. We not only get the work for this money, but the funds are left in the hands of poor colored men, who are thereby enabled to support their families.[141]

Perry's belief that the wealthier ABHMS should share its resources with the CABMC and other Black Baptist organizations working in the South echoed an argument he had made earlier in the *Michigan Christian Herald* when trying to raise money to emigrate to Africa. As he wrote in 1862, "if the Missionary Union cannot support a mission in Africa, I believe the State of *Mich., could;* that is, by *withholding* a little from the M.U. I do not believe in 'robbing Peter to pay Paul,' as they say down in Dixie, but I do believe in the other saying—'dividing the spoils.'" He further makes the point that thousands of Black members of White Baptist churches had made contributions on behalf of foreign missions.[142]

While Rufus Perry operated on a national level through the auspices of the CABMC, he was also influential locally. He and his wife Charlotte made their home at 999 St. Mark's Avenue in an integrated neighborhood near Weeksville, where they raised their family of eight children.[143] Perry was very active in the Weeksville community and among his many endeavors he took an interest in the public schools. The principal of the Weeksville grammar school was Junius C. Morel, a Black activist who Perry knew from their days in the African Civilization Society. Under Morel's leadership, Colored School No. 2, which was later renamed Public School 68, became "one of the earliest integrated public schools, not only in its student body but also in its teaching staff, in New York state."[144] In 1869, a dismissed Black teacher was replaced by a White teacher, a move that proved controversial. Rufus Perry was among those who opposed the appointment of the White teacher, saying, "she must necessarily lack sympathy with colored people and their children. She did not love any of them; would not nurse or fondle them; would not visit their homes, and become intimate with their parents."[145] Clearly, Perry believed that effective teaching involved a regard for and personal investment in students, attributes that had characterized the Stones' approach to education.

His position in that particular case, however, should not be construed as favoring segregation. Quite the opposite. In 1873 when the board of education moved to maintain distinctions between Black and White schools, some of which were naturally integrating as neighborhoods changed, Rufus Perry wrote a stirring editorial in the *National Monitor* calling for collective action to promote integrated schools:

> We earnestly appeal to the "leaders" among the colored people in . . . Brooklyn [to protest] against having our colored youth any longer proscribed in the matter of public schools . . . . We do not ask that the colored public schools Nos. 1, 2, 3 and 4 shall be closed. Not at all. What we reasonably demand is that these schools take numerical rank with the other schools simply as public schools, and not as public schools for colored children only; and that colored children be allowed to attend any of the public schools most convenient without regard to color . . . if we desire that our loved ones growing up shall be freed from the bondage of ignorance . . . if we would heed the voice of the colored child as it cries almost from the womb for intellectual freedom, . . . let us have a grand mass meeting and protest against a proscription, which unless abolished, will consign our children and their children to intellectual inferiority . . . . Agitate! Agitate! Agitate! Till right shall win the victory.[146]

Rufus Perry's strong support of integration extended to all segments of society, and he often complained about the segregation he experienced in the public sphere. In 1870, the *Brooklyn Daily Eagle* reported that "the Rev. Rufus L. Perry, the leader and pastor of the Weeksville colored people, rebukes the white Republicans of the Ninth Ward, and especially one Dr. R. O. Sydney, in keeping up distinctions in meeting between the two elements of the Republican party." Perry was quoted as saying, "when the association meet, the whites sit to themselves and the colored members to themselves. Sedentary demarcation strikingly prevails among them. Why is it? Doctor, we are precariously ill with social ostracism. Give us, therefore, a large dose of social amalgamation mixed up with our political amalgamation."[147]

Perry remained active in politics throughout his life and was an influential voice among the Black people of Brooklyn. Although loyal to the "party of Lincoln," he nevertheless withdrew his support from Republican president Benjamin Harrison in his 1892 reelection bid because of his "stand regarding Southern outrages." Perry had been among a delegation of Black Baptist ministers who had visited President Harrison and come away disappointed with his failure to protect Black people against White violence in the South. The *Brooklyn Daily Eagle* reported Perry as saying, "I am utterly opposed to Mr. Harrison's re-election to the presidency . . . . He is no good . . . . Any man who is unable to protect the rights of citizens of this country is unfit to be voted for."[148]

In 1870, Perry began publishing and editing the *National Monitor*, the "spicy" paper which would serve as his primary platform for advocacy. As William Wells Brown wrote in 1882, "The NATIONAL MONITOR is a wide-awake journal, edited by Rufus L. Perry, a live man, in every sense of the term . . . . The columns of the paper show well the versatile character of the gentleman whose brain furnishes the mental food for its readers, and the cause of its widespread popularity."[149] The paper circulated throughout the United States—with Perry donating hundreds of copies to missionaries in the South—as well as in Canada, Haiti, and parts of Africa.[150] An 1877 advertiser's handbook promoted the paper as "a politico-religious and family newspaper, earnest and fearless in advocating equal rights," and "the very best advertising medium among our 500,000 colored Baptists."[151]

It is a shame that out of the hundreds of issues of the *National Monitor* published between 1870 and 1895, only a few survive. However, the extant issues provide insight into the newspaper and the man behind it. The motto appearing in the masthead reads: "*'God hath made of one blood all nations of men': Hence their common origin, common destiny, and their equal rights*," a pointed rejection of the racist polygenesis theory and an assertion of Black equality. In a July 1875 issue, Perry calls for reparations in a short piece titled "The Colored People. Educate Them." in which he writes that education "should be regarded by all as a debt owed to the colored people . . . for their generations of unrequited toil under a national system of slavery."[152] In another piece in the same issue, "Yet in Bondage," he describes his idea of White allyship: "as God lives, there are good men and women among the whites, who long to see us educated, elevated, and reckoned with American citizens and in society without disparagement. They may be seen behind us *pushing*, but never before us pulling. Those who wish to keep *before us* and pull, are not our best friends; for they pull unto themselves, and retreat as we draw near, leaving us to fall back and be bruised."

Perry continued to wield a "sword dipped in wrath" when he or others were maligned for their race, as illustrated in an 1871 letter to the editor of the *Brooklyn Daily Eagle*, a paper that was sometimes disparaging of Brooklyn's Black community:

> I am induced by the assumption that you would publish the truth, if you knew it, about "darkey preachers," as you are pleased to call colored clergymen, to send you this communication; hoping that it may enlighten you, and generate in the minds of your readers a higher opinion of "negro preachers" than you allow them (your readers) to entertain in your spasmodic editorial in yesterday's EAGLE . . . .
>
> The "game" that Perry and his friends are trying to get on, is fully set forth in a published report of their doings, . . . a copy of which I herewith send you. Dig into it. Probe it as deep as your erudite cranium, your Caucasian acumen, wit and journalistic sarcasm—all combined—will enable you; and then I challenge any disparagement you can give it, or any just condemnation of what "Perry and his friends" are doing.
>
> I know the worth of, and can duly appreciate a live local paper whatever its politics be, but I detest a watchman who is so goaded on by his prejudices that he will imagine and report false things about his neighbors.[153]

Late in his life, Rufus Perry published a book titled *The Cushite, Or, The Descendants of Ham, As Found in the Sacred Scriptures and in the Writings of Ancient Historians and Poets from Noah to the Christian Era*, a comprehensive theological and historical work demonstrating how "the Negro's ancient ancestry *led the way, and acted as the pioneers of mankind in the various untrodden fields of civilization.*"[154] A primary motive for writing the book was to address the rupture of Black people from their historical and genealogical past by the Middle Passage as well as to refute the Enlightenment's erasure of the contributions of African civilizations. As Perry wrote:

> The most favored race of men preach about their own superiority till it becomes a kind of second nature. Then they piously incorporate it in their religion, and put it in their schoolbooks to be imbibed by their children; and they tax their highest artistic skill to make a pleasing pictorial illustration of themselves, and an abominable caricature of the people whom they would subordinate and rob. The poor Indian and the Negro have been here and there driven to the wall and tauntingly told that they are naturally inferior and that subordination is their normal condition . . . . This provokes the thoughtful Negro to look back to his remote progenitors and trace up his lineage in the hope of finding something of ancestral greatness with which to repel this goading taunt, and which may kindle in his breast a decent flame of pride of race.[155]

Two years after Perry published *The Cushite,* the *Brooklyn Daily Eagle* ran a short piece on June 18, 1895, reporting that Rufus Perry was dying at his home. He had sunk into a coma, and his physicians had given up his case as hopeless.[156] He died that same day at the age of sixty-one. The next day the *Eagle* published his obituary, describing Perry as "one of the best known colored clergymen in the country," who "enjoyed a considerable reputation outside of Brooklyn . . . . He was clear, concise and earnest in his speech, and wrote with ease and force."[157] The *New York Times* eulogized him two days later, writing "born a slave in Tennessee, he became one of the most prominent colored clergymen in the United States." The *Times* went on to note that Perry "delivered a scientific lecture on 'Light" before the State University of Louisville, Ky., May 16, 1887; and in recognition received the degree of Doctor of Philosophy."[158]

Indeed, not only was Rufus Perry among the most accomplished of the Stones' students, he is arguably among the most distinguished alumni in the history of Kalamazoo College. Given the energy and passion he devoted to the cause of Black equality, one can easily imagine Perry walking alongside Dr. Martin Luther King had he lived during the era of the Civil Rights Movement. In his own time, though he did not lead a movement, he helped thousands of Black Americans feel their worth and achieve much more than American society, left to its own devices, would have allowed. In many ways, Rufus Perry can be understood as a forerunner to King, a Black Baptist minister and rousing orator, fearless in his commitment to racial justice. Though he had close colleagues in the fight, it seemed that he often battled alone via the pulpit and the press. One wonders if the never-ending fight eventually wore him down physically. He did not live nearly as long as James Stone, who died at seventy-eight, or Lucinda Stone, who died at eighty-six. Like King, Perry found solace and courage in his religion. In May of 1890, Perry preached to his congregation at the Messiah Baptist Church: "Might may for a time trample right under foot; we may be abused at times by the baser sort on account of our color or previous condition, but if we be on the Lord's side and God be for us, neither men nor devils can prevent an ultimate triumph in our struggle for what is purely right and essential to our social happiness and spiritual salvation." He then went on to articulate what might well be understood as his personal creed: "Doing proves being. Action shows life; inaction, death. What we do shows what we are, and how we do it shows the degree of our interest and the measure of our intelligence."[159] By any measure, Rufus Lewis Perry was deeply committed to making the United States live up to its ideals of freedom and equality and displayed a powerful brilliance in all that he did.

The lives of James Andrus Blinn Stone, Lucinda Hinsdale Stone, and Rufus Lewis Perry intersected during a tumultuous time in both the history of the country and of Kalamazoo College. During those years, these three passionate souls burned brightly, and their glow illuminated the institution as well. They must have recognized in each other kindred spirits—dissenters and heretics—unafraid to stand up for what they believed was right. Rufus Perry's warm feelings for what he referred to as "the *much beloved* Kalamazoo Theological Seminary" were likely due in large part to his relationship with James Stone. Many years later, Perry would recall the Stones with fondness on the occasion of a reunion of former pupils in 1885, writing, "I thank you, and through you the invitation committee; but I cannot have the pleasure of being with you except in mind and heart. The quarter of a century spent by Dr. and Mrs. Stone in earnest, indefatigable and successful labor in the cause of Christian education, abundantly entitles them to the reverence and especial consideration of all their former pupils . . . . May God grant them yet many days of unalloyed happiness, and make your reunion a real blessing to all who shall be fortunate enough to be present."[160]

While these three remarkable people continued lives of engagement and activism after their time at Kalamazoo College, the institution retreated into provincialism, becoming in every sense of the term an ivory tower—insular, lofty, and predominantly White. It would be many decades before the College would again gain some national renown and come even close to being able to claim the mantle of progressivism.

Endnotes

1 William J. Simmons and Henry McNeal Turner, *Men of Mark: Eminent, Progressive and Rising* (Cleveland, OH: G. M. Rewell & Company, 1887), 620.

2 Simmons and Turner, *Men of Mark*, 620.

3 David Freedman, "African American Schooling in the South Prior to 1861," *Journal of Negro History* 84, no. 1 (Winter, 1999): 23.

4 Daniel Wadkins, "Origin and Progress Before Emancipation," in *A History of the Colored Schools of Nashville, Tennessee*, ed. G.W. Hubbard (Nashville: Author, 1874), 5.

5 Crystal A. deGregory, "Nashville's Clandestine Black Schools," *New York Times*, February 17, 2015, https://opinionator.blogs.nytimes.com/2015/02/17/nashvilles-clandestine-black-schools/.

6 Freedman,"African American Schooling in the South Prior to 1861," 24.

7 Wadkins, "Origin and Progress Before Emancipation," 5.

8 Rufus Lewis Perry, letter to the editor, *Michigan Christian Herald*, July 11, 1861, Burton Historical Collection, Detroit Public Library.

9 Simmons and Turner, *Men of Mark*, 620–621.

10 Suzanne Spellen, "The Tale of a Pioneering African-American Father and Son: Rufus L. Perry Sr. and Jr.," *Brownstoner*, February 1, 2017, https://www.brownstoner.com/history/brooklyn-black-history-rufus-l-perry-crown-heights/.

11 "Anniversary Week at Kalamazoo," *Michigan Christian Herald*, June 27, 1861, Burton Historical Collection, Detroit Public Library. A record of the Theological Seminary's 1861 commencement exercises lists Rufus Perry's hometown as Chatham, C.W. (Canada West, as Ontario used to be known).

12 Paul Heike, "Out of Chatham: Abolitionism on the Canadian Frontier," in *Abolitionist Places*, ed. Martha Schoolman and Jared Hickman (New York: Routledge, 2013), 32.

13 It is also possible that while in Chatham Rufus Perry crossed paths with John Brown, abolitionist and architect of the 1859 raid on Harpers Ferry. In 1858, Brown traveled to Chatham to request Martin Delany's assistance in carrying out a plan to establish Kansas as an alternative terminus to the Underground Railroad. Delany agreed to help, and gathered sixty to seventy Black men, most of whom were fugitive slaves, for a convention held on May 8, 1858, a time when Rufus Perry may still have been in Chatham. Frank A. Rollin, *Life And Public Services of Martin R. Delany: Sub-assistant Commissioner Bureau Relief of Refugees, Freedmen, And of Abandoned Lands, And Late Major 104th U.S. Colored Troops* (Boston: Lee and Shepard, 1883), 87.

14 Rollin, *Life and Public Services of Martin R. Delany*, 83.

15 In a letter to the *Michigan Christian Herald*, October 22,1862, Perry says that "every body acquainted with me knows that for the last four years I have been laboring for this special work [to go to Africa]." Burton Historical Collection, Detroit Public Library.

16 Heike, "Out of Chatham," 36.

17 Constitution of the AfCS, https://archive.org/details/constitutionofaf00afri/page/1

18 Ibram X. Kendi, *Stamped from the Beginning: The Definitive History of Racist Ideas in America* (New York: Nation Books, 2016), 146.

19 The Dred Scott Decision: Opinion of Chief Justice Taney, United States Supreme Court (New York : Van Evrie, Horton & Co., 1860, c1859), Library of Congress, https://www.loc.gov/item/17001543/

20 *Constitution of the African Civilization Society* (New Haven, CT: Thomas J. Stafford, 1861), Supplement to the Constitution, https://archive.org/details/constitutionofaf00afri/page/1

21 Rollin, *Life and Public Services of Martin R. Delany*, 84.

22 "History of Abeokuta," Egba Progressive Association, Inc., http://egbaprogressive.org/history_of_abeokuta.php.

23 Britannica, T. Editors of Encyclopaedia. "Abeokuta." Encyclopedia Britanni-

ca, July 12, 2019, https://www.britannica.com/place/Abeokuta.

24 Rollin, *Life And Public Services of Martin R. Delany*, 307–308.

25 "African Civilization Society," *Brooklyn Daily Eagle*, November 15, 1870, 6.

26 R. Lewis Perry, letter to the editor, *Michigan Christian Herald*, July 11, 1861, Burton Historical Collection, Detroit Public Library.

27 Charles True Goodsell and Willis Frederick Dunbar, *Centennial History of Kalamazoo College* (Kalamazoo, MI: Kalamazoo College, 1933), 198.

28 Gail Griffin, "'Heretic': Lucinda Hinsdale Stone," in *Emancipated Spirits: Portraits of Kalamazoo College Women* (Kalamazoo, MI: Ihling Bros. Everard Co., 1983), 52–53.

29 Belle McArthur Perry, *Lucinda Hinsdale Stone, Her Life Story and Reminiscences* (Detroit, MI: The Blinn Publishing Company, 1902), 309.

30 Griffin, "'Heretic'," 67.

31 Elizabeth J. Harris, "The Education of a Yankee Schoolteacher American Girls: From Vermont to the Michigan Frontier—Memoirs and Sketches," unpublished manuscript, 77, February 2019, in author's possession.

32 Conrad Wright, "The Dedham Case Revisited," *Proceedings of the Massachusetts Historical Society* 100 (1988): 19, http://www.jstor.org/stable/25080991.

33 Mary Elizabeth Day Trowbridge, *History of Baptists in Michigan* (Michigan Baptist State Convention, 1909), 75.

34 Perry, *Lucinda Hinsdale Stone*, 82.

35 Perry, *Lucinda Hinsdale Stone*, 82.

36 Perry, *Lucinda Hinsdale Stone*, 82.

37 Minutes of the Second Anniversary of the Kalamazoo River Baptist Association, June 14 and 15, 1843, 11, Kalamazoo College Archives, Kalamazoo River Baptist Association, 1842–1857, Box 21, Folder 7.

38 William Lloyd Garrison, *The Letters of William Lloyd Garrison: From Disunionism to the Brink of War, 1850–1860,* ed. Louis Ruchames and Walter McIntosh Merrill (Cambridge, MA: Harvard University Press, 1971), 265. "From 1841 to 1848, *The Signal of Liberty* was the organ of the Liberty party of Michigan as well as of the Michigan Anti-Slavery Society. Apparently, both organizations were then under more or less identical leadership. The Michigan Anti-Slavery Society passed out of existence with the demise of the state Liberty Party and *The Signal of Liberty*, which suspended publication on February 5, 1848."

39 "Michigan State Anti-Slavery Society," *The Signal of Liberty*, February 13,

1847, 170.

40 William Livingstone, *Livingstone's History of the Republican Party: A History of the Republican Party from Its Foundation to the Close of the Campaign of 1900, Including Incidents of Michigan Campaigns and Biographical Sketches* (Detroit, MI: Wm. Livingstone, 1900), 32.

41 Harris, "The Education of a Yankee Schoolteacher," 269.

42 "A Lamentable Picture," *Kalamazoo Gazette*, December 16, 1856, 2, Kalamazoo Public Library (microfilm).

43 "A Lamentable Picture," 2.

44 "A Lamentable Picture," 2.

45 Perry, *Lucinda Hinsdale Stone*, 10.

46 Perry, *Lucinda Hinsdale Stone*, 10.

47 Perry, *Lucinda Hinsdale Stone*, 92.

48 Lucinda Hinsdale Stone, *An Episode in the History of Kalamazoo College: Letter to Hon. J.M. Gregory, L.L.D.* (Kalamazoo, MI, 1868), 21, Kalamazoo College Archives.

49 Perry, *Lucinda Hinsdale Stone*, 28.

50 Perry, *Lucinda Hinsdale Stone*, 29.

51 Perry, *Lucinda Hinsdale Stone*, 30.

52 Perry, *Lucinda Hinsdale Stone*, 30–31.

53 Lucinda H. Stone, "Effects of Mental Growth," in *The Education of American Girls, Considered in a Series of Essays*, ed. Anna C. Brackett (New York: G.P. Putnam's Sons, 1874), 193.

54 Perry, *Lucinda Hinsdale Stone*, 32.

55 Perry, *Lucinda Hinsdale Stone*, 35.

56 Perry, *Lucinda Hinsdale Stone*, 47.

57 Joe Glickman, "Tracing Natchez," HistoryNet, https://www.historynet.com/tracing-natchez.htm.

58 Eugene R. Dattel, "Cotton in a Global Economy: Mississippi (1800-1860)," Mississippi History Now, October 2006, http://mshistorynow.mdah.state.ms.us/articles/161/cotton-in-a-global-economy-mississippi-1800-1860.

59 National Park Service, "Visit Forks of the Road," https://www.nps.gov/thingstodo/about-forks-of-the-road.htm.

60 Perry, *Lucinda Hinsdale Stone*, 35.

61 Perry, *Lucinda Hinsdale Stone*, 35–36.

62 Perry, *Lucinda Hinsdale Stone*, 36.

63 Perry, *Lucinda Hinsdale Stone*, 40.

64 Excerpts from a Hinsdale Genealogy, 167, Lucinda Hinsdale Stone name file folder, Local History Room, Kalamazoo Public Library.

65 Perry, *Lucinda Hinsdale Stone*, 42.

66 Perry, *Lucinda Hinsdale Stone*, 37–38.

67 Perry, *Lucinda Hinsdale Stone*, 41–42.

68 D. Jordan Winthrop, *Tumult and Silence at Second Creek* (Baton Rouge: Louisiana State University Press, 1995), 41.

69 Winthrop, *Tumult and Silence at Second Creek*, 343. Letter from Lemuel Connor to General Polk, near Natchez, Miss., Dec. 12, 1861.

70 Winthrop, *Tumult and Silence at Second Creek*, 326. Statement of Pleasant Scott, a former slave who had been brought before the Examination Committee.

71 Mary Savage Conner, *Mary Savage Conner of Adams County, Mississippi: A Young Girl's Journal* (Redwood, MS: 1982), n. pag. Lemuel Conner was the cousin of Mary Conner, a close friend of the Helm children, and his family was part of the Helm's social circle.

72 Winthrop, *Tumult and Silence at Second Creek*, 226.

73 Winthrop, *Tumult and Silence at Second Creek*, 125.

74 Winthrop, *Tumult and Silence at Second Creek*, 243, 245, 248, 259, 268.

75 Griffin, "'Heretic'," 64.

76 Griffin, "'Heretic'," 64.

77 Lucinda Hinsdale Stone, "The New South," *Kalamazoo Gazette*, August 11, 1898, Kalamazoo Public Library.

78 Perry, *Lucinda Hinsdale Stone*, 43–44.

79 Kendi, *Stamped from the Beginning*, 10–11.

80 "Anniversary Week at Kalamazoo," *Michigan Christian Herald*, June 27, 1861, Burton Historical Collection, Detroit Public Library.

81 Samuel Brooks, *Historical Catalogue of the Students of Kalamazoo College and of Kalamazoo Theological Seminary, 1851–1902* (Kalamazoo, MI: Ihling Bros. & Everard, 1903), 71, https://cache.kzoo.edu/handle/10920/5593.

82 R. Lewis Perry, letter to the editor, *Michigan Christian Herald*, July 11, 1861, Burton Historical Collection, Detroit Public Library.

83 R. Lewis Perry, "African Civilization," *Michigan Christian Herald*, March 12, 1862, Burton Historical Collection, Detroit Public Library.

84 Perry, "African Civilization."

85 *Constitution of the African Civilization Society*, Supplement to the Constitution.

86 Perry, "African Civilization."

87 *Constitution of the African Civilization Society*, Supplement to the Constitution.

88 R. Lewis Perry, letter to the editor, *Michigan Christian Herald*, October 1, 1862, Burton Historical Collection, Detroit Public Library.

89 Judith Wellman, *Brooklyn's Promised Land: The Free Black Community of Weeksville, New York* (New York: New York University Press, 2014), Kobo Books.

90 Wellman, *Brooklyn's Promised Land.*

91 Griffin, "'Heretic'," 70.

92 Hinsdale Stone, *An Episode in the History of Kalamazoo College*, 5.

93 Griffin, "'Heretic'," 70.

94 Perry, *Lucinda Hinsdale Stone*, 83.

95 Goodsell and Dunbar, *Centennial History*, 70.

96 Harris, *Educating American Girls*, 269.

97 Harris, *Educating American Girls*, 273.

98 Goodsell and Dunbar, *Centennial History*, 70.

99 Hinsdale Stone, *An Episode in the History of Kalamazoo College*, 6–8.

100 Goodsell and Dunbar, *Centennial History*, 198.

101 Griffin, "'Heretic'," 70.

102 Goodsell and Dunbar, *Centennial History*, 71.

103 Goodsell and Dunbar, *Centennial History*, 68.

104 Hinsdale Stone, *An Episode in the History of Kalamazoo College*, 6–8.

105 Griffin, "'Heretic'," 72.

106 Goodsell and Dunbar, *Centennial History*, 67.

107 Goodsell and Dunbar, *Centennial History*, 66.

108 Perry, *Lucinda Hinsdale Stone*, 54.

109 James Andrus Blinn Stone. (1864). *Protest of James A. B. Stone made before the*

First Baptist Church of Kalamazoo, April 1st, 1864 (Kalamazoo, 1864), 1, https://babel.hathitrust.org/cgi/pt?id=mdp.39015071398872&view=2up&seq=1.

110 Hinsdale Stone, *An Episode in the History of Kalamazoo College*, 6–8.

111 Hinsdale Stone, *An Episode in the History of Kalamazoo College*, 17.

112 Stone, *Protest of James A.B. Stone.*

113 Griffin, "'Heretic'," 80.

114 Hinsdale Stone, *An Episode in the History of Kalamazoo College*, 43.

115 Goodsell and Dunbar, *Centennial History*, 72.

116 Rufus Perry appears in the 1859–60 catalogue as a member of the junior class in the Preparatory Department and in the 1860–61 catalogue as a "resident student" not associated with any particular class. Yet Perry was listed among the graduates of the Kalamazoo Theological Seminary in June 1861 in the *Michigan Christian Herald.* Catalogue of the Officers and Students of Kalamazoo College, 1859–60, 12, https://cache.kzoo.edu/handle/10920/39134; Catalogue of the Officers and Students of Kalamazoo College, 1860–61, 7, https://cache.kzoo.edu/handle/10920/39133; *Michigan Christian Herald*, July 11, 1861, Burton Historical Collection, Detroit Public Library.

117 A Pastor, "An Inquiry," *Michigan Christian Herald*, October 1, 1862, Burton Historical Collection, Detroit Public Library.

118 R. Lewis Perry, letter to the editor, *Michigan Christian Herald*, October 1, 1862, Burton Historical Collection, Detroit Public Library.

119 Perry, "African Civilization Society."

120 Perry, "African Civilization Society."

121 R. Lewis Perry, "African Civilization," *Michigan Christian Herald*, May 28, 1862, Burton Historical Collection, Detroit Public Library.

122 Simmons, *Men of Mark*, 621–625.

123 Trowbridge, *History of Baptists in Michigan*, 75.

124 Griffin, "'Heretic'," 47.

125 "Kalamazoo women's rights pioneer Lucinda Hinsdale Stone honored by Congressman Upton," MLive, March 29, 2014, https://www.mlive.com/news/kalamazoo/2014/03/kalamazoo_womens_rights_pionee.html.

126 Perry, *Lucinda Hinsdale Stone*, 65.

127 Griffin, "'Heretic'," 86–88.

128 Griffin, "'Heretic'," 92.

129 Griffin, "'Heretic'," 113.

130 Wellman, *Brooklyn's Promised Land.*

131 Wellman, *Brooklyn's Promised Land.*

132 Wellman, *Brooklyn's Promised Land.*

133 "Rev. Rufus L. Perry Dying," *Brooklyn Daily Eagle*, June 18, 1885, 4.

134 Carol Faulkner, "'A Proper Recognition of Our Manhood': The African Civilization Society and the Freedmen's Aid Movement," *Afro-Americans in New York Life and History* 24, no. 1 (January 31, 2000): 41–62.

135 Faulkner, "'A Proper Recognition of Our Manhood,'" 8.

136 Faulkner, "'A Proper Recognition of Our Manhood,'" 11.

137 Consolidated American Educational Association, 1869, 10, microfilm, Reel R-82H, American Baptist Historical Society, Atlanta, Georgia.

138 James Melvin Washington, *Frustrated Fellowship: The Black Baptist Quest for Social Power* (Macon, GA: Mercer University Press, 1986), 85.

139 Washington, *Frustrated Fellowship*, 84.

140 Washington, *Frustrated Fellowship*, 95.

141 Washington, *Frustrated Fellowship*, 102.

142 Perry, "African Civilization."

143 Wellman, *Brooklyn's Promised Land*; also 1880 Census.

144 Wellman, *Brooklyn's Promised Land.*

145 Wellman, *Brooklyn's Promised Land.*

146 Rufus Perry, editorial in the National Monitor reprinted in the *Brooklyn Daily Eagle*, July 28, 1873, 4.

147 "Republican Troubles in the Ninth Ward," *Brooklyn Daily Eagle*, October 22, 1870, 6.

148 "Says Harrison Is 'No Good'," *Brooklyn Daily Eagle*, July 20, 1892, 10.

149 William Wells Brown, T*he Rising Son, Or, The Antecedents and Advancement of the Colored Race* (Boston: A.G. Brown and Co., 1874), 533.

150 "Free Distribution of Monitors," *National Monitor*, July 29, 1875, 2; William Cathcart, *Baptist Encyclopaedia* (Philadelphia, PA: Louis H. Everts, 1883), 829.

151 *Pettingill's Newspaper Directory And Advertisers' Hand-book* (New York: S. M. Pettengill, 1877), 29, https://babel.hathitrust.org/cgi/pt?id=umn.31951002264809d&view=2up&seq=49&size=175&q1=monitor.

152 Rufus Perry, "The Colored People. Educate Them," *National Monitor*, July 29,

1875, 1.

153 Rufus Perry, letter to the editor, *Brooklyn Daily Eagle*, January 27, 1871, 2.

154 T. McCants Stewart, "Introduction," in Rufus L. Perry, *The Cushite, Or, The Descendants of Ham* (Springfield, MA: Wiley & Co., 1893), iii–iv.

155 Rufus L. Perry, *The Cushite, Or, The Descendants of Ham, As Found in the Sacred Scriptures and in the Writings of Ancient Historians and Poets from Noah to the Christian Era* (Springfield, MA: Wiley & Co., 1893), 12.

156 "Rev. Rufus L. Perry Dying," *Brooklyn Daily Eagle*, June 18, 1895, 4.

157 "Dr. Rufus L. Perry's Death, Well Known as a Clergyman, Author and Journalist," *Brooklyn Daily Eagle*, June 19, 1895, 4.

158 "The Rev. Rufus L. Perry Dead," *New York Times*, June 20, 1895, 16.

159 "A Sermon by the Rev. Rufus L. Perry, D.D., at Messiah Baptist Church," *Brooklyn Daily Eagle*, May 19, 1890, 1.

160 Julia Gilbert Elder, *Reunion of Former Pupils of Rev. J. A. B. Stone, D. D., and Mrs. L. H. Stone* (Kalamazoo, MI: Kalamazoo Publishing Company, 1886), 51.

Chapter Three

The Shape of Things

After the fiery Stone years, Kalamazoo College's institutional identity, attitudes, and values cooled and hardened into a shape that would last for a very long time. It was a shape that brimmed with moral certainty and that held beliefs in American progress, the evolution of races from savage to barbaric to civilized, the rightful dominance of Christianity, and the universality of a Western White male truth. Implicit in its disposition was the superiority of White Americans, a belief so pervasive it was taken almost as a law of nature, reflecting entrenched racial and colonial hierarchies in the country at large.

Having formed a state (a political community governed by laws), White Americans during these years were seeking also to become a nation (a people who share a common ancestry).[1] The nation part was obviously more problematic, given the presence of an Indigenous population, freed people of African descent, a White population that had come from various parts of Europe, and a steady stream of new immigrants from across the globe. As a result, White Americans became intent on assimilating those whom they believed to be assimilable and banishing, in one form or another, those whom they believed were not.

It was in the late 1800s that Richard Henry Pratt established the Carlisle Indian Industrial School in Carlisle, Pennsylvania, to assimilate Native youth by isolating them from their families and stripping them of their language and culture. His catch phrase "Kill the Indian, save the man" resonated widely, and similar schools cropped up all over the country, including two in Michigan. Meanwhile, freed Black people and Chinese immigrants, seen as unassimilable, were shut out of mainstream society, their exile codified in the complex set of laws, ordinances, and policies comprising Jim Crow segregation and in the Chinese Exclusion Act of 1882.

While many openly espoused "America for White people," more progressive Americans, including many American Baptists, believed that Black people as well as Chinese and other immigrants could and should be part of American society, as long as they adopted Christianity and conformed to White social norms. Regardless of where White Americans stood on these issues, few disputed that the "common ancestry" that would define the U.S. national character should be some shade of Christian and White.

The New White City

As the turn of the twentieth century approached, White Americans basked in a self-congratulatory narrative of enlightenment and progress and marveled at their accomplishments as the Industrial Revolution spawned seemingly limitless new technologies and wealth. Nowhere was this braggadocio more on display than during the 1893 Columbian World Exposition in Chicago. Intended to celebrate 400 years of civilization's advance since Columbus's arrival in the Americas, the World's Fair, as it was commonly known, thrummed with the racial and colonial thinking of the time. The aptly named "White City," a complex of neoclassical buildings painted white, constituted a vaunting monument to Western Civilization. Juxtaposed against these gleaming edifices lay the Midway Plaisance featuring living dioramas of cultures from around the world arranged according to where Fair organizers believed they fell on the continuum from "savage" to "civilized."[2]

Intersecting at the Fair were three familiar nineteenth century activists, all well advanced in age and still advocating for their respective constituencies. Lucinda Hinsdale Stone had been invited by the Michigan Board of World's Fair Managers to serve on a committee of fine arts.[3] Frederick Douglass, former ambassador to Haiti and longtime acquaintance of Lucinda Stone, had been asked to represent Haiti, the only Black nation with a pavilion in the White City. And Simon Pokagon, a renowned

Potawatomi leader from southwest Michigan, whose father Leopold had negotiated a reprieve for his people during the 1833 Treaty of Chicago, had been invited to speak on Chicago Day, a nod to the fact that Chicago had been built on Potawatomi land.

Of the three, Lucinda Stone alone participated wholeheartedly. She wrote enthusiastically about the upcoming Fair, embracing its theme of progress and human evolution in which people of Western European descent were cast as the most advanced: "There will be Egyptian art representing the ideas of the oldest people of whom we yet know anything; there will be Indian art; Persian art; ancient Assyrian art; art of the American Indian, the Aztecs and Mexicans, the art of the Mound Builders and cliff dwellers, many masterpieces of each represented and all so arranged that one may trace the successive steps of improvement."[4] Picking up on her theme of "the Old White City and the New," she went on to compare the present moment in America to the European Renaissance: "this other rebirth of the world of which we celebrate by our Columbian Exposition . . . is but a hint of a time coming of which this World's Fair is a sure prophecy and an instrumentality to bring about the greatness and power of which I do not think any of us begin to apprehend."[5]

Though she had advocated for women's equality her entire life, she did not dwell on the social disparities lurking behind the New White City's façade. Forty-five years after the first women's rights convention in Seneca Falls, discrimination against women continued unabated, most egregiously in the denial of suffrage. Yet Stone was full of optimism and hope. Perhaps this was because she and other White women had had a hand in the organization of the Fair and were favorably represented in the Woman's Building, of which Stone was particularly proud. "The Woman's Building will afford a study for days in its exterior ornamentation and interior decoration," she wrote. "Every figure has its meaning and the same thought runs through all. The genius of woman, a factor in civilization!"[6]

Her enthusiasm was not shared by Frederick Douglass or Simon Pokagon, both of whom approached the Fair with a great deal of ambivalence. Where Stone perceived rebirth, Pokagon saw the death of a cherished way of life and Douglass the slow burial of Black hopes and aspirations. African Americans had advocated strongly for a role in planning the Fair and for an exhibit showcasing their accomplishments since Emancipation, but the Board of Managers had rebuffed their many overtures. Determined that fair-goers should know about this systematic exclusion and intent on drawing attention to rampant lynchings in the South,[7] the young journalist and activist Ida B. Wells and her future husband F. L. Barnett began assembling a pamphlet titled *The Reason Why the Colored American Is Not at the World's Columbian Exposition*, which they planned to circulate throughout the White City. Douglass provided the introduction to the pamphlet, in which he lamented that "this World's Columbian Exposition, with its splendid display of wealth and power," was for the Black people of America "a whited sepulcher." "Though [slavery] is now gone," he wrote, "its asserted spirit remains."[8]

Having seen his life's work as an abolitionist finally rewarded with the Emancipation Proclamation and the great strides made by freed people during the all-too-brief Reconstruction period, Douglass was now witnessing White supremacy's "redemption," which was birthing the repressive system that would come to be known as Jim Crow. Just a few years before his death, Black people were facing conditions not much different from slavery. No wonder his mood was somber.

Yet for Stone and other erstwhile abolitionists, the ongoing oppression of Black Americans had receded from front of mind, the issues muddied and eclipsed by impulses to "unify the country"—a euphemism for appeasing former slave-holders—and prevailing notions of "uplift suasion,"[9] which placed the onus on Black people to convince White Americans of their acceptability. What's more, the nostalgic Lost Cause narrative had begun to obscure the horrors of slavery and the South's bloody defense of it by spinning a gauzy tale of gentility, honor, and "states' rights." These ways of thinking foregrounded the needs of the White majority, obscured the effects of widespread and worsening racial discrimination, and blamed Black people for their struggles.

Douglass sought to confront these views in a speech on "Colored People's Day," a time set aside especially for Black people to attend the Exposition. Wells had urged him to boycott the occasion, which Barnett referred to as "the refinement of irony" given the Fair's ostracism of Black people in planning the event.[10] Douglass, however, was determined to make the best of it. So that afternoon under the glaring August sun, the seventy-five-year-old statesman ascended the podium to address "The Race Problem in America." Shortly into his speech, jeers from White hecklers caused Douglass to put aside his prepared remarks. He looked out over the audience of about 2,500 people and spoke from his heart. "Men talk of the Negro problem. There is no Negro problem," he declared, his voice rising. "The problem is whether the American people have loyalty enough, honor enough, patriotism enough to live up to their own Constitution." "We Negroes love our country," he went on. "We fought for it. We ask only that we be treated as well as those who fought against it."[11]

Like Douglass, Simon Pokagon hoped to use the Fair as a platform to advocate for his people while dreading the ways in which the Fair's organizers would choose to represent them. He had pushed for a delegation of American Indian tribes to participate in the Fair on the same footing as delegations from other countries and to portray themselves to the world on their own terms. Instead, Native people were represented by ethnographer Frederic Ward Putnam on the Midway Plaisance as anthropological studies "consigned to the past, along with other obstacles overcome along the path of progress."[12] Perhaps most painful to Pokagon was a *Chicago Daily Tribune* article titled "Return as Freaks," referring to the Potawatomi encampment on the Midway. The lead-in to the article read: "Descendants of Chicago's Original Settlers Come to Town. Indians of the Pottawatomie and Winnebago Tribes Arrive on the Plaisance and in Camp Will Be One of the Strange Features of that Queer Thoroughfare."[13]

The only future White people could imagine for American Indians was an assimilated one, and many applauded the Bureau of Indian Affairs' exhibit showcasing students from Indian boarding schools designed "to show the people what the Government of the United States is doing for the Indian."[14] An editorial in the *Chicago Daily Tribune* had praised the boarding schools as a viable solution to the "Indian Problem." "After Being Pushed from the Atlantic Coast to the Heart of the Continent," the subhead read, "the Noble Red Man Is at Last Willing to Sit at the Feet of His White Conqueror and Listen to the Words of Teachers."[15]

When it came time to speak on Chicago Day, Simon Pokagon was diplomatic, addressing his Native countrymen and beseeching them to "lay aside all bitterness of spirit" despite feeling "the sting of neglect because your rights have been ignored in taking part in the world's great Fair."[16] But like Wells, Barnett, and Douglass, Pokagon had written a pamphlet that was circulating among fair-goers and carrying a very different message.

Printed on birch bark, *The Red Man's Rebuke* sharply condemned American colonization of Indigenous lands. As Pokagon wrote, "in behalf of my people, the American Indians, I hereby declare to you, the pale-faced race that has usurped our lands and homes, that we have no spirit to celebrate with you the great Columbian Fair now being held in this Chicago city, the wonder of the world. No; sooner would we hold high joy-day over the graves of our departed fathers, than to celebrate our own funeral, the discovery of America."

While White Americans rejoiced in 400 years of "progress," Pokagon mourned the destruction left in its wake: "The cyclone of civilization rolled westward; the forests of untold centuries were swept away; streams dried up; lakes fell back from their ancient bounds; and all our fathers once loved to gaze upon was destroyed, defaced or marred, except the sun, moon, and starry skies above, which the Great Spirit in his wisdom hung beyond their reach." [17]

These counternarratives offered by Douglass and Pokagon revealed the White City as artifice. Indeed, the erection of the buildings had been rushed, the construction flimsy, their exteriors hastily painted to be ready in time for opening day. All that mattered was the image of American greatness being projected to the world. White Americans lovingly embraced this image and internalized it. Although Douglass and Pokagon both hoped for an America in which the promises of freedom, equality, and opportunity would extend to their people and believed that striving to make those promises a reality was the only viable path forward, their lived experiences had taught them a truth that White Americans could not grasp. The White City with its illusion of grandeur stood on shaky foundations, as did America's claims to equality. And yet the illusion was powerful and persistent.

The illusion dazzled a student from Kalamazoo College visiting the Fair in August of 1893. Caught up in the theme of human evolution from savagery to civilization, she provided a review of musical performances by various cultures for the *Index*, the College's student newspaper. Writing approvingly of the American Indian students from the Haskell Institute and their brass band, she noted that "one had to look closely at race characteristics to realize them different from any other student band in America. This was their attempt, as civilized Indians, to play our music and they did it well." The Javanese ensemble, however, made a less pleasing impression. "Of all monotonous sounds to an ear untrained in Javanese melody, these were the extreme," though, she allowed, "it may be lack of education on my part that prevents my appreciation of their efforts." The Japanese four-piece orchestra she found "as monotonous as the Javanese, only worse, accompanied by a droning nasal singing which set one's teeth on edge." As the editors of the *Index* summed it up, "music hath charms to sooth the savage breast, but that produced by the savage does not always sooth the civilized man."[18]

This was the racial and colonial context that permeated Kalamazoo College in the late nineteenth century and well into the twentieth. Assumptions of White superiority went unquestioned. Indeed, the narrative of White civilization and its mainstay, Christianity, served as an organizing principle for academic and social life at the College.

The Ivory Tower

In the late 1870s, the Kalamazoo College campus consisted of Lower Hall—originally Lucinda Stone's Female Department—on the corner of South Street and Michigan Avenue, and Upper Hall, the men's dormitory, later renamed Williams Hall, set on the other side of Michigan Avenue part way up a thickly wooded hill.[19] Arcadia Creek burbled along the railroad tracks at the base of the slope, opening up into Mirror Lake (more of a pond, really), which figured prominently in campus life and students' imaginations. With the addition of Ladies' Hall in 1887 and Bowen Hall in 1902, the College began to concentrate the campus on the wooded hillside that had been purchased by James Stone back in 1845 with financial assistance from his friend Leonard Slater, among others. As the years went by, new College buildings gradually ascended the slope until they formed the modern quadrangle. From atop the hill, one could take in an expansive view of the valley where the city of Kalamazoo grew a little more each year. As a student remarked in 1877 in the very first issue of the *Index*, "could the wild Indian of a hundred years ago return from his happy hunting-ground to look again from our high position upon the plain below, he would not recognize it as once his own happy resort. Here, where nature, for long years, greeted his dusky brethren with her sweetest smiles, the white man has chosen to dwell, and no trace of the aborigines is left save the name of the lovely village of Kalamazoo, nestling at our feet."[20]

It had not been that long since the forced removal of the Potawatomi, less than forty years, and many Potawatomi continued to live in Southwest Michigan. But they had quickly become the stuff of legend and were already being woven into the College's origin story as symbols of a wilder era tamed by the founders and other early pioneers.

Like many small liberal arts colleges, Kalamazoo describes itself as a tight-knit community, but the present campus culture does not begin to approach the closely woven social fabric of the late 1800s and early 1900s. The College was small, with no more than 15 faculty and a student body of under 200 for most of the nineteenth century. Student enrollment began to grow beginning in the 1920s, ranging from around 200 to as high as 700 by the late 1940s, with the size of the faculty increasing commensurately to around 50.[21] The community was also homogenous—White, Christian or at least secularly Christian, mostly from Michigan, and middle to upper-middle class. Students, then as now, took their studies seriously, and the academics were rigorous. Academic and social life were fully integrated, with faculty members chaperoning student social activities, hosting students in their homes, and serving as critics for oratorical competitions. Amusing in-class exchanges between popular professors and students were printed in the *Index*. Herbert Lee Stetson, who joined the faculty in 1900 as a professor of psychology and went on to serve as president from 1912–1922, was a particular favorite. Genial and witty, distinguished yet approachable, he was revered by generations of students. Presidents in general were much more involved with students in those days, often teaching classes and leading Bible studies.

Students were urged to join a literary society and virtually all did. These societies, Kalamazoo College's more staid versions of fraternities and sororities, drove the social life at the institution. They organized sleigh rides and skating parties in the winter and lakeside picnics and "field days" (athletic contests) in the warmer months, hosted teas and oyster suppers, held debates, and put on "spreads." There were friendly competitions between classes, including a tug-of-war every fall over Mirror Lake. Each class chose its own colors and class "yell," which reflected school pride and fostered a common identity. The yells changed every year, but this one, said to come from Aristophanes' play *The Frogs*, had lasting appeal:

Breck-ki-ki-kex! Ko-ax! Ko-ax!
Breck-ki-ki-kex! Ko-ax! Ko-ax!

Whoa-up! Whoa-up!
Paraballou! Paraballou!
Kalamazoo! Kazoo! Kazoo![22]

By far the most anticipated social event of the year, for students and faculty alike, was the Washington Banquet. Begun in 1889[23] when the still-young country was intent on building up its traditions and defining its national character, this celebration of George Washington's birthday featured a formal dinner with toasts and speeches. In the 1920s, during Allan Hoben's presidency, dancing was finally allowed.[24] Young men would save their money for weeks in order to afford the tickets for themselves and their dates. The Banquet foregrounded loyalty and patriotism and rehearsed American ideals forged during the Revolution and the early days of independence. The event proved impressively durable, lasting until about 1966.[25]

Students were aware that George Washington had owned slaves but were not much bothered by it. On the contrary, in some years Washington's slaves were featured as a means of evoking that earlier time. At the Banquet in 1894, a student read a ballad titled "Mt. Vernon," full of nostalgia for the genteel life enjoyed on Washington's plantation. In setting the scene for Washington's triumphant return from war, she described:

Little darkies, black as ink
With gleaming eyes and hair akink,
Huddled about together.
And when they heard the stately tread
Of Martha Washington they fled
Like leaves in windy weather.[26]

In 1913, the *Index* reported that the "much-looked-for and long expected social event of the college year took place at the New Burdick Hotel . . . Everything was in keeping with the occasion, from the picture of Washington in the first dress suit of the eighteenth century, to the chocolate-drop waiters, who fairly outdid themselves." "Washington, too, we are told, was partial to this kind of waiters," the writer noted, "having several around the house."[27] In subsequent years, the Banquet continued to be held at the Burdick Hotel, "where every luxury was enjoyed—from dress suits, cabs, and flowers, down to colored waiters in livery."[28] With the onset of World War I, some luxuries were sacrificed and the Banquet was moved to campus and held in Bowen Hall. "Colored waiters" may have been among the "luxuries" students gave up as they were not mentioned again in descriptions of the Banquet.

For the most part, Black people, American Indians, people of Asian descent, and other people of color were absent from thought and irrelevant to daily life at Kalamazoo College. The institution's identity was explicitly Christian and implicitly White. When people of color did come to mind, it was usually as social "problems," objects of missionary work, or sources of fun and entertainment, such as to provide scenery for events like the Washington Banquet or fodder for jokes that were sometimes printed in the *Index*. Now and then the societies would put on ethnically themed banquets or musical performances. Japanese and Chinese themes were especially popular. As part of the Junior Carnival in 1920, the "Kappa Pi girls ran a Japanese tea-room that was unique in its decorations to say the least," the *Index* reported. "Prettily costumed [J-p] girls were much in evidence and during the course of the evening Katharine Bennett and Genevieve Whalley presented a clever little Japanese dance."[29]

There was also the occasional minstrel show or blackface performance, an enduring fixation that would come into full flower on campus in the 1950s. The habit of seniors attending minstrel shows in town is mentioned in the *Index* as early as 1883.[30] As vaudeville grew in popularity in the early part of the twentieth century, blackface acts and full-blown minstrel shows became more common on college campuses, and Kalamazoo was no exception. These performances often occurred as part of events organized by the literary societies or concerts given by the Glee Club and Gaynor Club, the men's and women's singing groups. It would usually be one act in blackface or "in dialect," as in 1909 when the "Gaynor Girls, dressed as negro 'mammies,' carrying pickaninnies, gave 'Hush, Yo' Honey, Hush.'" "This selection pleased the audience especially," the *Index* reported, "because the make-up of the young ladies was so realistic and their rendition of the lullaby so perfect."[31] Similar acts appeared sporadically throughout the 1910s. Every now and then the concerts would include "American Indian songs."[32] In 1918, the Gaynor Club concert was to feature "a group of Indians, who will sing and Princess Red Feather will give a demonstration of Indian and bird calls."[33] As reported in the *Index* the following week, "the Indian songs and 'calls' were weird and effective."[34]

In April of 1919, the seniors put on a much-touted minstrel show. "Friday night in Bowen hall there was introduced to the college and friends talent, previously unheard of, displayed in the form of a minstrel show," the *Index* reported. "Soon after eight o'clock, the curtain arose (or rather was drawn aside) on some dozen handsome Negroes. Two wore fancy plantation costumes, while the rest wore dress suits. The men were sitting in a semi-circle with the interlocutor in the center. Harold Andrews (a white man) filled this place." Of course, they were all White men made up in blackface, but they seemed real enough for the audience. The article also referenced "the exquisite dancing of a Negro lady," also a White student.[35] That same year, the Regent, a vaudeville theater regularly featuring blackface acts, opened in downtown Kalamazoo.[36] The Regent was a sponsor of the *Index* and often ran advertisements in the paper. An ad in 1919 touted "A Japanese Revue" with "Six Gorgeous Girls in an Oriental Novelty" and "Kalamazoo's Favorite Comedians Adams & Guhl in their Blackface Comedy Riot, 'The Equinelent.'"[37] Between visits to the Regent and performances on campus, minstrelsy was a regular staple of student entertainment throughout the 1920s.

Students were not shy about employing blackface, but they sometimes referred to the practice coyly, as sort of an inside joke. In a review of the campus play *Seventeen* performed in 1923, the writer lauded the student who played the humorous role of the "negro servant," saying that "he certainly wins the hand-painted huckleberries in that part." In a review of the Kappa Karnival later that year, the *Index* mentioned "six Kappa tars who sang, danced, and joked." And an article in 1924 about an upcoming Kappa vaudeville show teased that one of the acts, "from secretly gained information, promises to be a 'corker,'"[38] perhaps referring to the burnt cork traditionally used in blackface make-up. Such performances continued through the 1930s and 1940s, though far less frequently.

In the 1930s, American Indian themes became popular in campus entertainment. The surge in interest came after the city of Kalamazoo put on a historical pageant featuring "Indians" as part of its centennial celebration in 1929. Several students played roles in the pageant as "bold bad Indians and dashing pioneers."[39] In 1931, students held a "Bucks and Indian Maids Pow-Wow." According to the *Index*, "Trowbridge [residence hall] parlors changed their color Saturday evening into the festive shades of an Indian village. Indian blankets, missed by residents of Williams hall on the crisp autumnal nights previous to the party, were found on the walls. There were tepees in the corners, and underbrush in which wild animals lurked—an earless rabbit, a bird, and one squirrel. The girls wore their war-paint, and Big Chief Duane Yates made much music."[40]

Four years after the city of Kalamazoo marked its centennial, Kalamazoo College held its own centennial celebration in 1933. As with the city's festivities, "Indians" were featured in a historical pageant held on the quad with actors in redface. Faculty, alumni, and students played roles in the drama, which was narrated by Charles Goodsell, vice president of the College and professor of history. According to the *Index*, the "presentation was cleverly and artistically handled in five scenes. The first was the 'Primitive Age,' opening with the muffled, rhythmic beat of the tom-tom of the somber American Indian ritual. The rites were interrupted by the rough and ready adventurous white men who pushed their way into the scene. These hardy men were led by Titus Bronson, the first settler of this district . . . Gun in hand he led the Indians to hunt and later with axe and pick began the conquest of the wild growth about them."[41] After the pioneers "make a conquest and drive the Indians out,"[42] Thomas Merrill arrives from the East "to introduce education and teach Christianity to the Western settlers."[43]

The centennial pageant was an example of how the College would use American Indians to add a sense of daring and adventure to the story of its founding. The Indians, seen as savage and benighted, cast into relief the "civilization" and illumination of Christian learning brought to the Michigan "wilderness" by Thomas Merrill and Caleb Eldred. The drama assumed White superiority and the inevitability of conquest. Though the White settlers were initially cast as interlopers who "pushed their way into the scene," their "rough and ready" and "adventurous" spirit was associated with American progress, whereas the "somber" and "primitive" Indians suggested a people in stasis. Serving merely as a prop, nothing about the generic "Indians" depicted in the pageant was authentic. But authenticity was not the point. By 1933, a romanticized myth of the American Indian had taken hold and was much more important to White Americans than the disquieting reality.

In many ways, the ivory tower replicated the vainglory of the White City in its reverence of Western Civilization and celebration of White

American accomplishments. Other cultures were often depicted as they were on the Midway Plaisance, as sideshows offering entertainment, the thrill of the exotic, and a foil to elevate the White protagonist in the great American saga.

"The Negro Problem"

When Black people and other people of color were not being conjured for entertainment, they were studied as "problems." In 1901, the *Index* held an essay contest, and the winning essay, "The Negro Problem," laid out one student's view of the issue. He began by asserting that White people had only themselves to blame for the character flaws he perceived in Black people, which were many. "The negro is but a mirror," he wrote, "and he but reflects his surroundings and the lessons we have taught him." The writer traced the problem back to slavery, making the unremarkable observation that "many a slave owner held no regard for the rights or the honor of those who were compelled to do his bidding." As a result, "the slave became the victim of his licentiousness and passion." This "licentiousness and passion" apparently stuck to its victims but not to its White perpetrators. The writer went on to describe "criminal negroes," who seemed to be his main concern, stating that "many of them are mulattoes, many come from homes (if they can be called such) where no regard is held for the sacredness of the marriage ties, many are of illegitimate parentage." Without citing his own credentials for offering solutions to the "Negro Problem," he asserted that "many schemes have been proposed, usually by theorists who knew nothing of the race except by hearsay." He went on to discredit these "many schemes" starting with the "theory" that "if the negro be freed and placed in the same circumstances as his master, he would soon become his equal." "Such a plan was, in a measure, adopted," he stated, referencing some mythical time and place in America when Black people were free from oppression, "and the failure has been a signal one."

Education, in his view, was also not the answer because "the negro is not a decendant [*sic*] of a cultured or scholarly race." Therefore, "when we put him in a school," the writer explained, "he lacks that inherent taste for study, his home surroundings are not such as to inspire him with a love for learning and, as a result, he makes an utter failure." Nor could the "Negro Problem" be solved "by the white absorbing the black race."

"The Caucasian race will never consent to be degraded by the infusion of Ethiopian blood," for "the greatest criminals come from the mingling of races. We must not combine the daring and audacity of the white with the passion and indolence of the black." The only remaining alternatives were, according to the author, to "educate the negro women" for "an army is no stronger than the mothers who bore them," and to "give the negro an industrial rather than an Academic education." "The black race is a burden and a disgrace which the Americans have brought upon themselves," he concluded, "and it is but just that they make amends."[44]

The *Index* editors assured their readers that for "the two essays that were awarded prizes in THE INDEX essay contest we have no apologies to offer, whatever . . . The essays speak for themselves, and show good work on the part of the authors. We are very much pleased with the result of this contest." The editors then thanked the judges of the essays, who were three clergymen from nearby cities.[45]

The appropriateness of an industrial rather than an "academic," or liberal arts, education for Black people was a popular idea at the time, one championed by Booker T. Washington, principal of the Tuskegee Institute in Alabama. The thinking was that Black people should be prepared for service work rather than leadership positions, an approach that appealed to White philanthropists who were investing in educational institutions for freed people in the South during these years. White philanthropists wanted to educate Black people so that they would not be a burden on society, but many also wanted to keep them from becoming too ambitious.[46]

When Booker T. Washington visited the city of Kalamazoo in January of 1896, many students went to hear him speak. This was just a few months after Washington delivered his "Atlanta Exposition Address," later referred to as the "Atlanta Compromise" by W. E. B. Du Bois because of its accommodationist message. Though Washington privately supported civil rights and Black empowerment, he publicly advocated for an approach that was more acceptable to White donors, namely, that Black people should start at the bottom of society and gradually, over time, work their way up.[47] In Atlanta, Washington assured his largely White audience that "the wisest among my race understand that the agitation of questions of social equality is the extremest folly, and that progress in the enjoyment of all the privileges that will come to us must be the result of severe and constant struggle rather than of artificial forcing."[48]

In Kalamazoo, Washington delivered a similar message that was recounted in the *Index*. "The race problem is one of the greatest, if not the greatest problem that confronts the American people," the article began, a typical opener when addressing the "Negro Problem." "There are many solutions proposed for this question," the student went on. "One says the only thing to do with the negro is to send him back to Africa, another would put all of the colored people in a part of our unoccupied territory and let them form a separate state. But these solutions are not practical." The only viable solution, then, was the one offered by Booker T. Washington—an industrial education. "At the close of the war the negroes began at the top; they wanted to go to congress or at least be governor," the student said referring to the brief time of relative freedom during Reconstruction when many Black men were elected to public office. "They had always worked and now they thought they could do without work." "Slavery took away the executive power from the negroes and it is going to take time to regain it," the writer continued, echoing a common refrain of that time. "When a black gets faith in himself and has a training to see and grasp opportunities, then he will stand on an equal footing with the white and the race question will be solved," the writer concluded, noting that "Prof. Washington won many friends in this city and will be remembered as an able orator, who speaks from the heart."[49]

In 1908, Dr. Arthur Billings Chaffee, a professor of history at the College, weighed in with his take on "The Education of the Negro." Chaffee had joined the faculty the year before after a six-year stint as president of Bishop College, a historically Black institution in Marshall, Texas.[50] He began by challenging certain beliefs about Black people that he assumed his audience would hold, asserting that "the Negro can learn, can think, can reason, can invent." He also defended Black people's claim to citizenship and rejected the common stereotype "that he is radically and hence essentially immoral." He then followed a more well-trodden path by assuring his audience that Black people did not aspire to "social equality," insisting that he had "met a great many colored men" and did "not recall an instance of presumption, except where a good explanation can be found due to ignorance."

Chaffee went on to assert that "with a fair chance [the Black man] will with time attain the best ideals." He emphasized that this process would take time due to "his ignorance regarding what he needs, his lack of independent judgment, due to inherited respect for another's opinions," among a list of other reasons. He concluded "that his education should have for its prime purpose the training due his manhood and not for any social status," and that "on account of present-day conditions, especially in the south, great emphasis should be laid on industrial education."[51]

Several years later, W. E. B. Du Bois visited campus and spoke in Chapel. Cofounder of the National Association for the Advancement of Colored People (NAACP) and editor of the NAACP's magazine, *The Crisis,* Du Bois believed that Black people should not be confined to an industrial education. His talk, as reported in the *Index*, addressed "all educational measures of worth" and "the great need of carefully trained men and women." He also "mentioned the fact that we generally think of the colored races of the world as inferior to ourselves." "Is this democracy?" he reportedly asked. "Two-thirds of the people of the world belong to the colorded [*sic*] races."[52] If Du Bois touched on "social equality," the third rail of the race issue in those days, it was not mentioned in the account of his talk. But the idea was certainly on his mind. Later that year, Du Bois published an article in which he stated, "THE CRISIS believes absolutely in the Social Equality of the Black and White and Yellow races and it believes too that any attempt to deny this equality by law or custom is a blow at Humanity, Religion, and Democracy."[53]

Fear of Black people attaining social equality nevertheless persisted. In 1924, a student named Harold Beadle won a series of intercollegiate oratorical contests addressing the "race problem." While in one speech titled "Free, but Not Equal," "Mr. Beadle emphasized the evil which exists in America in the discrimination against the negro,"[54] in a later oration titled "Inasmuch as Ye Do It Unto One of the Least of These," "Beadle [did] not advocate social equality for the negro, but merely political equality and the right to develop and educate himself."[55]

As African Americans began fleeing terror and oppression in the South in the early part of the twentieth century, a movement that would come to be known as the Great Migration, the "race problem" was felt more keenly at the College. In 1925, the *Index* editors expressed their anxiety, writing that the "migration of thousands of negroes to the north and west has served to stress the fact that the so-called race question has not yet been solved. The constitutional amendments, passed in the fever of war passions, and the nightmare of reconstruction, have not succeeded in giving to the negro that ideal freedom and equality which the spirit of the measures assured." "The negro question is one of national concern," they went on. "In the north and west, as well as in the south, friction develops whenever there is an influx of colored people. Economic rivalry has resulted in severe riots above the Mason and Dixie line, and few contend that the citizens of African descent are welcome brothers to the great majority of whites when the rubbing of elbows begins."[56]

Despite this anxiety, or maybe because of it, views on race at the College were beginning to shift. By 1926, the issue of "social equality" was suddenly up for discussion and addressed in an open forum held by the Kappa Pi society. The students reviewed an article in the *Nation* titled "Negro Segregation Comes North" by Walter White, who would go on to serve as executive secretary of the NAACP. As reported in the *Index*, the "article dealt with the conflict between the Negroes and the whites in Detroit resulting from the mingling of the two races in certain districts." The conclusion of the ensuing discussion was that "although social equality does not exist at present between all races, it ought to be developed by giving all equal advantages in education."[57] A few years later, students who had attended a Student Volunteer Convention in Detroit gave a short play titled *The Color Line* at a regular meeting of Methodist and Baptist students in Kalamazoo's First Baptist Church. Following the play, two international students from the College led a discussion on "Race Prejudice in Kalamazoo," which continued a discussion on "Negro Prejudice in Kalamazoo" held two weeks before.[58] Later that year a new sociology course addressing "race prejudice" was added to the curriculum.[59]

With the rise of the Nazis in the late 1930s, some began to draw parallels between the treatment of Jews in Germany and that of Black people in the United States. In a 1939 *Index* editorial, the writers pointed out that "we hate Hitler with a righteousness that sometimes borders on fanaticism, because of his persecution of the Jews. Yet, within our own borders we tolerate the persecution of a race that has known worse horrors than any revealed by even the most exagerarted [*sic*] 'eye-witness' accounts of Nazi maltreatment of the Jew. The reference is, of course, to the Negro." "Innocent Negroes have been literally torn to pieces," the writers continued, "and burned alive by cowardly mobs at the slightest pretext." "Even in this town," they stated, taking their argument locally, "when a Negro is murdered one hardly knows of it, because the newspaper account of the killing is buried among ads and filler news. In other words, a Negro doesn't count."[60]

Yet alongside this anti-racist passion, contempt for Black people could still be easily expressed without a second thought. Recounting a trip to the South with the tennis team, one of the players told of encountering "the dumbest Negro waiter that ever spilled soup on a vest."[61] And in describing a Black neighborhood in one of the Southern cities they visited, he wrote, "darkies, darkies, there were droves, herds, crowds, groups and individuals, all black. The pay-off came when we saw a little Negro, stark naked smoking a pipe on the front porch, while his mammy sewed up a hole in the seat of his pants."[62]

By the 1940s, racial issues were no longer being cast as the "Negro Problem" but were instead spoken of in terms of "race relations." Discussions about race, at least as reported in the *Index*, occurred mainly during Student Fellowship meetings, held at a local church. The Student Fellowship for several years held "an annual racial program" with the College Club of the Black-run Douglass Community Center, "composed of the negro students of Western State Teachers College."[63] In 1942, the two groups explored the topic "The Next Practical Step Toward the Improvement of Race Relations Among Us."[64] It was also during this time that the College began holding an annual "Religious Emphasis Week" featuring invited speakers, break-out discussions, and personal reflection. The event sometimes functioned as an avenue for exploring racial issues. In summing up the "Religious Week" of 1943, a student remarked on the impact made by the invited speakers and "their presentation of race, economic, and youth problems. They have 'made an impression,' a lasting one, on many of us."[65]

The rhetoric was shifting from casting Black people as the problem to promoting tolerance and mutual understanding. Some social scientists and biologists were now supporting this more egalitarian approach, in part as a reaction to the Nazis' persecution of Jews. In 1943, the *Index* ran an article about a sociologist who argued that race was a human invention. "Skin color, hair form, and the shape of the nose and lips enter into our awareness and become connected to our attitudes and judgments," Robert Redfield, dean of the social sciences at the University of Chicago, was quoted as saying. "Yet, except in terms of the attention paid to them, these characteristics have no consequence in human behavior."[66]

The following year, there was another article debunking biological racial differences, largely in response to Nazi propaganda. This time it was a professor of anatomy and physical anthropology from the University of Chicago who insisted that the Nazi idea of "pure blood" was a "misnomer." Based on his research, he believed that "6,000 years ago there was such a thorough race mixture that any claim of 'purity' today is not founded on historical fact and common knowledge." He then transitioned to a plea for mutual understanding. "If races are to get along with one another none can afford to have [a] chip on the shoulder. They must always be prepared to understand the viewpoint of the other. Doubt and suspicion are destructive no matter who kindles the flame." He went on to say that "progress of racial interfusion is a gradual and slow process." "Therefore the process of adjustment is one of reciprocal 'give and take,'" he explained. "Advancement is not made by exorbitant demands or by equally extravagant denials."[67]

This notion of "give and take" and the call for mutual understanding, though an improvement over the rhetoric of the "Negro Problem," obscured the role of White people as oppressors by making it seem like it was all a big misunderstanding between groups who stood on some imagined level playing field. Through this lens, the desire among Black people for fair treatment could be cast as an "exorbitant demand." And the necessarily "gradual and slow process," promoted mainly by White people, effectively maintained racial hierarchies. It was during this time that "tolerance" of other races began to be preached, a pretty low bar, but one that some White people found annoying nevertheless. "All I can say is nuts to the whole thing," one student was quoted as saying on his way into Welles dining hall at the end of Religious Emphasis Week in 1948. "They keep telling us to be tolerant of negros, but then what do they do about it? Nuthin'! If these people want to be friendly with negros, let 'em; but I wish they'd cut the talk and start to do something. As for me, I'm hungry!"[68]

"America for Americans"

Black people were not the only "problem" White people worried about when thinking about shaping a national identity. The country was, after all, largely made up of people who had emigrated from elsewhere. Anxiety about immigration mounted in the 1890s as European immigration shifted from Western Europe to Southern and Eastern Europe, bringing a "lower quality" immigrant considered harder to assimilate. In a speech that won the junior prize for oration in 1893, a student worried that the "valuable" immigration from Western Europe and Great Britain was declining while immigration "from races most alien to the body of the American people and from the lowest and most illiterate classes among those races" was on the rise. The "alien races" referred to were "Poles, Bohemians, Hungarians, Russians and Italians." "The population which came previous to 1860 was civilized," the student went on, while "that which comes to-day is, in some proportion, semi-barbarous . . . It is well known that individuals, benevolent societies and communities of Europe have furnished criminals and paupers with clothing and money and placed them on board steamers bound for the United States. How long will the American people permit this fair land to be the dumping ground for the human wrecks of other nations?"[69]

Another student expressed similar sentiments in a speech in 1895, arguing that nations flourish "only under a united and homogenous people, people living the same life, thinking the same thoughts" and warning that "we are today breeding diversity in religion, language, customs, conditions and sentiments such as never before existed in the United States, because foreigners will not adopt our institutions and become Americans." He reiterated the belief that the "class of immigrants that are taking up their abode together is different from those of fifty years ago. Many of those coming now are of the lower strata of society, paupers, criminals, men discontented with government and society. The tendency to crime already existing in these bands is increasing, and their habits of living disgust the ordinary American."[70]

Both students concluded their speeches by affirming that some well-regulated immigration was desirable and emphasizing the importance of assimilation to American institutions, values, and social norms. "That our nation should be dotted with these foreign communities, each diverging in its tendencies from the nation's perfection is a menace to its welfare," one of the students stated as he transitioned to a rousing conclusion. "But to have them all united with one purpose at heart, guided by that best effort of American minds, the constitution, armed by America's safeguard, an intelligent American ballot, eager to bear our flag, ready to strike down all who oppose it, . . . this will ensure a glorious and perpetual national life, and we shall have not America for the Americans, but Americans for America."[71]

The potential for assimilation, however, was generally not seen as possible for people of Asian descent. Chinese immigration had ground to a halt after the Chinese Exclusion Act of 1882. In response to increasing Japanese immigration beginning in the early 1900s, Congress passed the Immigration Act of 1924, effectively banning immigration from Asia. The following year, Japanese immigration was the subject of an intercollegiate debate contest. "The question is of very vital interest just now, and perhaps the consensus of opinion is slightly more with the negative side," the *Index* reported. Arguments in favor of Japanese immigration stated that "discrimination is un-American, violating the principle of political equality . . . The [J-ps] meet all the requirements of selected immigration. Discrimination is injurious to business and the maintenance of peace forbids it, as discrimination has broken treaties; it is also injurious to the prestige of Japan in the Orient. And lastly, the Japanese can be assimilated, to which end intermarriage is unnecessary." The arguments in opposition "maintained that the Japanese are undesirable and a menace, racially, economically, and politically; that they are attempting to bring about an invasion of the United States; that the present laws are not liable to cause war; and lastly that the Japanese are more dangerous than others whom we allow to come in."[72]

Later that year the *Index* ran an editorial titled "The New Japanese 'Peril'" about Japanese immigrants in Hawaii "who cling to their national and race customs and whose children become American citizens." "These 'Americans' could come into the United States as full-fledged citizens, and the immigration bar would be ineffective," the *Index* editors warned. "In a general way we are strong for the slogan 'America for white people' and would be willing to do something now to prevent the west from having its [J-p] problem to offset the Southern negro problem. If wise forethought and strong legislation can accomplish the end sought it ought not be opposed."[73]

Despite the presence of such anti-Asian sentiment on campus, the College enrolled students from Japan and other parts of Asia from time to time. When President Franklin Roosevelt ordered the internment of people of Japanese descent, including American citizens, during World War II, the College participated in an effort led by the American Baptist Home Missionary Society (ABHMS) to enroll Japanese American students in Baptist colleges. Going to college was one way to avoid detention, but very few Japanese students could afford this avenue because the government had frozen their families' assets and "few institutions were eager to enroll students of Japanese ancestry, much less provide financial assistance."[74] With support from the ABHMS, Thomas Sugihara '45, enrolled at Kalamazoo College in October 1942. As he later wrote, he "was the first of four Japanese-American students on the scene. Paul Hiyama came a few months later, followed by Yoshiya Igarashi and Leonard Yamasaki. By the fall of 1943, all four of us were there; there were not others before the end of the war."[75] In 1945, Sugihara and Hiyama tried out for the basketball team, undeterred by their relatively short stature. The team, with an average height of 5'8", gained fame as "The Shortest Basketball Team in the Nation" when a photo of the starting line-up appeared in more than 125 newspapers throughout the country.[76]

The initiative to enroll Japanese American students who would have otherwise been held in internment camps took place during the presidency of Paul Lamont Thompson, who served from 1938–1948. Thompson also played a pivotal role in helping a Japanese alumnus, Kiyonao (Kiyo) Okami '40, who was detained in the wake of the attack on Pearl Harbor. The two men were already corresponding with each other when Okami, then living in New York, was arrested and imprisoned on Ellis Island. His wife, Louise (Harris) Okami '42, wrote to Thompson asking for help and served as a conduit for letters between her husband and Thompson. In January of 1942, Okami wrote to Thompson saying that "you will be pleased to know that I had my hearing this afternoon. Much to my surprise, I was questioned for no more than 10 minutes, but Louise was separately closeted with the hearing board for nearly 20 minutes and was asked many personal questions. Our impression is that your views and your support will have a very important bearing on my case in as much as the board decided to give another hearing at which they are desirous of seeing you." Louise Okami added a postscript emphasizing that the "hearing board . . . made it plain much depends on your appearance as to Kiyo's release."[77]

Thompson traveled to New York to attend the hearing as a character witness. He also agreed to serve as Okami's sponsor and wrote letters on his behalf. After the hearing, Okami wrote to Thompson, saying that "there are no adequate words to express our sincere gratitude for what you have done for us. I have had the pleasure of many friendships and good associations with Americans as well as Japanese in the past, yet I had not known that there could be a friendship that ignores race, nationality and even the unfortunate fact that I am now classified as an enemy alien . . . I truly thanked God that I had been educated under a person like you."[78]

Kiyo Okami was finally released on April 10, 1942, shortly after Thompson wrote to U.S. Attorney General Francis Biddle at Okami's request. The friendship between the Okamis and the Thompsons would be lifelong. Okami later went on to establish "a successful career with the U.S. government using the very traits for which that government had imprisoned him in 1941—his dual knowledge of American and Japanese language and culture." At his sixtieth class reunion in 2000, Kiyo Okami was awarded a Citation of Merit from the Emeritus Club of Kalamazoo College.[79]

Missionary Mindset

The embrace of Japanese students on campus during World War II was consistent with a long tradition of interest in and concern for people from other cultures and countries. Many Kalamazoo students, though naive about racial and cultural differences and often reliant on stereotypes, had a sincere interest in engaging with people unlike themselves. As President Theodore Nelson described them in 1891, Kalamazoo College students were "earnest and progressive."[80] However, their earnestness combined with internalized ideas of White superiority and a belief in Christianity as the one true religion led many to consider other races and cultures as Leonard Slater had—through a missionary mindset. It was a mindset that was well-meaning as well as paternalistic and often dismissive of the religious and cultural beliefs of "heathen" people, seen as "benighted" and "superstitious." For those most devoted to the cause of uplifting the downtrodden and saving souls, missionary work held appeal. Baptists and other Protestant denominations had far-flung missionary enterprises during those years, spurred on by a belief in Christianity's ascendancy and an ardent desire to convert the "heathen" in every corner of the world. Driven by an unshakable conviction that acceptance of Jesus Christ was the only true path to eternal life, the "evangelization of the world in this generation" became a rallying cry among students in the late nineteenth century.[81]

The Kalamazoo College community was highly connected to these missionary efforts. Students and faculty read about them in Christian periodicals, and the College hosted regular visits from foreign missionaries who told of their experiences in the world's mission fields in hopes of inspiring students to devote their lives to the noble work of saving souls. For many years there was a Volunteer Band for Foreign Missions on campus, and the Kalamazoo College chapters of the Young Men's Christian Association (YMCA) and especially the Young Women's Christian Association (YWCA) studied far-off countries. The YMCA and YWCA were connected to the national Student Volunteer Movement, which sought to recruit college graduates to foreign missionary work. Many male graduates entered the ministry, and a small but steady portion of graduates, both men and women, went on to serve as missionaries abroad, most often in India, Japan, and China. In 1895, L. E. Martin, class of 1888 and a missionary in Ongole, India, wrote that "there were more graduates of Kalamazoo College in Ongole, than from any other college in the United States."[82] Several years later, the *Index* noted that twenty-five former students had entered the foreign missionary field in Bulgaria, Burma, China, India, Japan, Korea, the Philippines, and countries in Africa.[83]

Letters from alumni working as missionaries abroad were published in the *Index*, as were reprints of articles from other publications exalting missionary work. In 1900, L. E. Martin wrote of his experiences teaching in Ongole. Describing the difficulty of finding "properly qualified Christian men" to teach, he explained, "we get Christian men for positions in schools when possible, but when not possible we engage Hindus until we are able to do better." In terms of evangelizing, he wrote that the "class of people, among whom our work has produced results in open conversion, was of the very lowest, most degraded, most abjectly poor." Among the higher-caste Brahmins, they had been less successful. "We wonder sometimes at the obduracy of these higher classes," he went on. "So far as I know, not one of the old Hindu students here has come out as a Christian." "But we are by no means discouraged," he insisted. "We may be saddened by the awful darkness of the heathenism about us, but we are sure that the Lord Jesus is going to come into possession of His own here in India too, and that this wilderness of sin and ignorance and woe shall be made to blossom as the rose."[84] Martin would join the Kalamazoo College faculty later that year.[85]

The rise in foreign missionary work occurred alongside growing imperialism as Western nations, particularly the United Kingdom, France, and the United States, expanded their reach around the globe. Not surprisingly then, missionary work was often cast in imperialistic terms. A piece printed in the *Index* in 1880 declared that "missions contemplate the displacement of all other religions, to make Christ's the only one, to make it supreme; the creation of a new spiritual life in evil and dead souls and races; and prospectively of a new civilization of the world."[86] The writer went on to say, "the lines are formed, the orders are given, the field is set, the battle is joined; it is Christendom against Heathendom, and the one that carries the weight and the heaviest resources, wins at last." He then reiterated a notion prevalent among missionaries that the soul must first be cleansed by "civilization" before conversion to Christianity: "there remain great, sullen, sluggish masses of mind, impenetrable to the spiritual ideas, and incapable of the virtues of the gospel. At any rate, they must go through a preparatory dispensation of civilization, before they are ready for Christ."

Around the turn of the century, U.S. imperialism began to be debated on campus, especially with regard to Cuba, Puerto Rico, Hawaii, and the Philippines.[87] While colonization within the confines of the continent had been accepted as "manifest destiny," the expansion of American military and political power beyond the Pacific coast and into the Caribbean made many on campus uncomfortable. Religious imperialism, however, was seen as something else altogether. The rightful dominance of Christianity among the world's religions and the beneficence of evangelizing the "heathen" were taken for granted. As the millennium approached, "many foresaw a coming epoch of reason, peace, and godliness that would pervade the earth and lead to Christ's return."[88] In 1906, four Kalamazoo students attended the Fifth International Convention of the Student Volunteer Movement in Nashville, Tennessee. "Perhaps the most impressive and permanent thought," a student wrote about the impact of the convention, "was the great need and the unprecedented opportunity in heathen lands. Especially is this true in India, Japan, and China; these nations are awakening to their soul poverty and are stretching out their hands to us for help. With every tick of the clock a soul is going out into the dark, but whither? The responsibility rests on America; will she meet it?"[89]

Four years later at the convention in Rochester, New York, similar calls to action were voiced. "Ambassador Bryce emphasized the urgency of the motto of the Student Volunteer Movement, 'The Evangelization of the World in This Generation,'" the *Index* reported. "There never has been such a critical and auspicious moment as now. Never before have there been such changes and explorations. There is scarcely a spot where the influence of the ideas and habits of the white man is not being felt. Old ideas, customs, and religion have broken down. Is not this the time when, having destroyed these things, 'we of Christian nations should give them something to fill the void that we have made?'"[90]

Christianity was also seen as an antidote to domestic social problems. As a student wrote in a prize-winning speech in 1893, "when the masses are permeated with the principles of Christianity, then will moral darkness and inequality flee like night before the beams of the morning light."[91] Another student, writing in 1900, insisted that "Christian education . . . sends its heralds to live in the darkened slums of our great cities—vice is displaced by virtue and a higher life is attained; it lays its mantle on a poor negro boy and he becomes a Booker T. Washington, a prophet and champion of a benighted race; it takes the son of the meanest outcast of all Europe and teaches him to love the 'stars and stripes' and makes of him a worthy citizen of the grandest commonwealth under heaven."[92]

While it is possible that feelings of cultural superiority may have been tempered in some graduates after entering the mission field, alumni and students writing in the *Index* tended to express disdain or pity for "heathen" countries. A student and future missionary wrote in 1900 that "China, though she knows it not, is wretched and miserable and poor and blind and naked." "China has vast mineral wealth," he went on, "but on account of foolish superstitions which make it unlucky to disturb the ground she has made no use of coal though coal enough to supply the world for centuries is within easy reach . . . In education the Chinese appear a little better than in their industries, but even here they have little to teach to Western nations, and much to learn from them."[93] The following year a student who had grown up in Japan as a daughter of missionaries wrote an article about her summer travels in Japan with her family. Recounting a day-trip to a small village in the mountains, she recalled that "turning our gaze from the beautiful landscape, our eyes rested on something near us that seemed so out of harmony with its surroundings that we were filled with a feeling akin to pity. It was the shrine to some heathen God, and the stone idol with its horrible features seemed to cast a gloom over the entire region."[94] Several years later, writing from Assam, India, a former student decried "the ignorant and superstitious conditions of the great majority of these people." "I have seen signs enough of evil in its depths," he continued, "both within their very religious centers and apart from them, to convince me beyond the slightest doubt that they are in need of something better—that which alone the Christ in His saving power can give."[95]

The unflinching confidence in the righteousness of evangelizing "heathen" peoples around the globe faltered in the aftermath of World War I. The bloody conflict among Christian nations dealt a blow to the belief in continuous progress and the superiority of Western Civilization.[96] In late December of 1923, several Kalamazoo College students attended the International Convention of the Student Volunteer Movement in Indianapolis, Indiana. Like previous conventions, the event hosted speakers from all over the world with about 6,000 delegates in attendance. This time, prevalent among the topics were "racial problems."

As reported in the *Index*, the discussions were "frank." One student attended a session in which "a striking denouncement of the white race was made by a negro Y.W.C.A. worker, who made a stirring defense of the negro people, saying that they were not backward, but had not been given a chance." There was also a Chinese student who criticized "the attitude of the church in attempting to impose western civilization upon the East." George Sherwood Eddy, a prominent missionary popular on the speaker circuit who had presented a few times at the College, condemned rampant lynchings and the Ku Klux Klan.[97] He spoke of the more than four thousand lynchings that had occurred in almost every state in the union since 1885, noting that "in certain regions nearly all the lynchings had been Methodist or Baptist lynchings; that is, the majority of the mob were confessing Christian church members."[98] Eddy also noted the growing revolt worldwide against "racial autocracy." "It seems like hypocritical cant to speak of 'the white man's burden,' the so-called 'yellow peril,' the brown or black peril," Eddy stated, "when it is the white peril that has actually caused nine-tenths of the wars of the modern world, occasioned by the land-grabbing, the economic imperialism, the military exploitation and the colonial subjugation of peoples in the interest of a supposedly 'superior' white race."[99] "Despite a request that they refrain from applause," the *Index* reported, "the great evangelist's address so reached the hearts of the students that they spontaneously broke into a hand-clapping that continued for nearly five minutes."[100]

By the time of the next quadrennial convention in 1928, enthusiasm for the Student Volunteer Movement had dampened considerably, with only 3,500 delegates in attendance, down from the usual 6,000. The speakers were now advocating a more culturally sensitive approach to missions and trying to disentangle Christianity from Western Civilization. John R. Mott, a longtime leader of the Student Volunteer Movement, had significantly altered his message, saying that "the business of missions is not to get people to call themselves Christians, but to bring all people into one friendship." "At the close of the conference," the *Index* reported, "it was unanimously agreed that it would be far better and less embarrassing to American Christians if the two terms—'Western Civilization' and 'Christianity' were not understood as synonymous."[101] This change of heart was the beginning of the end for the Student Volunteer Movement, which petered out during the 1930s, both nationally and at Kalamazoo College. The YMCA and YWCA campus chapters eventually disappeared along with efforts to promote missionary work. But while the sheen of Western Civilization had been dulled by the war, it still formed the foundation of the students' worldview, and the missionary mindset would remain even though missionary work no longer carried its former prestige.

"A Sprinkling of Units from Other Ethnic Cultures"

White students for the most part interacted with their *ideas* of Black people and other people of color through blackface performances and ethnically themed entertainment, as subjects of study, and as targets of missionary uplift. Living in a racially segregated society and attending a small, elite Midwestern college, they rarely had opportunities to engage in authentic relationships with people of color. But as Arnold Mulder, a former faculty member, wrote in 1958, "while the student body was in very large part made up of young men and women from families that were typically native American [meaning White and born in the United States] constituting a somewhat closely knit homogeneous group whose attitudes and ideals might be expected in any American college community, there was usually a sprinkling of units from other ethnic cultures."

These "units from other ethnic cultures," as Mulder referred to American students of color and international students, enrolled at the College as "the result of administrative deliberation, not of mere accident," he explained. Indeed, most students of color who attended in the late 1800s and early 1900s came to the College through Baptist connections. "As long ago as in the middle of the nineteenth century the College had been hospitable toward Orientals and representatives of other ethnic groups," he went on, and "K-College graduates have played their part in the political and economic life of Japan and China, of Europe and other areas, returning to their native homes after receiving their academic training here." Many of these students were sponsored by Baptists with the idea, consistent with a missionary mindset, that they would acquire Christian religion and American know-how to take back to their communities. At the same time "it was held to be wholesome for Kalamazoo students to rub shoulders with young men and women from other cultures."[102]

One of the first students of color to enroll after the Civil War was Sam Song Bo, a student from China who attended in the early 1880s. He had immigrated with his uncle from Quang Tung Province[103] when he was fifteen and settled among a growing Chinese population in Portland, Oregon. Facing hostility from Portland's White community, Chinese immigrants lived concentrated in one area of the city. White anxiety about Chinese immigration fomented racist ideas about the Chinese as immoral, filthy, and diseased, and the popular media depicted Chinese people in menacing caricatures. While many White Americans sought to exclude Chinese people, progressive Baptists believed they could be included in American society by converting to Christianity, learning English, and adopting American values. Therefore, in an effort to save souls as well as the integrity of the nation, the American Baptist Home Mission Society established several missions during these years for Chinese immigrants on the West Coast, including a mission in Portland.[104]

Sam Song Bo saw the Baptist mission—a rare White-run organization extending a welcome to Chinese immigrants and offering classes in English—as a means of achieving social acceptability and improving his circumstances. Sam (the Chinese practice is to put the surname first) was among several Chinese who were baptized at the mission in 1875,[105] and soon afterward he sought to continue his education. The Baptist Home Mission in Portland sponsored his enrollment at McMinnville College (later Linfield College), a Baptist institution near Portland. After McMinnville, Sam came to Kalamazoo College, most likely through Baptist channels. College records show him enrolled for just one year, 1881–1882, but a *Kalamazoo Gazette* article suggests that he enrolled as early as 1878.[106]

An item in the *Index* under "Locals," which ran short updates on the doings of faculty and students, refers to Sam as "the genial Chinaman" and a member of the class of 1884.[107]

By casting his lot with the Baptists, Sam was able to gain the education he desired. But it also meant losing the connection to his home community and the relationship with his uncle. As reported in the *Kalamazoo Gazette*, when Sam converted to Christianity "his uncle refused to support or look after him farther, and was very angry with him." Sam defended his uncle, saying that "his uncle is a merchant and a very sensible man."[108] The same article states that "Mr. Sam Song Bo is being educated by the Baptists to become a missionary in China," but Sam's aspirations soon changed. He transferred to the University of Chicago, also a Baptist-affiliated institution, around 1882 to study medicine.[109]

Sam Song Bo would gain national fame a few years later when he published a letter in the New York City newspaper *The Sun* decrying the hypocrisy of erecting a Statue of Liberty in light of the discriminatory 1882 Chinese Exclusion Act, the first instance of Congress banning immigration based solely on nationality and race.[110] After receiving a letter sent to Chinese people in the United States soliciting funds for the pedestal of the Statue of Liberty, the bitter irony prompted Sam to speak out. "I consider it as an insult to us Chinese to call on us to contribute toward building in this land a pedestal for a statue of Liberty," he wrote. "That statue represents Liberty holding a torch which lights the passage of those of all nations who come into this country. But are the Chinese allowed to come? As for the Chinese who are here, are they allowed to enjoy liberty as men of all other nationalities enjoy it? Are they allowed to go about everywhere free from the insults, abuse, assaults, wrongs and injuries from which men of other nationalities are free?"

As one of a few Chinese people in the United States at that time who had attained a high level of education, his countrymen looked to him for help in navigating America's treacherous racial terrain. By this time, Sam had aspirations of becoming a lawyer, but the Chinese Exclusion Act precluded that possibility. "If there be a Chinaman who came to this country when a lad," he continued, "who has passed through an American institution of learning of the highest grade, who has so fallen in love with American manners and ideas that he desires to make his home in this land, and who, seeing that his countrymen demand one of their own number to be their legal adviser, representative, advocate and protector, desires to study law, can he be a lawyer? By the law of this nation, he, being a Chinaman, cannot become a citizen, and consequently cannot be a lawyer." In concluding his letter, Sam summed up the great American contradiction: "Whether this statute against the Chinese or the statue to Liberty will be the more lasting monument to tell future ages of the liberty and greatness of this country, will be known only to future generations."[111]

Flanking Sam Song Bo's time at Kalamazoo were two Karen students from Burma (now Myanmar). Myat Kyau attended from 1870–1878, just before Sam, and Koil Thabue enrolled a few years later in 1884. Kyau came to the United States at the age of twenty-three accompanied by Reverend D. L. Brayton, a Baptist missionary in Bassein, Burma, to attend college with the financial support of Michigan Baptists. He studied for several years at Kalamazoo College and later earned a medical degree from the University of Michigan. He returned to Burma in 1884, where he set up a medical practice in a village in Bassein. His marriage and the subsequent birth of a child were noted in the alumni section of the *Index*.

Kyau became something of a poster child for Baptists who believed that their proselytes should go on to spread civilization and Christianity to their people. Baptists who donated funds to support the education of promising converts also expected some sort of return on their investment. Reverend Jameson, a missionary in Burma, clearly felt that the investment in Myat Kyau had paid off, writing in 1886 that "the Baptists of Michigan proved themselves his friends, and he is proving that their gift of an education was wisely bestowed."[112] So impressed was Jameson by Kyau that he penned a long letter describing Kyau's medical practice and Christian work on behalf of his fellow Karen. The *Index* editors ran excerpts of the letter noting that it "will interest a great many of our readers who were acquainted with Myat Kyau."

Kyau had established a successful medical practice in a remote village and was "gaining the confidence of his people by the treatment of many kinds of disease." While Jameson expressed contempt for the Karen medicine men's "grotesque notions of disease and of remedies" and "utterly absurd native ideas as to the circulation of the blood," Kyau was planning "to gather these men . . . and give them elementary instruction in pathology." "It is my opinion," Jameson concluded, "that Dr. Myat Kyau is exceptionally approximating the ideal of what a Karen with an American education, may do for his people," and he "thanked God for such a man with an American education, who could go on and do a wise, grand, Christian work for his people, without missionary direction and control."

Koli Thabue spent at least fifteen years in the United States, attending a series of institutions. He first enrolled in the University of Chicago where he attained sophomore status and may have crossed paths with Sam Song Bo. He next entered Kalamazoo College in 1884, enrolling in the English-Scientific course of study. He was well known on campus and among Michigan Baptists. Thabue had formal photographs taken in Western as well as traditional Karen dress, and he traveled around Michigan giving public lectures on "the manners and customs of the Burmese" while "in costume" to raise money to support his education.[113] Though he was credited with work at both the preparatory and college level, the Kalamazoo College faculty asked President Wilcox to tell Thabue that "they have very grave doubts that he can complete a course in the college leading to a degree, but that they are willing to do for him all in their power, if he continue to study in the college."[114] Thabue remained two more years but did not graduate. He went on to earn a bachelor of science from Michigan's agricultural college (Michigan State University) in 1891 and later returned to Burma where he married and served as principal for the Pwo Karen School for a few years and then as an agent importing American agricultural machinery.[115]

Students of color would continue to enroll in low numbers, usually through church connections and one at a time. But in the early 1900s, there were a few years during which several students of color attended simultaneously and made their mark on the institution in ways that Sam, Kyau, and Thabue had not. They included Solomon Williamson, a Black student from Jamaica, who began in the Preparatory Department in 1903. His brother John joined him in 1906 as Solomon was preparing to enter the college course, and they graduated together in 1911. Also enrolling in 1903 were two African American students, James Thomas Rooks and Charles Lewis Williams, Jr., and the following year, two Japanese students enrolled, Katsuji Kato of Osaka and Sokichi Nagai of Tokyo.

Nagai was more worldly than the other students and stayed only a year. He would go on to earn fame as one of Japan's most promising literary figures in the 1920s and 1930s. Publishing under the pen name Kafu Nagai, he became "as famous in Japan as Hemingway is in America."[116]

Nagai grew up in Tokyo, the son of a wealthy authoritarian father whom he was expected to follow into the world of business. But Nagai, who described himself as "an emotional young man who has only the dream of beauty," longed for a more romantic life. After he dropped out of university, his father sent him to the United States, hoping the American entrepreneurial spirit would rub off on him. Nagai had already published three semi-erotic novels before coming to the United States and had written of wanting "dissipation, to destroy myself in dissipation . . . I want to see to what point unhealthy desires and pleasures can be pushed."[117] Given these proclivities, it is an odd twist of fate that he should wind up at a conservative Christian college in the Midwest.

Nagai first spent time in Tacoma, Washington, taking French classes and socializing with the Japanese working class there. According to Jeffrey Angles, professor of Japanese at Western Michigan University, "all of his stories written about that time were about these Japanese laborers and the unsavory characters of the Japanese underworld." After visiting the St. Louis World's Fair, Nagai noted in his diary that "upon people's recommendation I have decided to enter a school in a small town named Kalamazoo in Michigan." Angles believes that the people who recommended Kalamazoo College to Nagai may have been American missionaries in Tokyo whose own children were attending Kalamazoo College at the time. Nagai's mother and brother were both Christians who likely knew the missionaries.[118]

Nagai appreciated the pastoral nature of Kalamazoo as well as the more favorable racial climate compared to the West Coast. As he wrote to his brother soon after his arrival, "I am very happy here in Kalamazoo, as everybody is very kind to me. I'm no longer treated like a [J-p.]" While in Kalamazoo, Nagai continued taking French classes, was active along with his countryman Katsuji Kato in the Century Forum literary society, and worked on a collection of short stories that were later published under the title *Amerika Monogatari* (*American Stories*). Two of the stories are based on his time in Kalamazoo.

Angles and others have pointed out similarities to Kalamazoo College in the story "Atop the Hill" about a young Japanese man's time at a small Christian college in the Midwest.[119] "As people already know," the story reads, "American colleges are mostly denominational schools, established in the scenic countryside, far removed from the cities that are full of temptation, and the teachers as well as the students lead an ideally clean religious life. The school to which I went was one of them . . . " "As soon as the train reached a tiny station standing in the middle of a vast prairie," Nagai wrote, describing his character's arrival in the small college town, "I got off, and carrying a heavy bag, I walked all the way down a straight road of the provincial town, full of chickens and children at play, and called at the school, situated among leafy trees atop a small hill." The young Japanese man was greeted by a "kindly-looking elderly principal, . . . wrinkling his entire face in a big smile as if we were already good friends." The principal tells him of another Japanese student, a "Mr. Watano," who the protagonist describes as "leading a strangely anguished life there."[120]

Mr. Watano's character is thought to be loosely based on Katsuji Kato, who attended from 1904–1909.[121] Kato came to Kalamazoo College on the advice of a missionary and spent the first week in the home of Gaylord Slocum, president of the College.[122] During his time at Kalamazoo, Kato was very engaged, joining the Century Forum literary society and active in the YMCA. A devout Christian, Kato was elected chaplain of the Century Forum in 1905[123] and was a delegate to the YMCA Summer Conference in Niagara-on-the-Lake in Canada in 1907.[124] Kato contributed Japanese-style drawings to the *Index* as well as translations of Japanese poems and stories. He frequently delivered orations during meetings of the Century Forum and spoke in town from time to time as well.

Kato would become the first known student of Asian descent to graduate from Kalamazoo College. He went on to earn an MA, DB, and PhD from the University of Chicago, and an MD from Rush Medical College. He worked for many years as an assistant professor of pediatrics at the University of Chicago until he was sent back to Japan by the federal government in 1942 in the wake of the attack on Pearl Harbor.[125] In 1916, he was invited to represent Japan at the National Missionary Congress in Washington, D.C. There he delivered a critique of American missionary work in Japan, arguing that cultural insensitivity and a sense of superiority undermined the cause.

"I speak not in the spirit of criticism," he began, "but of absolute frankness. While I admit all missionaries are doing some good, I must say that there are some at least who, perhaps, are doing more harm than good to the cause of Christianity. I refer to those missionaries, well meaning and good-hearted, who, for lack of a certain insight into the situation, fail to interpret the spirit of Japan in the right manner, and come back to this country and paint Japanese life in darkest colors." While Kato believed Japan should have more missionaries, he insisted that "American missionaries must learn to trust 'indigenous leadership.'" "Money, of course, is power," he went on, "and, since the support of missionaries comes entirely from America, missionaries have a spirit of domination over the native workers. This has been, perhaps, the greatest single obstacle to the extension of the Kingdom in Japan."[126] Kato then pointed out aspects of American culture that he saw as counter to Christianity, including "race discrimination in California, which gives every Japanese in America a very unpleasant feeling . . . the extreme materialism with which many Americans are affected . . . [and] the seeming superficiality on the part of so-called Christians."[127]

The extent to which Kato experienced these negative aspects of American culture at Kalamazoo College is not clear. Christianity may have served simultaneously as a path to social belonging and a source of denigration of Kato's cultural identity, which perhaps contributed to a "strangely anguished life" at the College. Ultimately, however, Kato recalled his years at Kalamazoo fondly, and reminisced about "the good old days" during a visit to campus in 1949.[128]

Like Katsuji Kato, Solomon Williamson, from Wallingford, Jamaica, frequently appeared in the *Index*. He was active in the Sherwood literary society and the YMCA. Solomon published multiple poems and short stories in the *Index* and was a talented orator, winning first prize in a campus oratorical competition in 1910. As his fellow students wrote of him in the senior issue of the *Index* in 1911, "if Solomon of yore had it on our Soloman [*sic*], in the realm of wisdom, you will have to show us where . . . When it comes to getting away with the 'high-brow' stuff he is the peer of peers, and as an orator he is second to none. His favorite pastime is to sit by some babbling brook, on a warm spring day, and peruse Seneca's Morals . . . He is thinking seriously of going in for journalism and if he does his success is assured."[129] In contrast, Solomon's brother John was introverted and more interested in science than literary pursuits. After graduation, John Williamson enrolled at the University of Chicago, but within a year, Booker T. Washington had convinced him to join the faculty at the Tuskegee Institute, where he would spend the remainder of his career teaching chemistry.[130]

James Thomas Rooks and Charles Lewis Williams, Jr., had attended preparatory school at Virginia Union University, a historically Black institution originally established as a mission school for freed slaves by the American Baptist Home Mission Society in 1865. Coburn Dickey, Kalamazoo College class of 1899, went on to chair the Mathematics Department at Virginia Union and likely referred Rooks and Williams to the College. The year they enrolled at Kalamazoo, 1903, W. E. B. Du Bois published his well-known essay "The Talented Tenth," in which he wrote, "the Negro race, like all races, is going to be saved by its exceptional men. The problem of education, then, among Negroes, must first of all deal with the Talented Tenth . . . Men we shall have only as we make manhood the object of the work of the schools—intelligence, broad sympathy, knowledge of the world that was and is—this is the curriculum of that Higher Education which must underlie true life."[131] Elitist though his argument was, advocating for a liberal arts education was ground-breaking at a time when an industrial education was considered the only appropriate training for Black people. Although Du Bois popularized the concept of the "talented tenth," Henry Lyman Morehouse (for whom Morehouse College is named), a well-known Baptist and philanthropist, was the first to coin the term. "In the discussion concerning Negro education we should not forget the talented tenth man," Morehouse wrote in an 1896 article published in *The Independent* magazine. "An ordinary education may answer for the nine men of mediocrity; but if this is all we offer the talented tenth man, we make a prodigious mistake."[132] Morehouse was serving as president of the board of trustees at Virginia Union University when James Thomas Rooks and Charles Lewis Williams were students there,[133] and perhaps his views influenced Dickey in referring them to Kalamazoo College for a liberal arts education.

While at Kalamazoo, Charles Lewis Williams played on the football team and was elected captain his senior year. He was a member of the Century Forum literary society and participated in several oratory competitions, winning the prestigious Coopers Prize in Oratory in 1906. Williams was also active at the local YMCA along with Katsuji Kato, Solomon Williamson, and Thomas Rooks. Photos of Kato, Williamson, and Rooks are among the college memorabilia Williams saved in a scrapbook, suggesting that they were good friends. A laminated business card from 1906 notes that he was teaching business and English courses at the YMCA in the evenings. His business card states, "Special attention given to foreigners and those not having the advantages of early training." Perhaps it was his association with Kato that made Williams sensitive to the needs of people from other countries in learning English. Williams was mentioned in the *Index* numerous times for his prowess on the football field and for various speeches he gave. Among his memorabilia is a copy of his speech on the Irish rebel Daniel O'Connell.

Thomas Rooks roomed with Williams throughout his time at Kalamazoo. He also played on the football team and made the all-MIAA (Michigan Intercollegiate Athletics Association) team in 1905. That same year, he was elected president of the Century Forum and corresponding secretary for the YMCA. Handsome, athletic, and smart, Rooks drew the admiration of his peers and seemed to be the proverbial "big man on campus." His popularity is reflected by the many times he was mentioned in the *Index*, not only in articles about the football team and campus organizations, but also in the "Local, Personal, Exchanges, and Josh" section, which ran short quips about the doings of individual students and faculty. When Rooks's father died in 1906, the members of his class published a resolution in the *Index* expressing deep sympathy for their friend.[134]

Rooks's senior bio describes him as "the Goliath from North Carolina" who "thunders his stentorian voice in orations and hurls his massive weight against the football enemies of Kazoo." "Rooks has medical asperations [*sic*]," the bio continued, "and spends hours each day in the biological laboratory with the pretty girls whom he addresses as, 'my dears.'"[135] In June of 1906, Thomas Rooks became the first known African American graduate of Kalamazoo College; however, it is not clear whether his fellow students knew he was African American. With light skin and straight hair, he could easily have been perceived as White. Williams was also light-skinned, and one wonders if it was a coincidence that the two students Coburn Dickey referred to Kalamazoo College from Virginia Union University could have chosen to be "White passing."

Rooks went on to enroll in Rush Medical College in Chicago and realize his medical aspirations.[136] According to the 1930 census, he was living in Washington state and working as an eye, ear, and throat specialist. He had married a White woman and his race was also listed as White. Charles Lewis Williams pursued a number of careers, including a baker in Chicago and a teacher at the Asheville School, a college preparatory school in North Carolina. Later in life, he returned to Fauquier County, Virginia, where he farmed his family's eighty-acre plot.

Despite playing outsized roles at Kalamazoo College as students, neither Rooks nor Williams remained connected as alumni. In 1913, the *Index* staff listed them among those whom they had been unable to contact. "It is very strange that all the mail sent to the addresses given by Mr. Williams and Mr. Rooks, has been returned to the college unopened," the entry read. "Who can tell us about them?"[137]

In the late 1930s, three Native American students enrolled at the College. They had transferred from Bacone College, a two-year Baptist institution founded in 1880 to educate American Indian youth. Bacone was located on the Creek reservation in Muskogee, Oklahoma, and in close proximity to the reservations of the Chickasaw, Choctaw, Cherokee, and Osage—the Indian Territory created in the 1830s for tribes removed from their homelands east of the Mississippi River. For much of its history, Bacone had also enrolled White students, but during the 1930s, it was marketing itself as an institution exclusively for American Indians and attracting Native youth from all around the country. The three students who came to Kalamazoo were Dennis Groundhog, Cherokee, Jimmy Donaghey, Choctaw, and Willis Wood, Seminole. They had been fast friends at Bacone, and when two of them received scholarships to finish their baccalaureate education at Kalamazoo, the third friend decided to transfer as well.[138]

Though the original mission of Bacone had been to assimilate American Indians into the White population, Groundhog, Donaghey, and Willis attended during a time when Bacone was emphasizing the cultural identities of its students as a way to raise money from White donors. In their fundraising activities the school's leadership intentionally played to the expectations of White audiences by tapping into images of Plains and Southwestern Indians popularized in novels and westerns, but on campus students were encouraged to express their tribal identities and share their cultures with each other. The funds raised were used to hire Native American faculty and develop courses and programs on Indigenous arts, culture, and history.[139] As the scholar Lisa Neuman notes, "the romantic images of Indianness that Bacone's administrators, teachers, and students projected to the public were successful in generating income for the school and functioned to help them—to borrow an expression from Philip Deloria —'play Indian to Indian advantage.'"[140]

Being educated at Bacone during these years, Groundhog, Donaghey, and Willis would have entered Kalamazoo with a sense of pride in their American Indian heritage, and because both Bacone and Kalamazoo were affiliated with American Baptists, many aspects of institutional culture would have been familiar to them. These were clear advantages in adjusting to life at Kalamazoo College.

All three students played on the football team, and in October 1938 the *Kalamazoo Gazette* ran a story about them that invoked all the stereotypes White people had about American Indians. A photo of the three students wearing their football uniforms and Indian headdresses appeared with the caption "College R-----ns Ready to Scalp Hope's Gridders." "Dennis Groundhog, Willis Wood, and Jim Donaghey, Kalamazoo College's full-blooded Indians, plan to instigate a scalping party next Saturday afternoon," the article began. "Their intended victims are a band of Dutchmen from Hope College."[141]

The gimmick, racist as it was, would have been familiar to the three students. While at Bacone, Dennis Groundhog, and perhaps Donaghey and Willis as well, had participated in the men's glee club, the Singing Redmen,[142] which traveled the country as part of the school's fundraising activities. In interviewing Bacone alumni, including Groundhog, for her 2007 article "Selling Indian Education: Fundraising and American Indian Identities at Bacone College, 1880–1941," Neuman found that some former members of the Singing Redman recalled their experiences fondly while others were uncomfortable with "selling Indianness" to raise money.[143] However Groundhog, Donaghey, and Willis might have felt about "selling Indianness," they would have recognized the dynamic at play and seemed to use it to their advantage in finding their place in the Kalamazoo College community.

The students' American Indian identities at that time functioned as a vehicle for social belonging. In 1939, a columnist for the *Index* noted that "students come from all levels of life regardless of race, creed, color, or financial status . . . it certainly gives one a broader outlook on living to be associated with such fine characters as Jimmy Donaghey . . . a Choctaw Indian from Oklahoma . . . born and raised on the reservation there" and "Dennis Groundhog . . . another Indian from the Cherokee tribe of Oklahoma . . . [who] participates in his tribe's ceremonies in the summer."[144]

Dennis Groundhog, in particular, seems to have embraced, and been embraced by, the institution. In 1940, he became the first known American Indian graduate of Kalamazoo College. Donaghey and Willis appear not to have earned their baccalaureate degrees from Kalamazoo. Like Thomas Rooks before him, Groundhog was handsome, athletic, and popular while also excelling academically. The 1940 yearbook lists Groundhog among the senior class officers and notes that "he's a friend to everyone."[145] But unlike Rooks, Groundhog's racial and cultural identity served as an asset among his White peers. His American Indian heritage was often highlighted by fellow students in a positive (if naive and stereotypical) way, while Rooks's African American identity was never alluded to in the many mentions of him in the *Index*, and indeed, it is unclear whether his peers were even aware that he was African American.

Unbidden

Most students of color who attended in the late nineteenth and early twentieth centuries had been recommended by fellow Baptists. In addition to having been vouched for, these students had something else in common: they were all men. So, although the path for students of color at the College had been paved to some degree, Pauline Byrd, a Black woman, arrived in 1922 for her admission interview unbidden and without precedent.

Byrd had grown up in Kalamazoo, and her family, especially her mother and grandmother, had great ambitions for her education. "I always remember that [my grandmother] never talked to me without emphasizing the importance of an education," Pauline Byrd Johnson (her married name) told Ruth Moerdyk '83, during a series of oral history interviews conducted as part of Moerdyk's Senior Individualized Project. "I must learn. The only salvation for Negroes in America was education, was learning, and if I learned things nothing could make me a slave."[146]

She had always excelled academically, and her mother had over many years saved up money for her college education. Having endured the constant sting of racism in the predominantly White schools she attended in the city of Kalamazoo, Byrd hoped to attend Howard University. "I had never had any fun in school because I was ostracized socially, and I am a fun-loving person," Pauline Byrd Johnson recalled. "My intention was, when I got out of high school, to go south to a colored school where I could not only get an education, but also have some fun."[147] Her mother saw things differently, however. "If you go south to a colored school," Johnson recalled her mother telling her, "you're going to be separating yourself from the general population. That is segregation and it's the thing we have always tried to work against."[148] It was her mother's idea that she should attend Kalamazoo College.

"Negroes weren't able to do the work at Kalamazoo College, that was generally accepted," Byrd Johnson continued, "and my mother never thought that was a reasonable thing. I had gone all through school with white kids and had high grades; why couldn't I go there?"[149] Byrd was bitterly disappointed that she would not be going to Howard. "Inside I was angry for a long time, about a year, I think," she recalled. But her mother's word was law, so she submitted her Kalamazoo College application.

"In those days we had a personal interview with the president before we were admitted," Byrd Johnson explained. "Dr. Stetson interviewed every single student. I still remember the look of consternation and surprise on his face when I came in. Evidently he hadn't been told about me." As she was leaving Stetson's office after a successful interview, she turned suddenly to say something she had forgotten and caught him in an unguarded moment with a "look of surprise and amazement," eyes wide open and jaw dropped. "I'm sure he was shocked at what he had just done—letting a Negro into the College," Byrd Johnson concluded. "But he was a perfect gentleman and couldn't have done much else."[150] Pauline Byrd Johnson was unaware of the Black students who had preceded her, some of whom Stetson himself had admitted. So it was probably not the fact that she was Black that shocked him, but rather the fact that she was a Black woman.

The *Indexes* and yearbooks during Pauline Byrd's time at Kalamazoo College give the impression that she was well integrated in campus life. As a member of the Alpha Sigma Delta literary society, a staff writer for the *Index*, a member of the yearbook staff, and an honors student, her name appears multiple times in the *Index* during those years. But appearances can be misleading.

"I wasn't expected to do social things; I was just automatically excluded," Byrd Johnson said, describing her college years. "I was crazy about athletics and such, but by that time I had been ignored so much that I didn't even bother to go to the games. So I went to very few things of that sort. It was a matter of going to college and going to work." Recalling her involvement in the *Index* and yearbook, she said wryly, "it was hard to eliminate somebody as good as I was. It's interesting that some of the kids who were head of [the *Index]* didn't want me on, and never called me into staff or general meetings unless they just *had* to. So even with [the *Index],* whatever I did was mostly individual work. The same is true of the yearbook—the meetings to carry on the work—I was just automatically excluded."[151]

Setting aside any expectations of a social life, Byrd focused on her coursework. In 1925, Allan Hoben, who assumed the presidency of the College soon after she enrolled, established Honors Day as a way of encouraging and rewarding excellence in academics. Pauline Byrd was among the students recognized in the inaugural Honors Day celebration, receiving an award for outstanding scholarship in the French minor.[152] She was also selected to be part of a "scholars' group" that was allowed to take honors courses.[153] Yet, in her chosen major of English she had to contend with a hostile faculty member. "The English department head was one of the most prejudiced persons I have ever met," Byrd Johnson recalled. "I always had straight A's in English, never anything else, but he consistently gave me B's. One of the girls who worked with him and happened to be a good friend of mine asked, 'How does it happen that Pauline Byrd always gets B's when she's always been an A student?' He said, 'Because I wouldn't give a Negro an A, ever.'"[154]

"I have such a stubborn disposition that I went ahead and majored in English," Byrd Johnson continued. "And he never did give me an A." However, towards the end of her time at Kalamazoo, Byrd, without meaning to, wrote something that finally pleased her racist English professor. As Byrd recalled:

> Dr. Stetson asked us to write a paper telling of our plans for life, and I left that assignment for the last thing Sunday night. In order to get it done, just to have something to hand in, I remember so definitely writing what I didn't mean: "I'm going to go down south and work with my people and try to help them." And apparently Dr. Stetson read that and some of our letters at a faculty meeting. *Oh,* overnight I became the most popular person. I didn't know until some time afterwards what had happened, but that same Dr. Simpson who detested my race, and me, of course, met me in the hall and asked if I wouldn't like a copy of *Tess of the D'Urbervilles*

> that a publisher had sent him. Why, I almost fainted. That was the first time he had ever been decent to me.[155]

It is not hard to imagine the self-confident and accomplished Pauline Byrd carrying herself in a way that Simpson would have perceived as "uppity" and offensive to his sensibilities regarding social hierarchy. These were, of course, the years in which "social equality" for Black people was regarded as a radical idea, one that most White people were unwilling to accept. By playing into White expectations of how Black people should behave and what Black people should aspire to do, Pauline Byrd had inadvertently won the approval of her racist English professor. She was rewarded with a "fine recommendation" in which "he said, without knowing it, exactly what white people think about us," she recalled. Byrd Johnson went on quoting the letter, "'Miss Byrd is a fine student, she's punctual, she's accurate . . . ' and so on, all of these qualities, '. . . even though she's a Negro.'"[156]

Other faculty members were more friendly. "Miss Diebold is a woman I have always admired," Byrd Johnson said of Frances Diebold, a longtime member of the biology department, "though I didn't know her too well. I always felt she was unprejudiced—I felt that she was very gracious and friendly. Ernest Balch was the head of the history department, and he was a wonderful man. He was the first one who was very gracious and kind to me. Dr. Balch probably [made the greatest impression]. He was so kind and smart and warm." She also came to know Dr. Stetson well. After retiring from the presidency in 1922, Stetson continued to teach. "Dr. Stetson taught education and psychology, so I had him quite a lot," Byrd Johnson recalled. "He was a wonderful man . . . beautifully educated. It's an honor and a privilege to have known him." Byrd Johnson continued, recalling her conversations with Stetson, "I learned so much [from him] about seeing the good in people no matter how they treated me—seeing what they stood for aside from the race issue. To me that's important." And then she said something extraordinary: "Naturally you'd prefer that they accept you as a human being, but as long as that isn't likely, then you pick out the good and let the other go."[157] Letting go not being accepted as a human being. In order to get through Kalamazoo College, Pauline Byrd had to endure dehumanization as a regular fact of life.

In the several decades between the Civil War and World War II, many changes took place at Kalamazoo College under the leadership of ten different presidents. The curriculum evolved from a focus on the classics to the modern disciplines with majors and minors. Many buildings were erected, especially during Allan Hoben's presidency from 1922–1935, and by the 1940s the campus quadrangle looked very much as it does today. During all that time and amidst all those changes, however, the racial climate stayed remarkably the same. In the years before the first stirrings of the Civil Rights Movement, racial hierarchies remained firmly in place while campus life continued to unfold in an almost hermetically sealed world where being White equaled being normal and other cultures were studied as curiosities and tapped for entertainment.

The climate was such that the brilliant Pauline Byrd, who friends later described as "a stunningly beautiful young woman," "a delightful person," and "a conversationalist with great charm," suffered regular humiliations, large and small, which signaled at every turn her place at the bottom of the racial and social hierarchy. She later recalled a "little thing" that would sometimes happen at the end of the daily Chapel service. "The boys sat on one side and the girls sat on the other," she recounted, "and when we came to the aisle to march out we would walk with the person we met on that side. Well, some of those boys, when we would meet, wouldn't walk with me, and I would have to walk out alone."[158] "Then there were people who would be friendly [on campus] but not if you met them downtown," she went on. "A few were the same everywhere, and those girls were way outside of the social setting in which they lived."[159]

The social setting in which the White students lived assumed White superiority while also fostering a sense of White innocence. All sorts of behaviors that would have been considered rude, unjust, or downright mean if aimed at a fellow White student were automatically meted out to Black people as a matter of course. In such a setting, White students could feel magnanimous if they extended the most basic civility to a Black person, even if it was insincere. As a classmate of Pauline Byrd's recalled, still full of innocence decades later, "I never thought of her as different from anyone else . . . But she wasn't among those you invited to your home. I don't suppose any of us thought about it back then."[160]

In such a social environment, White people could live their entire lives without ever having to confront their inherent feelings of superiority or their dismissive treatment of people they saw as beneath them. All of their cultural touchstones were contained within the White world. Anything outside of those norms seemed insignificant by comparison. The degree to which White identity was centered is evident in a description of a course on race relations offered in the 1940s. Even students who were drawn to a class on race (who were mostly women) seemed to engage with other peoples and cultures in a light-hearted atmosphere ripe with opportunities for humor while their normalcy as White people was affirmed.

As a reporter for the *Index* wrote in 1943:

> If ever you are near Mandelle 12 on Monday, Tuesday, or Thursday mornings about nine o'clock and hear peals of laughter issuing forth from that vicinity, don't be shocked at such early morning vivacity, it's only the Race Relations class buzzing along at full speed with Dr. Hightower rendering his stimulating lectures on population, immigration, and race problems. He even shows off his talents along mathematics lines as he discusses the quota system while the class sits with mouths droping [*sic*] open, and a look of bewilderment envelopes the face of each member . . . The laughter and smiles come as a result of some of Dr. Hightower's droll side remarks for which the class is unprepared. After picking up dropped stitches and blotting pens . . . the girls once again resume thoughtful poses for the remainder of the lecture until another sharp quip is told . . . . This week the girls are going to start giving reports on minority racial groups in the United States. Each girl has selected a different group and it sounds like it will be an interesting venture comparing the many characteristics of each group . . . . Everyone learns a lot in Race Relations and also most of the girls add many rows to their knitting projects.[161]

The cold, hard shape of the College's institutional identity and ideas about race, which had persisted through several decades, two world wars, and the Great Depression, would hold for a bit longer. In the 1960s things would heat up again, creating the conditions for the shape to change. But first there would be the 1950s.

Endnotes

1. Jill Lepore, *These Truths: A History of the United States* (New York: W. W. Norton, 2018), 9.
2. Denton Jaques Snider, *World's Fair Studies* (Chicago: Sigma Publishing Company, 1895), 256–257.
3. Letter to Lucinda Hinsdale Stone from the Board of World's Fair Managers for Michigan, March 9, 1892, Kalamazoo Public Library.
4. Lucinda Hinsdale Stone, "Art at the World's Fair, the Old White City and the New," handwritten manuscript, lecture given at Birmingham, MI, March 3, 1893, Kalamazoo Public Library.
5. Stone, "Art at the World's Fair."
6. Stone. "Art at the World's Fair."
7. NAACP, History of Lynching in America, https://naacp.org/find-resources/history-explained/history-lynching-america.
8. Frederick Douglass, "Introduction," *The Reason Why the Colored American Is Not in the World's Columbian Exposition.* Manuscript/Mixed Material, 4. https://www.loc.gov/item/mfd.25023/.
9. Ibram X. Kendi, *Stamped from the Beginning: The Definitive History of racist Ideas in America* (New York: Nation Books, 2016), 264.
10. Douglass, *The Reason Why the Colored American Is Not in the World's Columbian Exposition.*
11. W. S. McFeely, *Frederick Douglass* (New York: W. W. Norton, 1991), 473, e-book; https://interactive.wttw.com/dusable-to-obama/1893-worlds-fair
12. Lisa Cushing Davis, "Hegemony and Resistance at the World's Columbian Exposition: Simon Pokagon and *The Red Man's Rebuke*," *Journal of the Illinois State Historical Society* 108, no. 1, (Spring 2015): 40.
13. "Return as Freaks," *Chicago Daily Tribune*, July 1, 1893.
14. "Indian Students from Carlisle," *Chicago Daily Tribune*, October 19, 1892.
15. "Indian Children Are Learning the White Man's Methods," *Chicago Daily Tribune*, August 14, 1892.
16. "Greetings from Pokagon," *Chicago Daily Tribune*, October 10, 1893.
17. Simon Pokagon, The Red Man's Rebuke (Hartford, MI: O. H. Engle, 1893), n. pag.
18. Miss Stevens, "Folk Music at the Fair," *College Index*, Volume 15, No. 2, November 1893, 17–18, 21.

19 Near the present site of Hoben residence hall.

20 "Kalamazoo as Seen from Prospect Hill," *College Index*, November, 1877, 1.

21 Kalamazoo College catalogues.

22 Kalamazoo College Student Handbook 1908–1909, 15, http://hdl.handle.net/10920/30814.

23 "Washington Banquet Custom for 46 Years," *Kalamazoo College Index*, February 14, 1936, 1.

24 Janice Kuenzli, "Dr. Bacon Recalls Washington Banquets," *Index*, February 22, 1946, 1.

25 The last mention of the Washington Banquet in the *Index* appears in the February 4, 1966, issue of the *Index*. "SUB Advances Washington Dance," *Index*, February 4, 1966, 1.

26 Maud Wilkinson, "Mt. Vernon," *Index*, March 1894, 81.

27 Chas. R. Cullen, "The Washington Banquet," *Index*, March, 1913, 11.

28 "Banquet Was Great Success," *Index*, February 27, 1919, 1.

29 "Junior Class Stages Carnival in Gym With Great Success Saturday Night," *Index*, January 22, 1920, 4.

30 Seniors attending minstrel shows is referenced in the April ("Locals," 81) and June 1883 ("Locals," 115) issues of the *Index*.

31 Donald R. Belcher, "Musical Notes, The Home Concert," *Index*, May 1909, 336.

32 Eurodelphian party featuring a "minstrel quartette" ("The Eurodelphian Party," *Index*, November 1911, 23); Kappas put on a "vodeville" show with the orchestra in blackface (Helen Bronson, "Kappa Pi," *Index*, April 1915, 37); Gaynor Club Program includes an American Indian Song ("Gaynor Club Ready for Spring Trip," *Index*, March 28, 1918, 1).

33 "Gaynor Home Concert In Bowen April 16th," *Index*, April 11, 1918, 1.

34 "Large Crowd Gives Gaynor Concert Enthusiastic Reception," *Index*, April 18, 1918, 1.

35 "Minstrels Are Huge Success," *Index*, April 24, 1919, 1.

36 The Regent opened in August of 1919 and operated as a vaudeville theatre until June 1930 when it was destroyed by fire, http://cinematreasures.org/theaters/54355.

37 Advertisement for the Regent in the October 2, 1919, issue of the *Index*, 4.

38 "Seventeen," *Index*, March 1, 1923, 2; "Kappa Karnival Meets All Expectations," *Index*, March 8, 1923, 2; "Herald Kappa Vodvil As Novel Attraction," *Index*, March 6, 1924, 1.

39 "College Represented in Notable Feature of Historical Pageant," *Index*, June 14, 1929, 2.

40 "Bucks and Indian Maids Pow-Wow," *Index*, November 27, 1931, 1.

41 "Quadrangle Festive Scene of College Historical Panorama," *Index*, October 14, 1933, 6.

42 "Historical Pageant Is To Be Colorful Event," *Index*, September 29, 1933, 1.

43 "Quadrangle Festive Scene of College Historical Panorama," *Index*, October 14, 1933, 6.

44 Carl D. Bushnell,"The Negro Problem," *Index*, April 1901, 185–188.

45 Editorial, *The Index*, April 1901, 205–206.

46 William H. Watkins, *The White Architects of Black Education: Ideology and Power in America, 1865–1954* (New York: Teachers College Press, 2001).

47 Kendi, *Stamped from the Beginning*, 277.

48 Booker T. Washington, Atlanta Exposition Address, September 1895, http://p1cdn4static.sharpschool.com/UserFiles/Servers/Server_10640642/File/bugge/Chapter%2017/washingtonvsdubois.PDF.

49 *Index*, February 1896, 72–73.

50 "New Faculty Members," *College Index*, October 1907, 15.

51 Dr. A. B. Chaffee, "The Education of the Negro," *College Index*, March 1908, 127–130.

52 "Dr. Du Bois Lectures to Student Body," *Index*, March 4, 1920, 1.

53 W. E. B. Du Bois, "The Social Equality of Whites and Blacks," *The Crisis* 21 (November 1920), 16.

54 "Beadle Is Men's Orator," *Index*, February 7, 1924, 1.

55 "Shirley Payne and Harold Beadle Are Kazoo's Entrants," *Index*, March 6, 1924, 1.

56 Editorial, *Index*, December 3, 1925, 2.

57 "'Social Equality' Discussed At Open Forum," *Index*, May 6, 1926, 2.

58 "Students to Give Short Play Sun.," *Index*, April 26, 1928, 4.

59 "New Course Is Offered," *Index*, November 9, 1928, 4.

60 The Right To Complain," *Index*, March 3, 1939, 2.

61 "Deep Down South with Doc," *Index*, April 7, 1939, 2.

62 Jack Grabber, "Deep Down South with 'Doc,'" *Index*, May 13, 1939, 2.

63 "Negro Students Will Conduct Fellowship," *Index*, April 28, 1939, 4.

64 "Race Relations Will Be Topic of Fellowship," *Index*, April 17, 1942, 4.

65 Ken Warren, "Aims of Religious Week Realized in Campus Talks," *Index*, March 5, 1943, 1.

66 "Says Most Racial Differences Are Human Inventions Not True To Biology," *Index*, April 2, 1943, 4.

67 "Chicago Professor Says 'Pure Blood' To Be Misnomer," *Index*, May 5, 1944, 4.

68 "Emphasis on Thought, Too," *Index*, March 12, 1948, 2.

69 J. E. Smith, "Immigration," February, *Index*, 1894, 67–69.

70 C. W. Oakley, "Americans for America," *Index*, June 1895, 144–145.

71 Oakley, "Americans for America."

72 "Dr. Griffith's Men Win Title in Debate League, Decisions Unanimous," *Index*, January 22, 1925, 1.

73 "The New Japanese 'Peril,'" *Index*, June 17, 1925, 2.

74 "Nisei Students at Kalamazoo College," *LuxEsto* (Summer 2000): 37.

75 "Nisei Students."

76 Thomas T. Sugihara '45, Letter to the Editor, *Kalamazoo College Quarterly* (Fall/Winter, 1992–1993): 5.

77 "From Enemy of the State to the State Department," *LuxEsto* (Summer 2000): 32–36.

78 "From Enemy of the State to the State Department."

79 "From Enemy of the State to State Department."

80 *Index*, November 1891, president's note at the beginning of the issue.

81 Dana L. Robert, "The Origin of the Student Volunteer Watchword: 'The Evangelization of the World in This Generation,'" *International Bulletin of Missionary Research*, October 1986, http://www.internationalbulletin.org/issues/1986-04/1986-04-146-robert.pdf.

82 "Locals," *Index*, December, 1895, 40.

83 "Alumni Notes," *Index*, June 1906, 180–181.

84 Louis Edwin Martin, "A Letter from India," *Index*, January, 1900, 156–159.

85 "Alumni Notes," *Index*, May 1901, 235.

86 President Caldwell, "Greatness of the Missionary Enterprise," *Index*, November 15, 1880, 4–5.

87 See for example R. W. Paltridge, "The Fifty-Sixth Congress," *Index*, January, 1900, 151–156; G. W. Sigler, "The Political Situation from the Democratic Standpoint," *Index*, October, 1900, 9–12.

88 John C. Barrett, "World War I and the Decline of the First Wave of the American Protestant Missions Movement," *International Bulletin of Missionary Research* 39, no. 3 (July 2015): 122–126, https://journals.sagepub.com/doi/abs/10.1177/239693931503900302?journalCode=ibmd.

89 "The Nashville Convention," *Index*, April, 1906, 133–134.

90 Alma Kurtz, "Rochester Convention, the Wonderful," *Index*, February 1910, 15–17.

91 G. M. Hudson, "Pure Christianity.—True Socialism.," *Index*, October, 1893, 1–3.

92 A. N. De Long, "Ultimate Supremacy of the American City," *Index*, June, 1900, 388–392.

93 Willard F. Dowd, "The Christian Conquest of China," *Index*, October, 1900, 3–6.

94 Ora V. Scott, "A Summer in the Mikado's Empire," *Index*, November, 1901, 44–46.

95 "Our Alumni," *Index*, April, 1912, 45.

96 Barrett, "World War I and the Decline of the First Wave," 122–126.

97 "World Hope Lies in Christ, Great Leaders Proclaim," *Index*, January 10, 1924, 3.

98 Report on the Ninth International Convention of the Student Volunteer Movement for Foreign Missions, Indianapolis Indiana, December 28, 1923, to January 1, 1924, 121, https://play.google.com/store/books/details/Student_Volunteer_Movement_for_Foreign_Missions_In?id=CEnPAAAAMAAJ.

99 Report on the Ninth International Convention of the Student Volunteer Movement, 114.

100 "World Hope Lies in Christ, Great Leaders Proclaim," *Index*, January 10, 1924, 3.

101 "College Students Attend Conference, Western Civilization, Christianity not Synonymous Is Vote of Volunteers," *Index*, January 12, 1928, 1.

102 Arnold Mulder, *The Kalamazoo College Story: The First Quarter of a Century of Progress 1933–1958*, (Kalamazoo, MI: Kalamazoo College, 1958), 39.

103 Samuel Brooks, *Historical Catalogue of the Students of Kalamazoo College and of Kalamazoo Theological Seminary, 1851–1902* (Kalamazoo, MI: Ihling Bros. & Everard, 1903), 75, https://cache.kzoo.edu/handle/10920/5593.

104 Derek Chang, *Citizens of a Christian Nation: Evangelical Missions and the Problem of Race in the Nineteenth Century* (Philadelphia: University of Pennsylvania Press, 2010).

105 Chang, *Citizens of a Christian Nation,*109.

106 College records are spotty during these years and the only mention of Sam Song Bo's attendance is from 1881–1882. A January 1878 *Kalamazoo Gazette* article (January 17, 1878, 4), however, mentions that Sam Song Bo had enrolled at the College and "proposes to take a full course."

107 "Locals," *Index*, December 1882, 24.

108 *Kalamazoo Gazette*, February 13, 1878, 4.

109 Brooks, *Historical Catalogue of the Students of Kalamazoo College*; photo of Sam Song Bo with his University of Chicago medical class in 1884, https://lawandborder.com/steve-miller-meet-saum-song-bo-statue-liberty-symbolizes/.

110 Sam Song Bo, "A Chinese View of the Statue of Liberty," *The Sun*, New York, NY, June 30, 1885, 2, https://www.newspapers.com/clip/16261363/letter-from-saum-song-bo-re-statue-of/.

111 Sam, "A Chinese View."

112 "Myat Kyau," *Index*, April 1886, 101–102.

113 "Locals," *Index*, February 1887, 55.

114 Faculty Meeting Minutes, January 8, 1888, Kalamazoo College Archives. Record Group 30/3. Faculty Meeting Minutes Ledgers. Box 1. Ledger 2.

115 Brooks, *Historical Catalogue of the Students of Kalamazoo College*, 81.

116 Margaret DeRitter, "Not lost in translation: Jeffrey Angles turns Japanese poetry into English: A challenge of rhythm, meaning," mlive.com, April 17, 2011, updated Jan. 21, 2019, https://www.mlive.com/entertainment/kalamazoo/2011/04/not_lost_in_translation_jeffre.html.

117 Michael Hoffman, "A Literary Loner," *The Japan Times*, April 26, 2009, https://www.japantimes.co.jp/life/2009/04/26/general/a-literary-loner/.

118 Margaret DeRitter, "Snow Tears," *BeLight*, January, 2012.

119 DeRitter, "Snow Tears."

120 Kafu Nagai, "Atop the Hill," *American Stories* (New York: Columbia University Press, 2000), 18–19. (Originally published in Japanese, 1908.)

121 DeRitter, "Snow Tears."

122 "Dr. Katsuji Kato," *Kalamazoo College Alumnus*, February, 1950, 13.

123 "Century Forum," *Index*, April, 1905, 186.

124 K. Kato, "Niagra [*sic*] Student Conference," *Index*, October, 1907, 16.

125 DeRitter, "Snow Tears."

126 Katsuji Kato, "Men and World Service," Addresses Delivered at the National Missionary Congress, Washington, D.C., April 26–30, 1916, 195–197, Google Books, https://www.google.com/books/edition/Men_and_World_Service/HYFUAAAAYAAJ?hl=en.

127 Kato, "Men and World Service."

128 "Dr. Katsuji Kato," *Kalamazoo College Alumnus*, February, 1950, 13.

129 "Soloman [*sic*] Jeffrey Williamson," *Index*, June 1911, 16.

130 Susan W. Allen, "New Scholarship Honors 1911 Graduate," *The Kalamazoo College Quarterly*, Winter 1991, 3.

131 W. E. B. Du Bois, "The Talented Tenth," *The Negro Problem: A Series of Articles by Representative American Negroes of To-Day* (New York: J. Pott & Company, 1903), 33–34.

132 Henry Lyman Morehouse, quoted by Henry Louis Gates, Jr., "Who Really Invented the 'Talented Tenth'?," https://www.pbs.org/wnet/african-americans-many-rivers-to-cross/history/who-really-invented-the-talented-tenth/.

133 Virginia Union University, Fourth Annual Catalogue, 1902–1903, Virginia Baptist Press, Richmond, VA, 1903.

134 Resolution upon the death of Rooks' father, *Index*, May, 1906, 147.

135 Rooks senior bio, *Index*, June, 1906, 160.

136 Emily Carder, "Alumni Department," *Index*, March, 1910, 37.

137 "Alumni Notes," *Index*, March, 1913, 25.

138 Newspaper clipping, "Kalamazoo College Will Turn Indians Loose Against Hope," October 23, 1938, RG 79/3, Scrapbook 40: May 1938–December 1938 All-campus activities newspaper clippings, Kalamazoo College Archives, Kalamazoo College, Kalamazoo, Michigan.

139 L. K. Neuman, "Selling Indian Education: Fundraising and American Indian Identities at Bacone College, 1880–1941," *American Indian Culture and Research Journal, [s. L.]* 31, no. 4, (2007): 51–78. https://doi.org/10.17953/aicr.31.4.bg82935727k15352,

140 Neuman, "Selling Indian Education."

141 Newspaper clipping, "Kalamazoo College Will Turn Indians Loose Against Hope," October 23, 1938, RG 79/3, Scrapbook 40: May 1938–December 1938, All-campus activities newspaper clippings, Kalamazoo College Archives, Kalamazoo College, Kalamazoo, Michigan.

142 Dennis Groundhog [obituary], Ancestry.com, https://www.fold3.com/page/111557426/dennis-groundhog-ogan.

143 Dennis Groundhog [obituary].

144 "A Thought or Two," *Index*, February 24, 1939, 2.

145 Kalamazoo College Boiling Pot, 1940, 15.

146 Ruth Ann Moerdyk, "Lone Wolf," *Emancipated Spirits: Portraits of Kalamazoo College Women*, (Kalamazoo, MI: Ihling Bros. Everard Co., 1983), 213.

147 Moerdyk, "Lone Wolf," 228.

148 Moerdyk, "Lone Wolf," 228.

149 Moerdyk, "Lone Wolf," 228.

150 Moerdyk, "Lone Wolf," 229.

151 Moerdyk, "Lone Wolf," 230.

152 "Honor Day Is New Occasion for Kazoo: Undergraduates Receive Scholarship Awards, to Be Held Annually," *Index*, October 15, 1925, 1.

153 "Number of Students in Scholor's [*sic*] Group Are Permitted to Enroll in Honor's [*sic*] Courses," *Index*, October 22, 1925, 1.

154 Moerdyk, "Lone Wolf," 234.

155 Moerdyk, "Lone Wolf," 233–234.

156 Moerdyk, "Lone Wolf," 234–235.

157 Moerdyk, "Lone Wolf," 229.

158 Moerdyk, "Lone Wolf," 230.

159 Moerdyk, "Lone Wolf," 230–231.

160 Moerdyk, "Lone Wolf," 224.

161 "Race Relations Class Amusing to Students," *Index*, November 19, 1943, 1, 4.

Chapter Four

Behind the Mask

The late 1940s were a sleepy time on the Kalamazoo College campus. Based on the content of the *Index*, very little was happening aside from the usual athletic events, dances, fundraising activities, and the occasional outside speaker. More space was dedicated to ads, perhaps to make up for a lack of content, and an issue in 1948 ran with some blank columns causing a frustrated reader to write, "last week's Index was a disgrace to this campus. Do you think that is the kind of paper I want to send home to my folks?"[1] The *Index* editors penned hand-wringing editorials about the purpose of the paper, the lack of interest in the *Index* among students and faculty, and the meager resources to support it. Then the next year, news of a novel event captured the campus's attention.

An Indian Prince

In February 1949, the following headline appeared among the otherwise banal content: "Indian Prince to Talk Here." According to the article, Prince Ali Kala Parishad, "the noted writer, lecturer, world traveler, soldier, and statesman," was to visit campus "under the auspices of the All India Congress" to seek aid for the Indian government under the Marshall Plan. The prince was to discuss current events in India and provide a detailed account of the assassination of Mahatma Gandhi, which had occurred the year before. "Having known Mahatma Ghandi [*sic*]," the *Index* reported, "he is especially well versed in the events leading up to the death of this famous personage."[2] The following week, another article ran, "Indian Prince Will Tell of Ghandi," again misspelling the name of the leader of India's independence movement.[3] The Men's Union was sponsoring the event and had cordially invited students, faculty, and friends of the College to attend.

Two weeks later, the *Index* reported that about 250 people had come to hear the prince, a large turnout for a campus of about 700 students. "Attracted by the advertising of a real live Indian prince," the article read, "they all rose in respect as the old gentleman walked down the aisle. He commenced his address with a few remarks about the general situation in India, and spoke of the Indians' desire to emulate our democracy."

However, it soon began to dawn on the audience that all was not as it seemed, especially when the prince displayed a very good sense of "strictly American humor." When an audience member asked the prince to reveal his "famous shock of hair," he "obligingly lifted his turban—to show a gleaming, white pate." The "prince," as it turned out, was a White actor, apparently in brownface. Far from being disappointed or offended by the hoax, audience members were delighted, and the actor's "excellent impersonation and snappy jokes kept the large crowd in an uproar most of the evening."[4]

Given the outlandishness of the stunt, one wonders if anyone actually expected a "real live" prince, but it seems the editors of the *Index* did. In the same issue that recounted the prince's visit, they published an editorial decrying the deceitfulness of the Men's Union and lamenting their own gullibility. Particularly upsetting to them was that "the very foundation of the fraud was direct lying, and lying is a violation of the Eighth Commandment." "We of the Index trusted the president of the Men's Union in accepting for publication the releases he gave us," they went on. "We here express our apologies to the student body for displaying such an unwarranted trust in its leaders. We are all the more concerned because this fraud was not only approved, but encouraged by certain members of the faculty. For the faculty of a Christian liberal arts college such conduct is almost inconceivable." As was common when White people impersonated people of other races or ethnicities, the event also included "off-color jokes."[5]

Bizarre as it may seem now, the "Indian Prince" episode held with a longstanding pattern of engaging with other cultures through exoticism, stereotype, and ridicule. Though the *Index* editors were indignant that the Men's Union had put one over on them, the deceit of brownface did not faze them. Use of brownface, yellowface, redface and, most commonly, blackface was a well-established tradition in American entertainment, and the practice had been employed at the College off and on since the early 1900s. Indulgence in such impersonations—for it seemed to hold an irresistible allure—projected White peoples' anxieties about and fascinations with race. As it turned out, the "Indian Prince" episode presaged an unrestrained embrace of blackface performance that would begin that year and continue through most of the 1950s.

Happy Days

In the years after World War II, White America embarked upon a period defined by optimism and economic growth. Having survived the harrowing years of the Great Depression and emerging victorious from the war, the country was now a world power with seemingly unlimited prosperity on the horizon. In those days, it was easy for White Americans to feel good about themselves. American soldiers had helped to vanquish an unmitigated evil abroad and had been hailed as heroes. In the new postwar order, America was seen, and saw itself, as a force for good in the world.

Yet the so-called "happy days" were not equally shared. Black veterans returned from fighting racial and ethnic hatred abroad only to face ongoing racism and violence at home. Oppressive Jim Crow laws continued in the South, while in the North, Black Americans confronted discrimination just about everywhere they turned. The GI Bill, a boon for White veterans in terms of access to higher education and housing, largely excluded veterans who were Black. For many Black veterans returning to families living in poverty, the urgent need to find a job took precedence over college. Those who did hope to attend college found themselves shut out of segregated Southern universities and facing quotas in the North, and inequalities in the public school systems meant that many Black veterans were not prepared for college-level work. Historically Black colleges and universities were overwhelmed with applicants and had waiting lists of a year or more.[6]

These were the years in which many White Americans attained their dream of home ownership, but discriminatory lending practices made it next to impossible for Black homebuyers to get a mortgage and restricted where they could live. It was common practice for predatory real estate agents to intimidate White families into selling them their homes at a price below market value by convincing them that an integrated neighborhood would drive down home prices. These agents would then sell the same home to a Black family at a much higher price. Black families were also charged higher interest rates on the loans they did get, making it difficult to afford the mortgage payments. As a result, racial disparities were keenly felt and feelings of anger, frustration, and resentment grew.

Though it probably did not cross their minds, racial discrimination characterized the all-White neighborhoods where many Kalamazoo College students had grown up. Redlining had been underway since the 1930s in cities throughout the country, including Kalamazoo,[7] and Detroit and Chicago were well on their way to becoming the most segregated cities in America.[8] The West Main Hill neighborhood adjacent to Kalamazoo College, where a good portion of the faculty and staff lived, was designated as "restricted" on the 1937 Home Owners' Loan Corporation (HOLC) map, meaning the neighborhood was limited to Whites only. HOLC agents were instructed to assess any "threat of infiltration of foreign-born, negro or lower grade population," and used notes such as "Negro-rapid" in describing the level of "infiltration."[9]

Throughout the 1950s, Kalamazoo College remained small, homogenous, and insular with enrollments ranging from around 400 to 700. About two-thirds of the students came from Michigan and 80 to 90 percent from the industrial Midwest.[10] The first professor of color, Dr. Wen Chao Chen, joined the faculty in 1950. Chen had been born in Shanxi Province, China. After receiving his bachelor's degree from Grinnell College, he went on to earn a master's degree in public administration and a doctorate in political science from St. Louis University. It would be eighteen more years before another professor of color was hired. The staff and students were likewise almost all White. From 1950 to 1960, a total of twenty-two Black students enrolled at Kalamazoo College. Eight of those students were from African countries and two were from Jamaica. Of the twelve African American students who enrolled during that period, six persisted until graduation, a rate consistent with graduation rates at the College overall.[11]

The students tended to be conservative, but many had no party affiliation, suggesting they were largely apolitical.[12] In those days, Kalamazoo was still very much a Baptist-affiliated college, and the Chapel, located in the middle of the quad, was literally and figuratively the center of campus life. As was common for institutions of higher education then, the

College functioned *in loco parentis* with many rules governing student behavior, especially the behavior of women.

Social life revolved around seasonal events, many of which had been going on for decades. Homecoming was the big event in the fall, with floats, a bonfire, and a formal dance. In December there was a Christmas Carol Service in the Chapel. The Washington Banquet, held in February in honor of George Washington's birthday, continued throughout the 1950s and featured a formal dinner and dance. In the early spring, Religious Emphasis Week brought outside speakers to campus, usually prominent Baptists, and fostered discussion and reflection. Sometimes Religious Emphasis Week included visits from Black clergy, one of the rare times when there were speakers of color on campus. The year wrapped up with the annual May Fete, which involved the election of a May Queen and her court as well as a formal dance.

The societies continued to drive the social life on campus. Having begun as literary and debate societies in the nineteenth century, by the 1950s they functioned mainly as social clubs. The three societies for men and three for women put on many events each year and held competitions for the best float and vocal performance. Almost all first-year students pledged a society and went through some form of hazing. One of the initiation practices was called "master-slave," in which pledging students had to do whatever the upperclassmen told them.[13]

For most White students of that time, this was all innocent fun. They were young, well off, in a setting that validated everything about them, and looking ahead to bright futures. They probably felt like they were living the American Dream, but they were actually living in a dream world. Disconnected as they were from a larger reality beyond the White monoculture on campus, they thought nothing of holding an annual, highly publicized minstrel show throughout most of the decade, even as the Civil Rights Movement got underway and people in the community registered complaints about the blackface performances.

"Flagrant Examples of Discrimination Are Everywhere Present"

From 1949–1956, the Century Forum, one of the men's societies, put on an annual minstrel show. There had been instances of blackface on campus for decades, but in the 1950s the Century Forum took blackface performance to a new level. The "Darktown Jamboree," later renamed the

"Century Showboat," featured White performers in blackface make-up projecting buffoonish images of Black people in one of the most anticipated and well-attended events of the year.

Minstrel shows had first become popular in the 1830s among northern White working-class audiences. Their heyday lasted from the 1840s through the 1880s, when minstrelsy constituted *the* popular culture of the United States. This was during a time when White Americans were concerned with establishing a uniquely American culture, one that was not derivative of Europe. They did this in part by appropriating culture from enslaved Black people and American Indians.

According to Eric Lott, author of *Love and Theft* (2013), northern Whites were fascinated by race in the antebellum years, and he provides a detailed analysis of how minstrel shows helped satisfy the curiosity of White people in the North, assuage their anxieties about race, and validate their feelings of superiority.[14] Some show-goers convinced themselves that they were actually watching Black people perform, and many of those who remained aware of the White actors behind the mask still assumed they were witnessing an authentic depiction of Black people and culture.[15] Minstrelsy was considered "low brow" entertainment and largely eschewed by the White elite. For working-class White people, however, minstrel shows served both to solidify their position in the nation's social hierarchy and safely lampoon the upper classes from behind a mask of "blackness."[16]

Many blackface performers purported to admire the musical traditions of enslaved people and to care deeply about their plight. They imagined that their performances were some sort of tribute. Yet, they were benefiting financially by expropriating and distorting Black culture at a time when Black people themselves were not permitted to appear on stage. Perhaps the Century Forum minstrel shows also involved a bit of "admiration." The society's other main contribution to the social life of the 1950s and early '60s was bringing jazz to campus. The society put on regular jazz concerts and brought Count Basie to perform twice.[17,18] There clearly was an appreciation of Black culture, but it was bound up with the racist jokes, distorted images, and mockery inherent in blackface performance.

The decades of minstrel shows in the United States had solidified in the minds of White Americans negative stereotypes of Black people. These included the docile, sexless "Mammy" and the shiftless, lazy "Coon."[19] The "Coon" character was often portrayed as a slick Northern dandy or a compliant Southern "Sambo." Harriett Beecher Stowe's 1852 novel *Uncle Tom's Cabin* popularized the "Uncle Tom" character,[20] a subservient older Black man, as well as the "pickaninny,"[21] an unkempt child dressed in rags who was subjected to all kinds of life-threatening dangers meant to be comical. Scenes of plantation life as depicted in Stowe's novel were often performed in minstrel shows. During slavery, these "black" characters were represented as happy-go-lucky and contented with their lot. They were also portrayed as foolish and slow-witted, and the White actors who played them spoke in "plantation dialect."

After Emancipation, the "Brute" caricature became prevalent as White people in the South promoted the fiction that freed Black men were reverting to barbarism without slavery's civilizing influences. The "Brute," shown as a menacing figure who preyed on White women, was used to justify Jim Crow laws and the frequent lynchings that terrorized Black people in the South from post-Reconstruction through World War II.[22]

Long after professional minstrel shows declined in popularity, these archetypal characters lived on in the motion picture industry and later in radio and television. Kalamazoo College students of the 1950s would have grown up listening to the popular *Amos 'n' Andy* radio show that aired from 1928 to 1955. Indeed, the names of two of the show's characters—Kingfish and Lightnin'—were used by student performers in multiple years of the Century Forum minstrel show. The lead characters in the *Amos 'n' Andy* radio show were portrayed by the White actors Freeman Gosden and Charles Correll, both of whom had a background in vaudeville and blackface performance. In 1951, the series was adapted for television and finally featured Black actors, although the actors were instructed to carefully imitate the speech patterns popularized by Gosden and Correll. The television show lasted only a few years before it was cancelled in response to a boycott organized by the NAACP. Among the reasons the NAACP cited for its opposition to the TV show was that "it tends to strengthen the conclusion among uninformed and prejudiced people that Negroes are inferior, lazy, dumb, and dishonest."[23]

After professional minstrelsy gave way to vaudeville and the movies, the genre was kept alive through amateur productions in schools, churches, and community organizations.[24] According to Susan Smulyan, author of *Popular Ideologies: Mass Culture at Mid-century* (2007), "just as professional minstrel shows played a part in working-class formation in the nineteenth century, amateur minstrels assisted in solidifying the self-identification of the middle class in the twentieth."[25]

Nationally marketed "how-to" books encouraged amateur productions by providing instructions for putting on minstrel shows complete with songs, jokes, and details on applying blackface make-up. The books drew their material from vaudeville, which had grown out of the minstrel tradition and frequently featured blackface acts. Nevertheless, vaudeville was considered more respectable than traditional minstrelsy. Therefore, these "how-to" books would have assured White middle-class performers that what they were doing was socially acceptable. "At the same time," Smulyan writes, "minstrel shows provided the historicity and nostalgic aura that allowed for an exploration and construction of race that so fascinated white Americans."[26]

Whether or not members of the Century Forum drew from these "how-to" books, the structure of their shows followed the pattern laid out in the manuals. The first part of the show typically featured the members of the chorus seated in a semicircle with the end-men on either side. The interlocutor, who functioned as emcee, stood in the middle. Following is a diagram from Harold Rossiter's 1921 book *How to Put on a Minstrel Show*[27] (Figure 4.1) along with a photo from Kalamazoo College's 1952 Darktown Jamboree (Figure 4.2).[28]

Figure 4.1. Minstrel Show Diagram. The numbered squares indicate where the end-men are to sit.

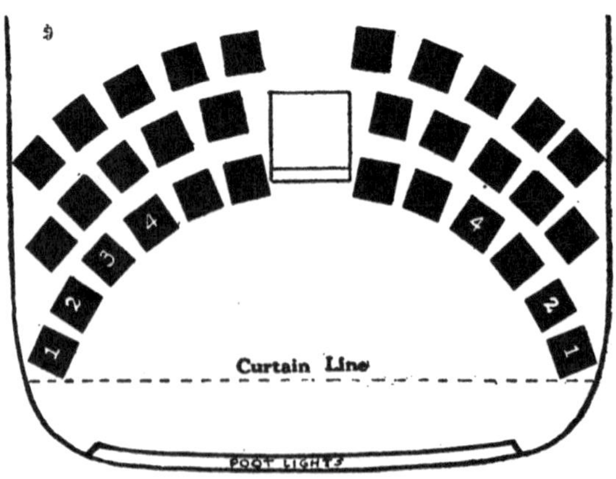

DIAGRAM.

Harold Rossiter, *How to Put on a Minstrel Show* (Chicago: Max Stein Publishing House, 1921), 8. Google Books. In the public domain.

Figure 4.2. A photo of Kalamazoo College's 1952 "Darktown Jamboree" with the performers arranged as shown in Harold Rossiter's diagram.

Kalamazoo College Archives. Reprinted with permission.

The chorus members and end-men were in blackface while the interlocutor was not. The interlocutor would banter with the end-men between musical performances that featured soloists with the chorus chiming in on cue. The end-men wore raggedy clothes, kept up a running dialogue of jokes with the interlocutor acting as straight man, and played the tambo and bones, traditional minstrel show instruments. Rossiter explains how the tambo and bones were to be played: "the idea is to make just as many grotesque *motions* while playing the instrument as possible. The feature can hardly be overdone . . . "[29]

The song "Here Comes the Showboat" typically opened the Century Forum minstrel shows. Many of the songs the students sang, such as "Down Yonder," "Waiting for the Robert E. Lee," and "Dixie," were nostalgic of a romanticized Old South consistent with Lost Cause ideology. The second part of the show, called the Olio, featured a variety of vaudeville-style acts. Some of the acts mentioned in the *Index* included a "torchy tune" by a "sultry singer"[30] and a quartet called "the Chocolate Four."[31] In 1953, one of the Olio acts was "The Faculty Harmony Trio."[32]

Harold Rossiter's how-to book instructed readers to bill a minstrel show like a circus,[33] and in 1952 the *Index* did just that with splashy headlines and Barnum-and-Bailey-style language. They also made use of "plantation dialect" in advertising the show. Under the headline "'Show Boat' Coming Again Tonight, Mad-Cap Minstrel Gang Brings Memories Of Dixie," the article began:

> Music, Music, Music! Yowsuh, dats what dere am gonna be plenty ob tonight at the Darktown Jamboree. Those illustrious characters of the Century Forum will be cutting up again in this fourth annual minstrel show with lots of song and dance (not to mention the so-called jokes which almost invariably incur a titter from the intelligentsia.) So take heed all you study-fatigued scholars (ah ah ah), and grab a riverboat down to Bowen's Dixieland Auditorium at 8:00 p.m. to spend the evening with . . . the blackfaced gang.[34]

The 1953 minstrel show featured a "chorus line" with male students in blackface wearing moplike wigs. Consistent with the minstrel tradition of sexualizing "black" female characters, they performed in drag wearing nothing but bandeau tops and shorts covered with balloons, laughing and dancing as the chorus sat in blackface behind them (Figure 4.3).

Figure 4.3. A chorus line in Kalamazoo College's 1953 minstrel show.

Kalamazoo College Archives. Reprinted with permission.

The book *Mahoney's Modern Minstrels*, published in 1945, included a plantation skit called "Echoes of the Old South." The tradition of acting out a plantation scene is perhaps depicted in a 1955 yearbook photo with a White character dressed as a Southern gentleman surrounded by kneeling characters in blackface (Figure 4.4).

Figure 4.4. Plantation skit in Kalamazoo College's 1955 minstrel show.

Kalamazoo College Archives. Reprinted with permission.

Over successive years the yearbook also featured photos of a character in blackface and wig wearing a sack-like outfit with "XXXX Flour" written on it, perhaps suggesting a "Mammy" character (Figure 4.5). The "Mammy" was typically portrayed as a rotund, maternal figure who was happy to care for her White "family," and the extra-large sack of flour may have been referencing these stereotypes. The costume may also have alluded to the fact that many enslaved women had to make their dresses out of old flour sacks.

Figure 4.5. Scene from Kalamazoo College's 1954 minstrel show.

Kalamazoo College Archives. Reprinted with permission.

Difficult as it may be to understand, in the early 1950s there was nothing in the White students' well-buffered world to indicate that the minstrel shows were anything but harmless fun. The stereotypes of Black people they uncritically embraced were commonplace in American popular culture, and the Century Forum must have been gratified and encouraged by the applause and accolades they received from their audiences. The performances were well attended, and it had to have been especially validating when members of the faculty participated in the show.

The first tugs at the fabric of their protective cocoon came in 1953 when the Centuries gave a performance of their show off campus. Afterward, several community organizations contacted the College to complain. The community objections were discussed in a meeting of the Student-Faculty Council in April of 1953. It is noteworthy that in the course of the discussion, community members were repeatedly referred to as "outsiders," suggesting the extent to which the students were isolated from, or felt unconnected to, the city in which they lived. According to the minutes, the vice president of the College had received a call concerning the minstrel show from a Mr. Duane Roberts of the Douglass Community Association in the city's predominantly Black northside neighborhood and had made an appointment to speak to Mr. Roberts in person. Mrs. Mills, a faculty member, had "received letters from the various intercultural groups in town," and one of the student members said that, "he had talked with Mr. Benjamin Graham, Director of the Bureau of Social Aid, and that Mr. Graham is also very much opposed to the minstrel show." Another student reported that "the Centuries gave a 'pre-view' of the show at dinner one night, it was extremely offensive, and certainly the Negro students would not go to see more of the same type of thing." After a lengthy conversation, the Council voted unanimously to "recommend to the faculty to recommend to the Social Committee that the Century Forum minstrel show not be given another year."[35]

The following fall, minutes from another Student-Faculty Council meeting recounted a follow-up discussion of the minstrel show issue. Word of community complaints had indeed reached the Social Committee, and members of the Committee had subsequently met with the officers of the Century Forum. The outcome was that the Centuries promised that there would be "more whiteface and no jokes that would be in poor taste." They were reluctant to give up the blackface, however, because it gave "the actors something to hide behind so they would feel more at ease before their audience."

A student member of the Council, trying to wrap his mind around the community complaints, "asked if the objection was to the minstrel show or to the black face." As he thought about it more, he "wondered if outsiders looked on the student body as a group of discriminators who are trying to discriminate against Negroes." "If this is the case," he asserted indignantly, "these outsiders have a very wrong idea."

The vice president of the College reported that he had met with "a representative of the Negroes in town," presumably Mr. Roberts of the Douglass Community Association. He tried to set Mr. Roberts's mind at ease by explaining "that there were different types of jokes; some Irish, some Scottish, some Negro, etc.," an explanation that failed to allay Mr. Roberts's concerns.[36]

The following spring, the Centuries went ahead with their annual minstrel show. Based on yearbook photographs and *Index* articles, the only discernible change was that they were no longer calling the show the "Darktown Jamboree." It was now referred to as the "Century

Showboat."[37] The students were still in blackface and the performance continued to follow the typical minstrel show structure.[38] The Showboat went on in this same vein through 1956 despite ongoing complaints from people both on and off campus.

In January of 1954, Weimer K. Hicks assumed the presidency of Kalamazoo College. Hicks was socially conservative and maintained high standards of propriety and decorum. During a faculty meeting in the fall of 1955, he raised the issue of the "societies, especially their public productions and their initiations,"[39] perhaps referring to the minstrel shows.

Later that fall, Hicks received a letter from an alumnus and former member of the Century Forum who had recently been on campus for homecoming. As a student, he had directed two minstrel shows and participated in two others. During his visit, he learned that the administration had changed the date of the annual minstrel show, a move that concerned him greatly because the new date required that rehearsals be divided before and after spring break. He felt this would have deleterious effects on the quality of the performance.

In his letter he argued that the minstrel shows built community, not only among the Centuries but among the entire campus. He also stated his belief that the shows improved the College's standing in the larger community—either he was unaware of complaints made by community members or he did not take them seriously. The letter's tone was vaguely threatening. While he congratulated Hicks for aspiring to raise the College's profile, he also insinuated that he would not have the support of Century Forum alumni as long as the show remained scheduled as it was.[40]

In Hicks's reply it becomes clear why the minstrel shows troubled him. "At the very beginning may I say that all of us very much appreciate the efforts and quality of the Annual Minstrel Show," he opened diplomatically. "It was really the first presentation that I saw after I arrived on campus two years ago. I was most delighted with the performance, particularly in the work of the chorus." "Last year's presentation was likewise very very good," he continued. "However, out of it did grow certain problems for during the second semester the quality of the academic work of our students was at an all time low."[41] It was not the nature of the show, then, that concerned Hicks, but rather its impact on academics. And so, the show went on. It went on in spite of offended community members, and it went on in spite of the growing Civil Rights Movement.

The Civil Rights Movement as Seen from the Kalamazoo College Campus

In 1954, the Supreme Court finally struck down the "separate but equal" doctrine in its landmark *Brown vs. the Board of Education* decision. The following year, while visiting family in Mississippi, fourteen-year-old Emmett Till was kidnapped, tortured, and murdered after being accused of flirting with a White woman. His grief-stricken mother insisted on displaying his mutilated body in an open-casket to show the world the depth and brutality of racial hatred in America. Tens of thousands of people viewed his body, and the story of Till's lynching was widely covered by the media. A few weeks later, his killers were acquitted by an all-White jury. Later in 1955, Rosa Parks was arrested for refusing to give up her bus seat to a White man, launching the Montgomery Bus Boycott, which lasted over a year.

While these events did not manage to create enough cognitive dissonance on the Kalamazoo College campus to put an end to the minstrel shows, they had begun to slowly raise awareness of ongoing racial injustice among at least some students. However, the distorting lens of the White monoculture led to flawed analyses of the country's deep-seated racial issues and held in place some colossal blind spots.

In February 1956, a student published a piece in the *Index* commenting on two invited speakers who had addressed the legacy of the Civil War with respect to the current "Negro Problem."[42] He summarized one speaker's remarks by saying that "the most important cause of the Civil War was the uncompromising attitude of both the southern states-righters and the northern abolitionists." The student went on to further falsely equate abolitionists and Confederates by saying, "both demanded rights for a group of people and both wanted every concession granted immediately." To alleviate tensions brought on by the recent Supreme Court decision, the writer of the article suggested letting "the enforcement of the Court's decision hang fire until both sides cool off and become a little more rational." "The Negros have been denied many of their rights in the south (and the north) for many, many years," he continued. "One more decade of some denial that might prevent hardships, riots and bloodshed does not seem to [*sic*] much to ask of them."

The following month, the same student wrote an article about a trip a group of Kalamazoo College students had made to Washington, DC. While there, they met a White student from Alabama who they felt had enlightened them on racial issues. "Most Southerners actually have very close relationships with the Negroes," the writer assured his readers, referring to the bond White Southerners imagined they had with their Black servants. "The Negro performs many more services in the South than he does in the North; cooking, keeping house, waiting tables, maid and chauffer services are a few," the writer continued, as if this was evidence of progress. "Many [of the students] were ashamed of themselves when they discovered that their treatment of the northern Negro was actually on a lower par than the treatment the southern Negro received," he continued, edging a little closer to some sort of personal revelation. He contrasted how much the Southerners "love Negroes who come into their households to care for their children and help them cook and clean house" with "the greater percentage of the righteous long-nosed north who won't hire a Negro because 'they can't be trusted,' or they won't let them take care of their children because 'they might be dirty,' or they won't let them into their homes because 'a Negro must know his place,' or they won't talk to them on the street because 'they might injure their social position.'"[43]

Although they were beginning to discern the hazy contours of their own racism, the students managed to come away from the experience feeling greater empathy for White Southerners with the writer putting forth the following defense: "The average Southerner realizes that a change is inevitable and that the Negro is coming into his own. Perhaps he is jealous; the South is proud and doesn't want to be pushed around by someone else."

As the 1956 minstrel show approached, the *Index* ran a story about the upcoming Showboat with a photo of the students who were to play the end-men and the interlocutor. True to form, the interlocutor is shown looking straight into the camera with a serious expression on his face with the six end-men positioned around him hamming it up.[44] Appearing in the same issue was an emotional editorial denouncing racial discrimination and urging White students to support the Civil Rights Movement. The article had been written by one of the end-men pictured in the article about the Showboat.

Upset by a recent incident in which a group of Kalamazoo College students were turned away from a local restaurant, apparently because one of the students was Black, the editorial writer (and minstrel show performer) expressed shock that such discrimination could occur in his community. "We have heard of similar incidents in Detroit or Chicago," he wrote, "but we never thought very much about them. We told ourselves it couldn't happen here. Well it did, and it hurts. We have suddenly realized how much discrimination and prejudice there is present."

"Of course, discrimination is not very obvious here," he continued. "We don't make the negroes sit in the back of busses, we don't have separate rest-rooms for them, but the discrimination is still there; we just hide it under a blanket of hypocrisy.... We clamor against race prejudice while flagrant examples of discrimination are everywhere present."

He concluded by calling on White people to "stand side by side with the Negro and put an end to discrimination where ever it occurs." "It is a job that requires a great deal of patience and tact," he wrote. "Our civic leaders, our press, our professional men, our professors, and we students must take an active part in this fight to really establish equal rights for all."[45]

The day after publishing this eloquent plea for racial justice, the writer blackened his face, acted the fool, and sang nostalgic songs about the Old South. Although he clamored "against race prejudice," he himself was part of a "flagrant" example of discrimination. It seems no one saw the irony because at the time there was nothing ironic about opposing racial discrimination and also employing blackface. Dafina M. L. Stewart, author of *Black Collegians' Experiences in US Northern Private Colleges: A Narrative History, 1945–1965* (2017), notes that blackface acts were common at many Midwestern colleges during these years and that these performances and other forms of racist stereotyping often coexisted with calls to end racial discrimination.[46] The case of the student who wrote the editorial shows how such contradictions could coexist not only within institutions but also within individuals.

"A Great Deal of Patience and Tact"

The next fall, Paul Collins, a new member of the administration, decided to tackle the issue of the minstrel shows once and for all. Collins had been hired as dean of men the previous year. He likely had a more sophisticated understanding of racial issues than most people on campus, having worked at a historically Black college in Tennessee.[47] In October of 1956, he took it upon himself to write to Hicks:

> I have been aware for some time of the criticisms leveled by members of the faculty and the community at the Showboat . . . I felt that it would be helpful if we could meet with the officers of the society, several faculty members and several from the community who were concerned with a show which offended a particular group and seemed to perpetuate a stereotype of that group.
>
> In opening the meeting [with the students] I stressed the importance of our position as a church-related college, our belief that all societies are a part of the college and that their activities must represent the best for which we stand . . . I stated that the purpose of the meeting was not to reach a decision regarding the show. That decision would have to be made by the society. For two hours we talked over the entire problem.
>
> I believe that the young men present came to have a broader understanding of the wider implications of their type of show . . . .They did reach the point in the discussion where they wondered if they omitted the black faces and the phraseology, whether the show would be acceptable. We did also emphasize that a showboat could be and was often something quite different from the type of show they have had.[48]

Collins certainly appears to have used "a great deal of patience and tact," as the writer of the editorial suggested would be necessary in putting "an end to discrimination where ever it occurs." He seemed to want to ensure that the Centuries not only stopped producing the racist shows but that they also understood why and took ownership of the decision. Still, it is striking to what degree and for how long the administration tiptoed around the Centuries, even with repeated complaints from the community and the intensifying Civil Rights Movement. Whose interests were being protected and whose feelings were being taken into account? Much energy and thought went into how to handle the issue with the Century Forum delicately, but what of the feelings of people in the larger community and, more importantly, the feelings of the small number Black students on campus?

Hicks wrote a short note back to Collins saying that he greatly appreciated his memo and believed Collins was approaching the matter constructively. He congratulated him for making progress and wished him luck. Though Hicks appeared pleased that Collins was handling the issue, it hardly seems as if the minstrel show was topping his list of priorities.[49]

The Century Forum ultimately decided to end the use of blackface and substantially revise their annual production. Though they continued to put on a "Showboat" well into the 1960s, it was transformed into a variety show with skits satirizing campus life. Hicks wrote to the president of the Centuries in January of 1957 saying, "word has reached me of the decision of your Club to alter the established pattern of your annual show. I realize that a change of this nature is not easy. I know, too, that it has been made in deference to certain individuals who have felt that the previous productions have been offensive to a minority group." Hicks went on to congratulate them on their "understanding attitude" and "co-operative spirit," concluding that "your action certainly reflects credit upon your organization and the individuals who comprise your membership."[50]

College minstrel productions had reached their peak in the 1920s, so it is somewhat mystifying why minstrelsy burst forth in the 1950s at Kalamazoo and similar colleges, including Albion and Hope in Michigan, Denison and Wooster in Ohio, and Wabash in Indiana.[51] Although minstrelsy's legacy was kept alive in radio, television, and movies, and most any Black character was forced to conform to the stereotypes popularized by the minstrel tradition, by the 1950s minstrel shows had become old fashioned and were rarely performed on college campuses, at least not in such a public way. In some respects, the students of the 1950s were less sophisticated than their counterparts of the 1920s, who at least seemed somewhat aware that they were using the mask of blackness to cross the lines of propriety and engage in something not altogether on the up-and-up.

The 1950s are often portrayed as a carefree time, at least for White people, but that characterization is in many ways misleading. White society in the 1950s was very repressed, with strict adherence to traditional gender roles, rules governing social class, and racial hierarchies that kept Black people relegated to the lowest rung of society and separated from White people. As a small, Christian institution, Kalamazoo College emphasized conformity to these norms. Though in certain ways the College could sometimes seem more progressive about race than White society in general, Black students and other students of color had to negotiate the appearance of equality layered on top of deep-seated notions of White superiority. In such an environment, it is not hard to see minstrelsy's appeal to White students. The mask of blackness allowed them to transgress these rules and hierarchies. In the context of a minstrel show, there could be sexual innuendo, cross-dressing, and a bizarre sort of race mixing as the White performers inhabited "black" bodies, which both fascinated and repelled them. Under the cover of a minstrel show it became acceptable to perform an Apache (pronounced Ah-PAHSH) dance, a routine popularized in Paris in the early 1900s that looks like choreographed intimate partner violence. It also became permissible for male students to cross-dress and for a student at a Baptist college to transform into a "sultry singer" and offer a "torchy tune."

The mask of blackness also made the minstrel shows acceptable to the socially conservative faculty and administrators of the 1950s. It allowed them the conceit that it was not White students putting on these transgressive performances, but White students pretending to be "black," and it was to the blackness, not the students, that all the social taboos were attached. It meant everyone could laugh and say, "just kidding," after slipping for a brief time the bonds of a restrictive social order.

As for the racist stereotypes and denigration of Black people, the students did not get it. They considered it all a big joke, intending no harm to anyone. In fact, in many ways, minstrelsy allowed the students to maintain their "innocence" with regard to issues of race. Ralph Ellison wrote in 1958 that minstrelsy "constituted a ritual of exorcism." "Other white cultures had their gollywogs and blackamoors," he explained, "but the fact of Negro slavery went to the moral heart of the American social drama, and here the Negro was too real for easy fantasy, too serious to be dealt with in anything less than a national art."[52] This elaborate exorcism meant, according to another scholar of blackface, "that white Americans could consider themselves and their nation as good and decent while still engaging in racist behavior."[53]

Minstrelsy is so complicated and fraught because it reflects all the contradictions, fascinations, desires, and anxieties inherent in a "free" country born of slavery, an "equal" society organized around a racial caste system, and an "innocent" White population perpetuating or at least tolerating these evils. The unsettled and largely unconscious feelings about race that gave rise to the minstrel shows had been in place for a long time and they did not go away simply because the shows did. The minstrel shows were an instance of deeply held racial prejudices and anxieties being released in a very public way through a time-honored outlet for White people. As Ellison wrote, "the Negro looks at the white man and finds it difficult to believe that the 'grays'—a Negro term for white people—can be so absurdly self-deluded over the true inter-relatedness of blackness and whiteness. To him the white man seems a hypocrite who boasts of a pure identity while standing with his humanity exposed to the world."[54] According to Eric Lott, "minstrelsy brought to public form racialized elements of thought and feeling, tone and impulse, residing at the very edge of semantic availability, which Americans only dimly realized they felt, let alone understood."[55] In the coming decade, the ongoing Civil Rights Movement and the rise of the Black Power Movement would finally force White students to confront their thoughts, feelings, and fears about race and attempt to put words to the confusion within.

Endnotes

1 "Letters," *Index*, Friday, December 10, 1948, 2.

2 "Indian Prince to Talk Here," *Index*, February 11, 1949, 1.

3 "Indian Prince Will Tell of Ghandi," *Index*, February 18, 1949, 1.

4 "Prince Pulls Punches, Turns Out American," *Index*, March 4, 1949, 1.

5 "Union Turns Joker," *Index*, March 4, 1949, 2.

6 Hilary Herbold, "Never a Level Playing Field: Blacks and the GI Bill," *Journal of Blacks in Higher Education*, no. 6 (Winter, 1994–1995): 104–108.

7 This website shows how Home Owners' Loan Corporation (HOLC) maps of the 1930s led to the segregation seen in many Michigan cities today: https://www.bridgemi.com/michigan-government/michigans-segregated-past-and-present-told-9-interactive-maps.

8 Aaron Williams and Armand Emamdjomeh, "America Is More Diverse than Ever—But Still Segregated," *The Washington Post*, updated May 10, 2018, https://www.washingtonpost.com/graphics/2018/national/segregation-us-cities/.

9 Mapping Inequality: Redlining in New Deal America, University of Richmond Digital Scholarship Lab, https://dsl.richmond.edu/panorama/redlining/#loc=13/42.291/-85.598&city=kalamazoo-mi&category=5-e.

10 Kalamazoo College catalogues, Kalamazoo College Archives.

11 Kalamazoo College catalogues, Kalamazoo College Archives .

12 "Majority Favor Nixon, Adlai Distant Second," *Index*, May 20, 1960, 1. 51 percent favored Nixon while only 16 percent were for Stevenson. Students' party affiliations were recorded as Independent (48.9 percent), Republican (37.9 percent), and Democrat (13.2 percent).

13 "Women's Societies to Accept Frosh, Master-Slave Relations Soon Follow," *Index*, February 13, 1948.

14 Eric Lott, *Love and Theft: Blackface Minstrelsy and the American Working Class*, 20th anniversary ed. (1993; New York: Oxford University Press, 2013), 67.

15 Lott, *Love and Theft*, 20.

16 Lott, *Love and Theft*, 69–71.

17 "Centuries Bring Count Basie Here," *Index*, February 14, 1958, 1.

18 "Centuries Bring Count Basie to City," *Index*, January 11, 1961, 1.

19 "The Coon Caricature," Jim Crow Museum, https://www.ferris.edu/HTMLS/news/jimcrow/coon/homepage.htm.

20 "The Tom Caricature," Jim Crow Museum, https://www.ferris.edu/HTMLS/news/jimcrow/tom/homepage.htm.

21 "The Picaninny Caricature," Jim Crow Museum, https://www.ferris.edu/HTMLS/news/jimcrow/antiblack/picaninny/homepage.htm.

22 Between 1882 and 1951, an average of 50 Black people were lynched each year. "The Brute Caricature," Jim Crow Museum, https://ferris.edu/jimcrow/brute/.

23 Joshua K. Wright, "Reflections on Black Image in Amos 'n' Andy," *Abernathy: An Online Magazine for Black Men*, March 1, 2017, https://abernathymagazine.com/reflections-on-black-image-in-amos-n-andy/.

24 Susan Smulyan, *Popular Ideologies: Mass Culture at Mid-century* (Philadelphia: University of Pennsylvania Press, 2007), 18.

25 Smulyan, *Popular Ideologies*, 22.

26 Smulyan, *Popular Ideologies*, 26–27.

27 Harold Rossiter, *How to Put on a Minstrel Show* (Chicago, IL: Max Stein Publishing House, 1921), 8. Google Books.

28 *Boiling Pot*, Kalamazoo College yearbook, 1952, 100.

29 Rossiter, *How to Put on a Minstrel Show*, 15.

30 Larry Vickery, "Shufflin' Songsters Part Curtain With 'Jamboree,'" *Index*, March 27, 1950, 1.

31 Ed Hall, "Music, Dancing, Laughter Head Tremendous Bill," *Index*, March 16, 1951, 1.

32 "CF Minstrel Show Once More a Roaring Success," *Index*, March 25, 1953, 1.

33 Rossiter, *How to Put on a Minstrel Show*, 23.

34 Nan Wilcox, "Mad-Cap Minstrel Gang Brings Memories Of Dixie," *Index*, March 15, 1952, 1.

35 Kalamazoo College Archives, John Scott Everton Papers, Student-Faculty Council 1951–54, Box 6, Folder 17, meeting minutes of April 23, 1953.

36 Kalamazoo College Archives, John Scott Everton Papers, Student-Faculty Council 1951–54, Box 6, Folder 17.

37 "Here Comes The Century Showboat!" *Index*, March 17, 1954, 1.

38 *Boiling Pot*, Kalamazoo College yearbook, 1954, 107, Nancy Swanty; "Here Comes The Century Showboat!" *Index*, March 17, 1954, 1.

39 Marilyn Hinkle, *On Such a Full Sea* (Kalamazoo, MI: Kalamazoo College, 1982), 27.

40 Ed Staren to Weimer K. Hicks, November 19, 1955. Kalamazoo College Archives, Weimer K. Hicks Papers, Social Committee 1955–56, Box 35, Folder 11.

41 Excerpts from Hicks' letter to a Century Forum alum, November 25, 1955. Kalamazoo College Archives, Weimer K. Hicks Papers, Social Committee 1955–56, Box 35, Folder 11.

42 "Connors Column," *Index*, February 17, 1956, 3.

43 Bill Connors, "Washington Trip Reviewed," *Index*, March 28, 1956, 5.

44 "Showboat is Coming," *Index*, April 20, 1956, 1.

45 J.A.F., "Editorial: Discrimination and Prejudice," *Index*, April 20, 1956, 2.

46 Dafina-Lazarus Stewart, *Black Collegians' Experiences in US Northern Private Colleges: A Narrative History, 1945–1965* (New York: Palgrave MacMillan, 2017), 166. [Note: "Dafina-Lazarus" is now a deadname.]

47 Collins, who was White, had previously been dean of instruction at LeMoyne College (now LeMoyne-Owen College), an HBCU in Tennessee.

48 Excerpts from Paul Collins (Dean of Men) Memo to President Hicks, October 26, 1956, Kalamazoo College Archives, Weimer K. Hicks Papers, Paul E. Collins 1955–59, Box 109, Folder 11.

49 Kalamazoo College Archives, Weimer K. Hicks Papers, Paul E. Collins 1955–59, Box 109, Folder 11.

50 Weimer Hicks, letter to the Century Forum, January 30, 1957, Kalamazoo College Archives, Weimer K. Hicks Papers, Miscellaneous Correspondence, Century Forum, 1956–58.

51 Stewart, *Black Collegians' Experiences*, 172.

52 Ralph Ellison, "Change the Joke and Slip the Yoke," in *The Collected Essays of Ralph Ellison* (New York: Random House, 1995), 137–138.

53 Michael Millner, "Why Blackface?" *The Conversation*, February 14, 2019, https://theconversation.com/why-blackface-111404.

54 Ellison, "Change the Joke and Slip the Yoke," 144.

55 Lott, *Love and Theft*, 6.

Chapter Five

"There Is No Innocence"

In August of 1960, seventeen-year-old Walter Hall stepped onto the lush green quad of the Kalamazoo College campus. Raised in Memphis, Tennessee, during the Jim Crow era, he had turned down early admission to Fisk University to attend a small liberal arts college in the North that his mother had read about in *Good Housekeeping* magazine. He had also considered DePauw University, but crossed it off his list after his uncle warned him about Klan activity in the area. Hall was the only African American on campus that year out of about 680 students. Soon after arriving, the president of Kalamazoo College, Weimer K. Hicks, approached him with hand extended. "How do you do, Walter Hall," he greeted him warmly. "I was shocked," Hall recalled, wondering, "How does this man know my name?" He soon found out that Hicks knew everybody. "That was his thing," Hall said. "He knew every student by name."[1] During his time at Kalamazoo College, Hall would witness the final years of a campus culture that had changed little since the turn of the century, from the student societies to May Fetes to required Chapel services. He would also experience the birth of the K-Plan and the stirrings of student unrest, graduating just before dramatic social movements reverberated through the College's cloistered halls, shaking up traditions and norms.

"Our Uneasy Silence"

In coming North for college, Walter Hall had escaped the virulent, explicit racism of Jim Crow, but he had entered a strange and unfamiliar environment where racism lurked just beneath the surface, expressed in confusing ways by well-meaning White people who did not understand their own prejudices. "I struggled when I first came to K," Hall remembered. "I was an exceptional student in a Black school system. I got an early entry into Fisk because of what I was academically. That didn't measure up the same when I came to K. So, without Paul Collins constantly channeling me, I probably wouldn't have made it through the first year." Coincidentally, Paul Collins, dean of men, had served as dean of students at LeMoyne-Owen College in Memphis when Hall's parents had attended, so he had a personal connection to Walter Hall and was invested in his success. As Hall recalled, "he did a great deal in terms of setting me on the right path to get through K College."[2] In Collins, Hall had found what most Black students at Kalamazoo College did not, a mentor to help navigate the unknown and often alienating terrain.

While Collins helped him adapt to the academic environment, Walter Hall, outgoing and affable, did his best to participate in the College's social life. "During the sixties," Hall explained, "a time of tension and turmoil from a lot of sources, interracial dating was not the norm . . . I remember the first big dance they had at Welles Hall, I forget what they call it, May Dance or whatever. I asked a girl to go . . . She told me later that she couldn't believe the inquisition she had to go through because she had gone to the dance with me." As a sophomore, Hall faced outright racism when he pledged one of the societies, meant to be the vehicles for social belonging on campus: "I tried to pledge Phi Lambda, and they told me 'no.' My roommate at the time said he was one that voted against me . . . He said, 'I don't think you're Phi Lambda material.' So, I was an independent for a half year. And then Century Forum asked me to join." Hall would go on to be elected president of the Century Forum his senior year.[3]

It had been only a few years since Paul Collins had convinced the Century Forum to end their blackface minstrel shows. And although the blackface performances had quickly disappeared from the student body's short institutional memory, the internalized racial stereotypes and notions of White superiority that allowed the shows to flourish during the 1950s persisted. Due to widespread segregation in the United States, few among the White students, faculty, and staff had authentic interactions with Black people or other people of color to challenge their stereotypes and assumptions. Though many White people at the College sincerely believed in racial equality, their conscious convictions were often at odds with their unconscious beliefs, leaving them innocent of their own prejudices and arousing a deep disquiet when engaging in issues of race.

Many Black alumni from the early to mid-1960s do not recall the Civil Rights Movement having much of an impact on campus. "We were pretty insulated," Donna (Coleman) Odom, '67, explained. "Just the physical placement of Kalamazoo College in Kalamazoo [made] that the case. And, also, because it was . . . a rigorous academic schedule, you were pretty much fixated on what was going on on campus and your studies and that kind of thing."[4] Although Odom discussed the movement with the few other Black students in her class, it was not something most people on campus talked about. But every now and then the Civil Rights Movement would manage to penetrate the prevailing indifference.

In 1960, a group of students typed up a flyer describing the lunch-counter sit-ins in the South and the violence being unleashed against peaceful Black protesters. At the top of the flyer was the handwritten heading "Are We Concerned?" The question was phrased more ambiguously at the bottom: "Does This Concern Us?" It could have meant "Are we worried about this?" or "Does this have anything to do with us?" Perhaps they intended it both ways.

The flyer, with its purple mimeographed type, did indeed communicate concern, along with discomfort and intellectualism. "In order to fully understand this situation," they began earnestly, "we must consider the problem completely . . . .Whether or not Kalamazoo College gives support to this movement will not be a simple question of apathy. This problem will only concern the question of racial discrimination. Is the oft-practiced doctrine, 'separate but unequal,' morally right," they asked as if to stimulate intellectual debate, "and is the method of protest (sit-ins) the proper way to protest?" they wondered, as if it was their call to make. Ending on a stronger note they asserted, "If you sincerely believe that the recent occurrences are right and necessary in the march to eliminate racial supremacy, you will assist this movement in every way possible."[5] It was a call to action, but an uncertain one.

Perhaps due to the growing prevalence of the Civil Rights Movement, the College began inviting Black thought leaders to campus, among them Thurgood Marshall, who delivered the commencement address in 1961, and James Baldwin, who visited in November of 1960 as a promising young writer. Hosted by the English Department, Baldwin spent a week on campus giving talks, visiting classes, and engaging in "fireside chats" with students and faculty. What a rare place Kalamazoo College must have seemed to him, so very earnest in its enveloping Whiteness. Baldwin had been asked to give a lecture on "minority rights," but after spending a few days on campus he gave a talk titled "In Search of a Majority" instead.[6]

"I am supposed to speak this evening on the goals of American society as they involve minority rights," Baldwin began, "but what I am really going to do is to invite you to join me in a series of speculations. Some of them are dangerous, some of them are painful, all of them are reckless. It seems to me that before we can speak of minority rights in this country, we've got to make some attempt to isolate or to define the majority." "What is honored in a country is cultivated there," he continued. "If we apply this touchstone to American life we can scarcely fail to arrive at a very grim view of it."

Baldwin went on to place the country's racial pathology not on "minority groups," as was so often done, but squarely on the majority. "When we think of the American boy, we usually think of someone who is a cross between a Teuton and a Celt . . . Outrageous as this image is, in most cases, it is the national self-image. It is an image which suggests hard work and good clean fun and chastity and piety and success," Baldwin said, likely describing the self-image of many male students in attendance. "It leaves out of account, of course, most of the people in the country, and . . . has almost nothing to do with what or who an American really is. It has nothing to do with what life is. Beneath this bland, this conqueror-image, a great many unadmitted despairs and confusions, and anguish and unadmitted crimes and failures hide."

Baldwin suggested that in America social status had substituted for cultural identity, and "if this is one's concept of life . . . , when one slips, one slips back not a rung but back into chaos and no longer knows who he is." This fear of losing status was, according to Baldwin, "one of the real reasons for the status of Negroes in this country. In a way, the Negro tells us where the bottom is: *because he is there,* and *where* he is, beneath us, we know where the limits are and how far we must not fall."[7] In effect, Baldwin was saying that without Black people, and more specifically without Black people "in their place," White people would not know who they were.

A brief item in the *Index* titled "Our Uneasy Silence" suggests that Baldwin managed to get White students to look inward, perhaps for the first time, rather than assuming that racism was something that existed outside of themselves, something that they watched on the television news rather than participated in. The thought left them literally dumbstruck. "We had no evaluation or even comment about the visit of James Baldwin immediately after he left the Campus," the editors of the *Index* wrote. "The INDEX readers who became acquainted with Baldwin probably found this a surprising omission—to say the least. Our silence was not one of indifference, but instead the inability to adequately express the rather profound effect we believe James Baldwin had on many students. His forthrightness, integrity, and insight aroused in many of us an uneasiness and a questioning of our own attitudes and values."[8]

Baldwin's visit occurred during the fall of Walter Hall's freshman year, when they were quite possibly the only two Black people on campus. Whereas Baldwin had left White students in stunned silence, Hall described the experience of hearing Baldwin speak as a "seminal moment."[9]

"As a freshman I was just trying to find my way and how I could best fit in," he later explained. "Having been raised in the South during the 40s and 50s, adjusting to an 'All White' environment socially was something I was ill prepared to handle. I found myself questioning who I was . . . Do I totally embrace white culture and norms of campus life or try to adhere to the standards that I was raised by?"

"Then James Baldwin came to campus," Hall went on. "He was a black man who was small in stature but projected larger than life imagery. Baldwin came across as someone who was comfortable in his own skin and exuded supreme self confidence. During the Fireside Chat he challenged his white audience to think differently about race relations. That empowered me to be myself and not be someone that I thought might be more accepted by the white campus majority."

"I remember meeting with him afterwards to thank him for being so inspiring and speaking truth to those that had been shielded from facts,"

Hall continued, and "for giving me the courage to be comfortable with being Black at K College."[10]

"Boiling Water" College

James Baldwin's impact, profound though it may have been for some students, was not enough to keep White people at the College focused on issues of racial injustice. The main concern during the 1960s was—interestingly, given Baldwin's remarks about status—institutional prestige. From the beginning of his presidency in 1954, Weimer Hicks had been determined to make Kalamazoo a nationally known college, but first he had to save it from financial collapse. He had inherited an institution in decline, "fueled if not ignited by the depression, which brought the College down to its knees by the end of 1952," in the assessment of Dr. Richard Light, chair of the board of trustees. The faculty was divided, student enrollment had dropped from a high of 654 during World War II to just 356, and the endowment had plummeted from $1,800,000 in 1932 to around $750,000.[11]

Seemingly undaunted by the dire state of affairs, Hicks assumed the work of building up the College with enthusiasm. "I have accepted this challenging responsibility with humility, realizing that I have much to learn," Hicks said during his first public appearance on campus in the fall of 1953. "I pledge to you every moment of my time and every ounce of my energy to make certain that Kalamazoo College continues to grow and prosper."[12] Hicks would prove to be as good as his word, investing himself completely in the College and gaining widespread admiration as a talented, hands-on administrator, respected and liked by students, faculty, and staff. In many ways, the wind was at his back with the Baby Boomer generation beginning to reach college age, a robust (White) middle class, and a thriving economy. He made the most of it.

Over the course of the 1960s, Kalamazoo College's student body almost doubled, growing to over 1,300 by 1970. This growth was made possible by the K-Plan, an innovative approach to higher education that integrated off-campus programs with on-campus study. It was a bold and risky step, initially motivated by the financial gains of operating the institution year-round. Laurence Barrett, dean of faculty, took it upon himself to ensure there would be educational gains as well. When the K-Plan was implemented in 1962, the calendar changed from semesters to quarters to accommodate its experiential components. After their first year, students attended year-round on an on- and off-campus pattern. Sophomores spent their spring quarter engaged in a Career Service internship and then returned to campus for summer classes. Juniors spent the fall and winter quarters studying abroad and finished the year on campus taking classes in the spring and summer. In their senior year, half of the students were off campus in the fall doing their Senior Individualized Project while the other half were off in the winter. All the seniors were back on campus in the spring, and then, if all had gone well, they graduated.

The K-Plan would turn out to be transformative for both the College and the students, and for a time attracted national attention. *Time* magazine ran an article in 1961 titled "Boiling Water College," making use of one translation of the College's Potawatomi name. Written in the voice of the confident White man from the old news reels, the article began, "After 128 tepid years, Kalamazoo this fall cooked up a year-round operation that gives students, at no extra cost, a remarkable range of educational experience in the standard four years . . . " "A college can no longer give a broad education in its little oasis," Hicks was quoted as saying. "We're trying to use the whole world as our campus."[13]

Kalamazoo College was indeed bubbling with activity in the 1960s. Greater geographic diversity among students, mind-expanding experiences abroad, and growing engagement in national and international issues ushered in the fresh air of new perspectives, stirring up, if not completely sweeping out, the cobwebs of provincialism. The social turmoil of the times led students at Kalamazoo and elsewhere to chafe at the *in loco parentis* model of higher education that closely regulated their lives. By the early 1970s, the ten o'clock curfew for women students and required Chapel attendance had been abolished.

In the nascent years of Foreign Study, as the program was originally called, the vast majority of students studied abroad. Most went to Europe, where there were programs in France, Germany, and Spain, but the College had also established programs in Latin America and Africa. During this time, there was growing interest in Africa on campus, as many countries were shaking off colonial rule, while in South Africa apartheid was stripping away the rights and liberties of the Black majority. The College began adding courses on Africa to its curriculum and in 1969 established the African Studies program.[14]

Students studying abroad began seeing the United States through the eyes of the world. This international lens helped White students begin to grasp the evils of Jim Crow segregation as they found themselves needing to answer for America. In 1963, a student studying in France wrote a letter to the *Index* about watching a French rendition of *Uncle Tom's Cabin* in one of her classes. At the end of the film, violent scenes from Birmingham, Alabama, flashed onto the screen as the credits rolled. "It lasted no more than a minute," she wrote, "but it was like a slap in the face. There was Birmingham, complete with riot scenes; Negroes being forced into police vans, Negroes being kicked, Negroes lying in the gutter. Negroes being insulted and degraded. Alabama looked worse from this side of the Atlantic than it did from Kalamazoo."[15]

Black students who studied abroad in Africa had a different kind of awakening. As Bertha Doleman, '65, wrote of her time in Freetown, Sierra Leone, "I felt very much at home there, so free to be myself, so accepted. Suddenly, for the first time in my life, my blackness was an asset and not a liability; my skin served to include me in the mainstream of life rather than set me apart." "A person who has never experienced racial discrimination cannot possibly understand what this means," she continued, "what it means to know that you are in your own house and if another man cannot tolerate your blackness then it is he who must leave, what it means to be able to associate with whites and feel that you are on absolutely the same level—without the nagging discomforts and suspicions than often hinder such relationships in the States."[16]

"You Have to Be 'Somebody'"

Even before the K-Plan was instituted, President Hicks had begun the work of raising the institution's academic profile by investing in faculty and becoming more selective in admissions. Through grants and budget reallocations, he made sure that professors were highly compensated and sought to recruit faculty with Ivy League pedigrees. Current faculty would be astonished to know that in 1960 "Kalamazoo College stood fourth in mean salaries among twenty-five leading liberal arts colleges in the country."[17]

The Hicks administration took a similar approach with students. "In recent years we have been trying vigorously to lift the quality of our student body in two areas," he wrote in 1962. "First, we have sought to be more selective intellectually and have made excellent strides ahead. Second, we have tried to bring to the campus students from more significant backgrounds, individuals whom we frequently refer to as VIP's."[18] That approach needed to be delicately balanced against another priority: cultivating good relations with Michigan Baptists, who continued to be an important source of support. This would at times present a dilemma when a prospective student from a Baptist family did not have the desired academic profile or financial means. As an alumnus wrote to Hicks in 1962, "many people are getting the idea that you have to be 'somebody' before getting any attention from the College."[19]

Although Hicks raised this concern with the admissions staff, he was loath to alter the strategy. "Obviously this is a delicate area," he wrote. "We want to concentrate our emphasis upon the 'important' student, the one who can help to build the reputation of the college simply by our having him on our campus." "I have no suggestions to our admissions staff," he concluded, "beyond that of extreme caution."[20]

Hicks also had strong opinions about how the student body should be shaped in order to maintain the institution's "character." The campus in the 1950s and early to mid-1960s reflected the mores of a conservative Christian college in which a certain decorum and propriety were expected. In the 1950s, there had been heated debates in faculty meetings about whether male students should be allowed to wear Bermuda shorts[21] (the propriety of minstrels shows, however, was not questioned). No one was more concerned about maintaining conventional standards of dress and behavior than Hicks, who believed that such things should be considered in admission decisions.

"As we become increasingly selective from year to year, I think it is important that we place increased emphasis upon personality and social qualities of the young men and women we accept," Hicks wrote to the admissions staff in 1960. "The Kalamazoo College education has a way of fostering independence of thought and action . . . We never quite reached the 'beatnik' category, but we are so dangerously near to it that I think we should take every possible precaution." He urged the staff to "report those qualities of character and social adjustment which are negative." How to spot such qualities? "With the men," Hicks explained, "this is most likely to express itself in beards, the long hair, the blue jeans or sloppy dress, etc. With the young ladies it is found in the bleached hair, the absence of lipstick, the accentuation of dark colored clothing, etc."[22]

Changing times were shaping a new social landscape, one which Weimer Hicks did not recognize. One October weekend a few years later, Hicks walked over to Welles Hall to chat with students lining up to enter the cafeteria and learn a few more of their names. What he saw disturbed him. As he wrote to the Admissions Committee afterward, "I did come away with the impression that we have a few more 'beatniks' or long hairs or Bohemians than is normal. This raised in my mind the question of whether the admissions committee should not sit down and attempt to spell out what they may want in the way of an entering freshman class . . . Are we going to welcome everyone," he asked, "providing they are intellectually superior, with no thought of the Protestant evangelical tradition which has built and dominated the college? Since we know that the intellectual college is more likely to draw the Bohemian student, are we therefore going to admit students without regard to some of the qualities which still characterize the wholesome Midwest communities like our own city?" "I for one feel," he concluded, "that we will soon reach the stage that we will be screening students in light of many of the above mentioned qualities . . . . If we do not, then our college in five years will be a changed institution."[23]

"Black Is Beautiful"

The institution was indeed changing, and not even the meticulous monitoring of Weimer Hicks would be able to keep the social revolution at bay. The beards and more casual dress that so concerned him were reflections of the largely White counterculture movement beginning to take hold. With just a few Black students on campus in 1963, the Black Campus Movement that would rock higher education in the late 1960s was something he could not even begin to imagine.

In 1964, President Lyndon Johnson signed the Civil Rights Act outlawing discrimination on the basis of race, color, religion, sex, or national origin, which led more Black students to enroll in predominantly White colleges. Ron Spann and Bertha Doleman, both in the class of 1965, noticed the change after returning from study abroad. "We saw a definite uptick in the number of Black students coming in," recalled Spann. "And, we were both very impressed by that. And, I think that added to our happiness because even though we didn't get real close to some of them—just the coming and going made that very hard," he commented referring to the K-Plan's on-off campus pattern, "we knew who they were and they knew who we were . . . It sweetened the pot a little bit for us in those last years. We didn't feel so alone."[24]

During the 1960s, the visibility of Black students in some ways increased on campus. Grace Hayes, '60, who had grown up just blocks from Central High School in Little Rock,[25] was chosen as May Fete Queen in 1960. Hayes had entered Kalamazoo College at the age of sixteen, and in 1958 she was selected as one of about ninety delegates nationwide to represent the United States at the Brussels Universal Fair in Belgium.[26] Bertha Doleman was elected May Fete Queen in 1965. She graduated summa cum laude and was inducted into the Phi Beta Kappa honor society. Ron Spann, the only other Black student in the class of 1965 with Doleman, cofounded the *Cauldron* literary magazine in 1962. Walter Hall, in addition to being elected president of the Century Forum, served as general manager of the College's radio station, WJMD. "'I played music that normally wouldn't be played on the K College campus,' laughed Hall, who offered up a mix of jazz, blues, and R&B on his show "The Beachcomber."[27]

But growing visibility did not necessarily translate into social acceptance or a sense of comfort on campus. "Looking back," Hall recalled, "I was the first Black student of the sixties at Kalamazoo College, 1960 when I entered. I was the only Black student at Kalamazoo College . . . My first year was difficult because of, the standpoint socially, it was different, and if it hadn't been for Western Michigan University, I probably wouldn't have made it," Hall said referring to the larger institution next door. "Socially I can adapt to a certain level, but to really enjoy myself socially, I had Western."[28]

The few Black students on campus in the early 1960s looked out for each other. Walter Hall was befriended by Jesse Dungy, '59, who had returned to Kalamazoo to pursue graduate work at Western. According to Hall, Dungy served as "sort of a sounding board for adjusting to Kalamazoo College."[29] Hall paid the favor forward when Ron Spann and Bertha Doleman enrolled the following year. As Spann recalled, "we got some good solicitude, some mentoring from the upperclassmen, people like Walter and Jesse . . . So that's who we had for kind of putting a friendly arm around the shoulder, guiding you this way and that . . . but it felt very isolated."[30]

The social atmosphere was particularly isolating for Black women. Denise Strong, '67, recalled the alienation of not being recognized for who she was. "The White students on this campus could never figure out my name. They could not tell the difference between me and Donna," Strong said, referring to one of the two other Black students in her class. "So, I could distinguish, you know, 890 people, but you can't distinguish between two people? That's annoying." Both Strong and her classmate Donna (Coleman) Odom felt particularly invisible at the "mixers," informal dances held for students to get to know each other. "If I went to a dance," Strong recalled, "they were playing music I didn't like, I didn't have a date, and no one asked me to dance . . . So, it was not fun."[31] White men asking Black women out seemed to be taboo. It may not have been easy for Walter Hall to ask a White woman to a dance, but it was at least within the realm of possibility. Donna Odom realized early on that dating was not going to happen during her time on Kalamazoo's almost all-White campus. "The first weekend that we were here as freshmen," she recalled, "they had a kind of a welcoming party . . . , kind of an outdoor party. And, one young man actually asked me to dance. And we talked and he invited me to a little after party they had at the guys' dorm. And I think he probably got in trouble after asking me there because he never asked me again."[32]

Odom, who had studied French all through high school, had been attracted by the College's study abroad program. In those days, students crossed the Atlantic Ocean on a ship, a five-day voyage that Odom recalled as "being between two worlds" where "people felt a little freer . . . , the freedom just to be themselves." In that space of possibility, she and the young man who had asked her to dance "buddied up a little bit, and every now and then, in the cafeteria, we would talk and that sort of thing. He was one of the people who just really made me feel comfortable."[33]

By 1967, forty-two Black students were enrolled at Kalamazoo College, though they still comprised just 3 percent of the student body. To combat social isolation and indifference from the administration to the challenges they faced in adjusting to a White institution, Black students banded together for support and some relief from the ascendancy of White people, White culture, White traditions, and a White curriculum. Clyde Solomon, '71, a student from Cincinnati, later recalled the difficulties of his first year. "I did poorly," he said of his academic performance, "and it wasn't because I wasn't smart. I think it was the impact of being there and making adjustments to that college . . . There wasn't any support for us.

There was nobody there, no faculty, no coaches, or anybody of color that could say, 'hey, you know, this is going to be okay.'"[34]

"Most of us suffered that first semester," he continued. "It took me about a year to sort of figure things out and to make the social adjustment. Then after the social adjustment, the academic stuff just came." Thinking about his freshman-year GPA, he added, "some people probably thought that we just weren't smart enough to do the work. 'Look at them,'" Solomon could imagine them thinking, "'we got them here and they can't do the work.'"[35]

Many Kalamazoo College students were now thoroughly engaged in the issues of the times as the Civil Rights Movement persevered and the United States was drawn into the Vietnam War. The counterculture students Hicks had worried about in 1963 were in full activist mode, protesting the war, racial injustice, sex discrimination, and restrictive social norms. As the Black Power movement took hold in the late 1960s, it was increasingly covered in the *Index*. The Black Panther Party for Self-Defense had formed in 1966 on a platform of "land, bread, housing, education, clothing, justice, and peace." The Party's activism took the form of armed patrols to police the police in Black neighborhoods, community service work, and advocating Black power, Black pride, and Black separatism.[36]

A 1967 speech by Stokely Carmichael in nearby Grand Rapids, Michigan, received extensive if not approving coverage in the *Index*, the writer declaring that Carmichael's logic was "geared to the emotion rather than the intellect," leaving the White listener with "a vague feeling of frustration." "This is not true for the Negro listener," the writer explained, "who quickly identifies with Carmichael and who feels the emotional impact of the speech more strongly and lastingly than the white listener. The difference is the key to the value of the speech and the only thing which gives it a positive worth." Carmichael's three-fold approach to confronting systemic racism—for Black people to learn about their culture and history, feel self-pride, and unite as a people in self-determination—was characterized by the writer as "Negro retaliation."[37]

This discomfort with anything "emotional" was a common theme in White students' reactions to Black activism. Most White students, well-meaning as they tended to be, tried to support movements for racial justice, but the confrontational approach of Stokely Carmichael and other proponents of Black Power unsettled them. They dealt with their anxieties by calling for "calm" and "rationality," proxies for control.

Early in 1968, the Student Senate announced that it was hoping to bring the Reverend Albert Cleage, Jr., a Black nationalist from Detroit, to speak during the Student Senate's Chapel program. In the wake of the 1967 Detroit uprising, Cleage had cut ties with the Congregational Church and established a new church known as the Shrine of the Black Madonna, which was becoming "an important center for black theology and political power."[38] An *Index* article announcing Cleage's visit described his work in "trying to build a church that emphasizes an unfailing Black faith in Black people; to restore the destiny and control of Black affairs, rejecting the 'outsiders,' regardless of their sympathy or intentions."[39]

The week after Reverend Cleage spoke in Chapel, the *Index* ran three articles by White students describing their takes on Cleage's talk. Under the overarching headline "Black Power from White Perspectives . . . ," the opinion pieces were titled "Oppression Yields Profit," "Civilize the Suburbs," and "Mista Charlie Is Dead," the latter referencing a term in the Black community for an arrogant, condescending White man. All three writers noted that his talk had made the largely White audience uncomfortable, and though they attempted understanding, they could not shake their uneasiness.

Cleage's "bleak conception of American society is bitter to accept, but it is probably ruthlessly true," one student wrote. "Provided the black power advocates accomplish their aims, their dignity, my concern is still the result of the process," he went on. "I fear the capacity of white ugliness to accept their integrity. Or," he concluded more honestly, "I fear that the superstructure black power would create might be as unsatisfactory as the one against which it grew."

Another writer summed up Cleage's message to well-meaning White liberals as follows: "If you care and if you understand as well as you as a white person can understand, then don't bother any longer to sign up for work in the inner city ghetto or the rural south. Go to the suburbs, make these people understand, CIVILIZE them." Casting aside the oft-deployed shield of "good Whites" in the North versus "bad Whites" in the South, Cleage pointed to places like Cicero, Illinois, where a Black teenager had been beaten to death by a group of White youth on his way home from a job interview. "You can't redeem white men with love or anything else," Cleage was quoted as saying. "Only Power."

Unaccustomed to being judged by their race, two of the writers took exception to Cleage painting White people with a broad brush. "Many sympathetic Whites are offended by Cleage generalizing their status as that of 'enemy,'" wrote one. Another characterized Cleage's statements as "a hatred for the white man not based on the white man as an individual but as an overgeneralized symbol," missing the irony that being cast as an "overgeneralized symbol," and a negative one at that, was what Black people confronted on a daily basis.

Cleage's message for the White people of Kalamazoo College was challenging to be sure. It was one thing to sympathize with peaceful Black protesters calling for equality and quite another to face the specter of Black Americans seeking power and self-determination on their own terms. Most White people could only experience the thought as threatening. "It is my hope," one of the students summed up shakily, "that representative black power and black interest can emerge before frustration, emotion, and irrationality racially polarize the problem into hating, armed camps bearing death, destruction, and futility."[40] Again, the fear of emotion and a looming sense of chaos, perhaps the same sense of chaos James Baldwin had suggested White Americans feel when experiencing a loss of status. Many White people may be slow to accept the existence of systemic racism, but they instinctively shudder when they imagine the tables being turned.

While on campus, Cleage met with Black students and, according to DeMonte Johnson, '71, encouraged them to organize. As Johnson recalled, "he taught us we were some backwards Negroes because we didn't have a Black Student Organization."[41] Indeed, by this time Black students at many colleges and universities across the country had already established what were typically called "Black Student Unions," which had begun to form in 1966.[42]

The relatively late formation of Kalamazoo's Black Student Organization was probably due to social disruption caused by the K-Plan's on-off campus pattern and the intensity of the quarter system. But even though they had not created an organization, Black students at Kalamazoo were talking about Black consciousness and Black power. Both Clyde Solomon and DeMonte Johnson recall a student named Linda Jordan as a driving force. "[The College] brought in a sister, girl from Newark, New Jersey," Solomon recalled. "She actually worked with Amiri Baraka, he was Leroi Jones before he changed his name . . . She just really was helping us understand this whole Black power aspect and raising our level of consciousness."[43]

As Sharon (Greene) McWilliams, '72, recalled, "I was in school during a very turbulent time in the country. So, it was challenging to figure out who I was at the same time that Black people were developing an identity as Black people as opposed to Negroes. And, challenging in that women were beginning to step up and say, 'No, we're not just here to support men. We have something to offer as well.'"[44]

DeMonte Johnson remembered how manifestations of racial pride among Black students disturbed their White peers. One day he and Solomon walked into the cafeteria "wearing these short sleeve sweatshirts that were yellow, which had a Soul Brother on it . . . Now, as far as I'm concerned, it was just a sweatshirt. Had the brother on it, so that means I'm proud of being who I am. It doesn't mean I dislike you or, but it's just for me. But for the White kids, it was like, 'Whoa.' We walked in the cafeteria, and it was like somebody turned the sound off."[45]

A week after the *Index* ran "Black Power from White Perspectives," Clyde Solomon published an article describing what Black consciousness meant to him:

> Going to a predominantly white school presents a problem for the Negro. There has been a tendency for the black person to lose his identity and become assimilated into the white man's culture . . . and many times I feel sort of left out as far as the social atmosphere is concerned. This wasn't because of any racial tension; the students at Kalamazoo are very friendly, but there is nothing which has any appeal to my needs. The bands that played at the mixers don't play the kind of music I'm accustomed to. Few people dance the way I do. I suppose I could change my taste and my style of dancing so that I could fit in with the rest of the people; but this is exactly the trap I don't want to fall into . . . . I am black and I want to remain black physically and mentally . . . . I do a radio show where I play mostly soul music, music by Negro artists. I stick to my own informal

> language in informal conversation and when I do go to mixers, I dance the way I always have danced. This attitude that I have . . . is shared by most of the black students in the freshman class. A statement that has stuck in my mind was made by an upperclass black student who said that our class of Negroes is really different . . . . I do believe that black is beautiful and I am proud that I am a black man.[46]

"Our Time Is Extremely Valuable and Can Be Wasted No Longer"

Less than three weeks later, Clyde Solomon was watching TV in the Harmon Hall lounge when news of Martin Luther King's assassination broke. "I remember . . . when it came on that King was shot, and thinking, 'Wow, people must really hate me, you know? I'm here in this White environment, and they kill King. They must really hate me because I'm Black, because how could you kill King?' And then, it just sort of took off and the next thing I knew we were over at Western Michigan occupying a building."[47]

Within two weeks of King's assassination, Black students at Kalamazoo College formed the Black Student Organization (BSO), now the longest running student organization on campus. The purpose of the BSO as stated in its constitution was brief and to the point: "We, the black students of Kalamazoo College for the purpose of learning more about ourselves and relating our experiences to the black community as a whole adopt this constitution." Membership would include "all those deemed by the group to be beneficial to the purpose."[48]

The same day the BSO constitution was ratified, a piece President Hicks had written for the alumni magazine was reprinted in the *Index*. In it, he rose to the defense of the student activist, "the one with the beard and the long hair." Though still bothered by their appearance, Hicks had grown more sympathetic to their cause. "Ten years ago I thought I understood the philosophy and the goals of the small, church-related college," Hicks wrote. "But the whole world of my thinking has been shaken at its very foundations." He praised students for being service oriented, highlighting participation in the Peace Corps and a tutoring program in Kalamazoo's predominantly Black northside neighborhood. He defended the students' right to protest U.S. involvement in the Vietnam War, even though he did not always approve of their tactics. And, he commended them for their embrace of racial equality and integration. "They judge individuals primarily by their intrinsic qualities, not by the color of their skin," he wrote. "One has difficulty in finding on our campus any evidences of the prejudices of the past."[49]

Hicks may not have perceived racial prejudice on campus, but Black students experienced marginalization daily in Kalamazoo College's White-dominated culture. It did not take long for the newly formed BSO to insist that Kalamazoo College make itself relevant to Black students.

On May 6, 1968, the BSO issued its first set of demands. Noting "stalling and confusion" in the Student Senate regarding approval of the BSO constitution and budget request, their first demand was that their funds come directly from the Business Office instead of going through the Student Senate. According to the scholar Ibram X. Kendi, many "BSUs demanded higher appropriations for their ambitious and expansive campus and community projects. Some groups demanded a separate budget allocation or financial autonomy," and, he notes, "activists at U-Houston and Kalamazoo-C (MI) demanded fiscal independence."[50]

Second, they demanded "increasing the number of non-white administrators and faculty members" in order that the academic program "include adequate emphasis upon the contributions of non-white peoples throughout the world." They prioritized the humanities, "specifically philosophy," the social sciences, "specifically history," English, and physical education. "Progress in employing non-white instructors especially in the Social Sciences Department must be seen by fall, 1969," they specified, with representation in all four areas by 1970. The demand also called for BSO participation in the hiring decisions.

Third, "in a psychologically unconscious attempt to abet the Crime of Assimilation into a spiritually barbaric melting pot, Kalamazoo College has exposed its students to only one side of the cultural coin," they wrote. To rectify this imbalance, the BSO demanded equal representation of students of color on the Committee on Academic Visitors, and that "campus speakers competent in relating objectively and truthfully the histories and cultures of the Third World be engaged in equal numbers for college programs and lectures by spring, 1969."

Finally, they demanded action on the program proposed by the BSO Higher Education Committee to connect with students of color in the region and advise them on attending college, at Kalamazoo or elsewhere.[51]

The memo concluded with a sense of urgency consistent with Black Power principles. "Our time is extremely valuable and can be wasted no longer," they wrote, "therefore we of the BSO must be informed of the College's decision(s) on our demands by 4 p.m. Thursday, 9 May 1968." The communication was signed by BSO cochairs Linda Jordan and Edwin Taliaferro. Jordan, who had been instrumental in raising the consciousness of her fellow Black students, did not return to campus the following fall, while Taliaferro, known to his friends as "Tally," emerged as a leader among Black students on campus.

Edwin Taliaferro, who later changed his name to Chokwe Lumumba, had grown up in a housing project on the west side of Detroit and, like other Black students, had struggled in adjusting to Kalamazoo College's predominantly White environment.[52] "Kalamazoo College to me the first two years . . . it was a bit of a cultural shock," Lumumba told Eduard Avis, '89, who interviewed Lumumba for his Senior Individualized Project. "People used to think I was real withdrawn and introverted."[53] King's death was a defining moment in tipping him toward activism, but Lumumba was careful to point out that "it would be unfair and unsound to believe that people are transformed to any particular kind of activity because of one event." "I can recall Emmett Till's death," Lumumba went on. "That was a traumatic experience . . . I can remember times me and my parents [were] sitting in restaurants, drive-ins, and wouldn't be served, things of that nature and I wondered about it . . . When King died a lot of these things began to come back to me, they began to fit into a system I guess we'd say of political thought."[54]

The activism sparked in Lumumba at Kalamazoo College would remain a lifelong passion. He earned a law degree from Wayne State University and joined the Republic of New Afrika, a Black separatist organization advocating for an independent Black republic in the South and $400 billion in reparations. He went on to become a prominent civil rights lawyer and "earned a reputation as an aggressive defense lawyer, particularly in police brutality cases." At the time of his death in 2014 at the age of sixty-six, he was serving as mayor of Jackson, Mississippi. "Mr. Lumumba hardly moderated his views" in later years, according to his obituary in the *New York Times*. "In an interview last year he continued to defend the Republic of New Afrika. The day after his election, he raised hackles by questioning Columbus's historical importance. And at his inauguration, he could not resist raising his fist in the black power salute and shouting an old slogan: 'Free the Land!'"[55]

"Taliaferro was clearly one of the most influential factors in the formation of the BSO," according to Elvin Caldwell, '11, who also interviewed Lumumba for his Senior Individualized Project. "He had personally adopted and genuinely subscribed to the ideas of urgency, Pan-Africanism, black independence and power."[56] Caldwell goes on to detail how the principles of Black power shaped the BSO's purpose and demands. Their constitution's emphasis on "learning more about ourselves and relating our experiences to the black community" was consistent with the teachings of activists like Malcolm X and Stokely Carmichael "that blacks had to first learn about themselves in order to redefine themselves as black, strong and energetic . . . in contrast to what whites have told blacks throughout their time in this country."[57] Furthermore, "as students at a prestigious institution like Kalamazoo College, blacks had to relate their acquired experiences back to the black community" instead of remaining removed from their communities after graduation, a phenomenon Ibram Kendi refers to as "ladder altruism."[58] "As stated in Black Power articulated by Carmichael," Caldwell explained, "it was the duty of these blacks to remain relevant to the black community by giving back and maintaining their racial identity and cultural integrity."[59] Black Power activists also warned that "college institutions were 'whitewashing' blacks into losing their racial identity." According to Caldwell, "the BSO used their demands to make Kalamazoo College recognize their identity. The BSO defined themselves in their racial pride, urgency, black unity and black independence" and "used these concepts to formulate their demands."[60]

Whether or not Hicks and those advising him recognized these Black Power principles at work in the BSO's demands, the shock and sadness they felt over King's assassination led them to give the demands prompt, serious, and sympathetic consideration. Hicks was in New York when the demands were issued on May 6. When he returned on May 8, he devoted the entire day to discussing the demands in a series of meetings, including one with the BSO leadership to make sure that he fully understood the nature of the demands. Hicks drafted his response that evening in order to meet the BSO's deadline of May 9. The next day, after being vetted and commented on by colleagues, the final draft of the response was delivered by a group of senior administrators and faculty to the BSO.

The administration's response tried to strike a tone of understanding and agreement while resisting any departure from College policy. As Hicks wrote, "May I begin by expressing deep sympathy for the status quo of the Black people in our country. America has failed to evolve a society in which all individuals are judged by their intrinsic worth. Therefore I am determined to do all I can to further the cause of equality in which I believe. I am determined that the educational program on this campus speak to this conviction, this commitment." The memo went on to communicate complete agreement with demands 2 and 3, hiring more faculty of color and bringing more speakers of color to campus. About demands 1 and 4, Hicks wrote, "our only differences are minor, involving the means and technique of achieving the desired ends." On demand 1, Hicks agreed to the full amount of funds requested by the BSO, but he insisted that they be appropriated by the Student Senate instead of the Business Office. On demand 4, complying with the Higher Education Committee's program, Hicks agreed, but only to allocating $500 instead of the full $900 requested. Whether this was intentional or a misreading of the demand is not clear.

Hicks closed his response by "expressing again our desire to help in whatever way we can. Our interest in Black students, inadequate though it has proved to be, dates back to the early 1900's. Concerns like yours are not new; only the degree of intensity is new. Now our common task is to capitalize upon the opportunity to build together for the future."[61]

The Black Student Organization met that evening to discuss Hicks's reply. They decided to "accept the attempt at meeting the demands concerning (1) faculty, administration and curriculum improvements and (2) visiting lecturers and chapel speakers (demands 2 and 3)" and "reject the attempt at meeting the demands concerning (1) BSO financing and (2) the Higher Education Committee proposal pending further negotiations with the appointed BSO representatives (demands 1 and 4)."[62]

The following day was the annual Mother's Day Celebration with over 400 parents and family members on campus. The BSO took advantage of the occasion to publicly voice their concerns by picketing in the dining hall, the Light Fine Arts building, and the president's house, drawing the attention of the local media and prompting Hicks to write to the executive committee of the board and local trustees. "In their protests they were most respectful and they conformed to the patterns of propriety," he wrote, "though naturally we are disappointed that they took this particular stance."[63]

On Monday, Hicks wrote to the BSO suggesting a plan to set demands 2 and 3 in motion while urging further negotiation on demands 1 and 4, about which he "sincerely believe[d] that we have agreement in principle."[64] Three days later Hicks again wrote to the BSO, this time agreeing to all of the demands in full, including having their funds come directly from the Business Office.

The bypassing of the Student Senate in appropriating funds to the BSO proved controversial. The Student Senate had voted on May 13 to relinquish its constitutional control over funding to student organizations in the case of the BSO, perhaps smoothing the way for the administration to agree fully to demand 1. To inform the student body of their decision, the Student Senate issued a position paper in which it laid out two perspectives on the demand, one in opposition and one in support. The former worried about "setting a precedent" and "reverse discrimination, an unethical means to an ethical end." "The 'uniqueness' of the organization is obvious, but is it relevent [*sic*]?" the writer asked. "We must evaluate the demand for finances not with regard for 'blackness' but for the campus community."

The argument in support placed the demand in historical context: "This altering of regular channels may be viewed by some as special treatment. Discrimination in this country against the Blacks has gone on for nearly four centuries—it is deeply rooted . . . Since the Blacks were forced into this situation by Whites using unethical means, one should not be overly concerned about using unconventional means to help rectify the situation—especially when many are going to use the excuse that ethical means must be used in an attempt to maintain the status quo."[65]

Individual students also wrote letters and articles for the *Index* expressing a wide range of views. On May 22, two students penned a joint letter objecting to the administration's response to the BSO's demands. "Preferential treatment of the BSO involved a sacrifice of democratic process," they complained. "Students may now assume that if tradition, policy, and ideals can be so readily set aside for 'uniqueness' and 'emergency,' any cause or organization need only threaten campus calm to sidestep customary procedures and effect desired change."[66] In contrast, Terry Brown, one of the more radical White students on campus, wrote in the May 17 issue, "Black and White must meet as equals and not as Negroes being given the gift of entrance into White society. For, 'Negro' is a White term as is integration. We demand that the Negro accept our culture before we accept him, but baby, White does not make right."[67]

Despite the controversy, the BSO prevailed in attaining their initial aims and, more importantly, in bringing issues of racial equity in higher education to the fore for the first time in Kalamazoo College's history. Their actions led the College to hire its first African American faculty member, Dr. Romeo Phillips, who began the following fall as a professor in the education department. Phillips would remain at Kalamazoo College for the rest of his career, retiring in 1993. He later recalled the scrutiny he received from the BSO. "They wanted to know if I was an Uncle Tom," he explained. "But, I'm from Chicago and we're pretty tough . . . so, after a while, the word came out, said, you know, 'Dr. Phillips, don't mess with that man. He's from Chicago, and he will not take any foolishness.' And, so we got along beautifully."[68]

The BSO's cause had been helped by the national mood in the wake of King's assassination. Black students all over the country were making similar demands, and the White higher education community, sufficiently shaken by King's death, was willing to listen. It was one of the rare instances in American history where the door leading to racial equity opened just a crack. The BSO had made the most of the moment, but it would prove fleeting. A document summarizing the BSO's actions in the spring of 1968, likely penned by Hicks, acknowledged the need for institutional change, admitting that "for years we have brought Negroes to the campus and saturated them with a white culture. Basically, we have tried to make them over. We have actually befriended them without making them our equals." But he also intimated the limits to what the administration probably saw as its indulgence. Noting that they had been "most, most patient and understanding," the document reflects the conflicted feelings of the College's leadership. "We must recognize that we must add to our faculty a representative number of Black professors," the writer conceded. "We must alter our curriculum to include Black history and culture, for the benefit of our white youth as well as our Black. And in the near future our Black youth must come to see that the tragedies of this spring and the indifferences to their people over the years do not justify continuing preferential treatment."[69] A stunning statement when one considers the centuries of preferential treatment afforded White people.

"You Must Attempt to Stand Where We Are Standing"

After the spring of 1968, the BSO embarked upon an intense period of activity, attending conferences with Black students from other colleges, working in the Black community locally and regionally, and continuing their own education on Black history and culture. This they did on top of their regular course load while continuing to raise issues of concern with the administration and following up on progress in meeting their demands.

In late January 1969, the BSO wrote to Hicks to "state the black students who desire to live together spring quarter and to set up a mechanism to perform this function every quarter."[70] The memo also requested Black resident assistants to work with Black students. The BSO wrote again in March "to clarify what should be and has been done in [the] area of hiring Black professors,"[71] noting also that "there should be a recruitment agent and counselor for the Black students" as well. "We are becoming increasingly disenchanted with the slow progress in this area," wrote Jasper Jones and Thom Seavers, cochairs of BSO that quarter. "We are aware of the difficulties encountered by you because of established procedures in hiring new professors, but we cannot tolerate this or anything else to stand in the way of necessary change."

Hicks replied that "we take strong exception to your statement that the Administration has made 'slow progress' in the hiring of Black professors," noting that the College had hired Dr. Romeo Phillips, was planning to make one-year appointments with two professors from Sierra Leone, and had "secured a Professorship in Urban Studies to support a Black appointee for a five-year period."[72]

Memos went back and forth between the BSO and the administration throughout the winter and into the spring. The BSO raised concerns about racist programming policies at the College's radio station, meeting space in the planned renovation of the student center, admissions procedures, and control of the Westab building, a facility in the city's mostly Black northside neighborhood that had been donated to the College. The BSO wanted the Black United Front (BUF), a confederation of Black-run organizations in Kalamazoo, to determine how the building could best be used to serve the city's Black residents.

The administration honored some requests while rejecting others, often citing policy and precedent. A particular point of contention turned on the request to house Black students together in the residence halls. While the Dean of Students was willing to accommodate to a degree, he and Hicks saw the request as "segregation" and worried that creating an all-Black space within the residence halls would violate the 1964 Civil Rights Act.

As tends to happen at Kalamazoo College, tensions accumulated as the year wore on, and by May of 1969 the BSO again found it necessary to issue demands. "In the past twelve months the Black Student Organization has constantly impressed upon this college administration the necessity of adjusting, changing, or adding to its judicial, residential and admissions procedures, its academic curriculum, its faculty and administrative personnel and its budget," they asserted in a memo detailing the conditions that must be met before fall 1969. "That which we demand now, we have requested before."

This time, there were seven demands instead of four, reflecting additional issues that had arisen over the past year. The first demand called for several new courses on Black history and culture along with a plan for who would teach them, at least in the short term. The second demand called for altering admissions procedures and giving the Black membership on the Admissions Committee ultimate authority over decisions about Black applicants. The third demand concerned the BSO budget allocation of $5,500, which they wanted to come directly from the Business Office as it had the year before. The fourth demand centered on "Black control of the Westab Program as recommended to the President by the Student Faculty Committee on Westab in March of 1969." The last three demands centered on housing Black students together in the residence halls, with the fifth demand restating earlier requests that there be an "adequate number of suites grouped together to accommodate all Black male students (both upperclassmen and incoming freshmen) in either Crissey or Severn, and that this space be adjusted in future quarters to insure accommodations for all Black male students, and a complete section in Mary Trowbridge or Crissey or a house for both upperclass and freshmen Black women." The sixth and seventh demands were aimed at changing policies that were keeping the administration from fully honoring the fifth demand.[73]

On May 15, Hicks shared the administration's official response in a meeting with the BSO leaders and, because the demands were about to be published in the *Index*, copies of the response were also sent out to the College community. Whereas Hicks began his response to the demands of the previous spring by "expressing deep sympathy for the status quo of the Black people," stating his determination "to do all I can to further the cause of equality," and assuring the BSO that "we have studied your requests with care," the response to the demands of 1969 had a distinctly different tone. "Your letter of May 12 was duly received and considered," he began unceremoniously. "Since its receipt I have consulted with a cross section of individuals and groups in order to assure consensus on the principles which must determine our replies."[74]

The BSO noted the change. The magnanimity present after King's assassination had waned. As Chokwe Lumumba later recalled, "it's interesting to me, you have to excuse me, but we've been going through oppression as Black people for some . . . at least 200 years, you know what I'm saying? And to think that people, [after] we have one year of demonstrations, are beginning to get fed up, I don't have a great deal of sympathy for that."[75]

The administration's response rejected out of hand Internal Colonialism and Racism in Culture, courses to be taught by Edwin Taliaferro and Richard Sutton, a graduate student and leader in Western Michigan University's Black Action Movement. "It is a principle of the faculty that all courses must be as objective as is humanly possible, representative of all points of view," Hicks explained. "The readings proposed by the BSO do not meet this requirement, nor do the proposed teachers have the training in the disciplines required for these courses." During an earlier meeting of the Administrative Committee, made up of faculty and administrators, to consider the response to the demands, a faculty member had said that "courses to be introduced should be based on truth and reason." Romeo Phillips, the newly hired Black professor, diplomatically "pointed out that there may be a need to bring the full segment of American society—the truths [as] blacks see them."[76] Black students across the country had demanded similar curricular changes, often being told, as the BSO was, that such courses were not "objective." However, "what the universities have failed to realize in almost every case," wrote two academic deans in the *Educational Record* in 1969, "is that the American educational experience is a *white* experience, an experience based on white history, white tradition, white culture, white customs, and white thinking."[77]

Laurence Barrett, acting dean of academic affairs, had also expressed strong opposition to undergraduates teaching college-level courses, yet Edwin Taliaferro was already teaching a 100-level course that spring,[78] and the following year, when he would teach the proposed Internal Colonialism course, he would be a college graduate. Richard Sutton was likewise a graduate student at Western Michigan. Both were well versed in the proposed topics.

The administration agreed to having the English Department propose a course on "Black writers" to be offered the following year. "Its content and structure will be developed by the instructor," the reply read, omitting reference to the demand for two Black teaching assistants. The administration also found it necessary to point out that the "proposed course will be open to all students," though the BSO had not suggested otherwise.

The Black History Seminar demanded by the BSO was "not to be offered in 1969–70." No explanation was given, but there was a promise to begin a search "for a Black historian to be added to the Department as of September, 1970." The administration skirted the demand for three individualized courses—Plays and Poetry of Black America, The Black Psyche, and The Music of Blackness—to be added "as soon as competent non-white instructors can be obtained to teach them," citing the policy that "individualized courses are not determined by the administration," but rather "are provided at the discretion of individual members of the faculty."

Out of the seven courses proposed by the BSO then, only one, a course on "Black writers," as the administration termed it (the BSO had called for a course on the Afro-American Novel), was to be taught the following year. No commitment was made to having Black teaching assistants, as stipulated in the demand, nor was that part of the demand even acknowledged.

On demand 2, regarding admissions, the administration agreed to hiring a Black recruitment agent and to a BSO member working on the admissions staff during their Career Service quarter. In response to the demand that four Black students be added to the committee, an open invitation for "a Black student" on the committee was reiterated. The administration rejected the demand that the Black membership have ultimate authority over decisions regarding Black applicants, insisting that the "authority to admit or reject a student rests with the entire membership the Admissions Committee in all cases."

With regard to the BSO's budget request, the administration pointed out that the direct allocation the previous year was due to "unusual circumstances" and "now insists that the normal procedures be followed." They side-stepped the demand for Black control of the Westab building stating that "the College is interested in working with other groups within the community surrounding the Westab facility."

On demands 5 through 7, concerning the residence halls, the administration remained rooted in the position it had held all year and, instead of responding to the details of the demands, reproduced excerpts from previous memos.[79]

Appended to the administration's response were four guiding principles that the Administrative Committee had put forth as "essential to the effective functioning of any liberal arts college." Namely that:

1. The College authorities must retain final responsibility for determining the academic and nonacademic programs of the institution.
2. They must retain final responsibility for determining who matriculates at the College and who serves as its faculty and staff.
3. Although any teacher's experiences, ethnic or otherwise, will bear upon his competence to teach certain subjects, the College cannot accept the idea that a teacher's race automatically determines his competence to teach any particular subject matter or any particular group of students.
4. They cannot adopt deliberately a policy which is illegal, or which provides special privileges, regulations, or procedures for any group within the student community.[80]

In unilaterally determining these rules of engagement, the administration set up a bulwark that allowed it to distance itself from the conditions motivating the BSO's demands. Their reaction had little to do with an attempt to understand and everything to do with appeasement. The first two principles stated the obvious, that College authorities were in control of the College, a fact of which the BSO was no doubt fully aware. Their demands, therefore, were pushing for the administration to depart from the usual course of action in order to create a better experience for Black students. The third principle conflated the call for the College to hire more faculty of color with the idea that only Black faculty could teach the courses proposed by the BSO. Though the BSO clearly preferred that the courses be taught by faculty of color, they were not insisting on that. This was evident in the demand for a course on the Afro-American Novel, which would need to be taught by a White professor given that the entire English Department was White. They were, however, with good reason, concerned about the capacity within the faculty to teach courses from a Black perspective given that the faculty had shown no inclination to do so up to this point nor did they exhibit an understanding of the Black experience, hence the demand for two Black teaching assistants. The fourth principle was likely driven by a communication issued in March by President Richard Nixon's Department of Housing, Education, and Welfare warning "all colleges and universities receiving federal assistance not to institute separate Black Studies programs, 'separate housing,' or 'separate social activity' spaces that excluded white students,"[81] in effect turning the 1964 Civil Rights Act against Black students by equating these requests with forced segregation. Whereas the Kalamazoo College administration used the threat as a shield in its stance vis-à-vis the BSO demands, the president of Antioch College pushed back, claiming that a "literal interpretation of the Civil Rights Act in this 'deliberate and crucial question' might deny black students rights that white students have long had."[82]

"We believe that a liberal arts education should be beneficial for Black as well as white," Hicks wrote in concluding the response to the BSO demands. "Each group very much needs exposure to the culture and values of the other, and each group needs to examine its own assumptions and values from the perspectives and values offered by the other," he went on, drawing a false equivalence by not understanding that Black people had always been steeped in White culture and values and had always needed to understand the "perspectives and values offered by the other" simply to survive in the United States.

Not surprisingly, this response did not land well with the BSO. The ensuing stand-off galvanized the campus and a rush of events ensued. The following day, the administration held an all-campus meeting in the Chapel to clarify their stance, and the Student Commission issued a position paper mostly in support of the BSO. "Ignoring the basic problems and frustration which brought about these demands will not make them disappear," the Commission admonished. "Rather we must face the problems and work towards equitable solutions. The Commission feels that on the whole the response of the administration was inadequate to what it felt were meaningful demands."[83] Meanwhile, meetings were taking place between the administration and Student Commission, and various individuals and groups from across campus were weighing in with their opinions. As Hicks later wrote, "the President opened his door for one and all who wished to express himself. It became obvious that the BSO represented one group. There was a second group which strongly supported anything which the Blacks demanded, but there was a sizable quiet but determined group of white backlash. There then was the large majority who were not deeply troubled and appeared to be neutral."[84]

That Saturday, May 17, was the annual Mothers' Day celebration, and as they had done the year before, the BSO used the occasion to protest the administration's response to their demands. At two o'clock, the leaders of the BSO read a statement to Hicks at the opening of the Mothers' Day concert: "Your reply to our demands was totally inadequate. We reject it. Your response is evidence that the racism that permeates American society is present in the administrators and faculty of this college. Our demands must be met by 6:00 Saturday, May 17, 1969,"[85] later that same day.

Realizing he would not have time to formulate a response by six o'clock, Hicks invited the BSO leadership to meet with him that afternoon. "We spent an hour and fifteen minutes together," Hicks wrote in a summary of events a few days later. "Nothing was solved but at least we talked and discussed things quietly and the Blacks got some of their 'hang-ups' off their mind." Later that evening, about twenty-five Black students converged on the Mothers' Day banquet. As they approached the speakers table, Hicks "jumped up with microphone in hand and asked if they wished to speak." According to Hicks, "their representative, Emmett Deans, spoke briefly and then the group departed after giving the Black counterpart of the Heil Hitler salute,"[86] which was Hicks's way of describing the raised fist symbolizing Black power.

With nothing resolved, the conflict continued to play out over the next few weeks as the academic year hurtled toward closure. In the midst of hastily scheduled meetings, campus forums, position papers, petitions and protests by White students supporting the BSO, and a flurry of memos, a BSO member named Genna Rae McNeil sat down to pen a statement to the faculty and administration in an effort to get them to understand the BSO's perspective. McNeil was well known and respected on campus. A highly engaged student, she had been president of the Alpha Lambda Delta honor society, a soloist in the College Concert Choir, a participant in the Northside tutoring program, a dormitory counselor, a senior fellow in the Philosophy Department, and a member of the steering committee for the Africa Institute to be held on campus that summer. She had been elected Homecoming Queen that fall and had recently been awarded a Ford Fellowship for graduate study, which she planned to use at the University of Chicago to pursue a doctorate in history.[87] Her views would have carried weight with many students, faculty, and administrators.

"As Black students there is but one conclusion we can draw from your most recent reply to our demands, your addendum of guiding principles, and the clarification forum of Friday, May 16, 1969," she began. "That conclusion is that you must not have understood the full meaning of our demands. We understand your standpoint; we have shared it for 300 years. It is now imperative that you understand that we no longer share it."

She appealed to their proclivities as academics by placing the demands in philosophical and historical context, quoting John Dewey, Paul Tillich, and Alfred North Whitehead alongside Stokely Carmichael, Charles Hamilton, and LeRoi Jones. "Black people are not demanding the impossible," McNeil asserted. "Black people are affirming the need to look at reality again. For in looking more closely with us you, too, may build a construct of more details from which you, too, may see new patterns of possibilities. There is but one way for you to understand and comprehend what we say to you. You must choose to transcend your limited perspective; you must attempt to stand where we are standing. If you do not try we can not begin to talk."

The preamble to the BSO's demands had been brief, but freighted with meaning. "Our underdeveloped communities must be built," they had stated, "and to accomplish this, educational skills and resources must be secured from you—the immediate part and representative of the oppressor which has retarded our development." McNeil quoted those words and then provided a full explication of their meaning, pointing out the "principles regarding ends and means, extended moral responsibility, and ultimate concerns implicit in the statement cited."

Beginning with ultimate concerns as expressed in the demands, she quoted Whitehead and Tillich on the inadequacy of language, in effect asking the administration to make "a leap of imagination to understand [their] meaning." She then took aim at "custom and precedent"—powerful forces in maintaining the status quo—citing Dewey on the need for habits "more flexibly responsive than those now current" and Carmichael and Hamilton on the need to question "old values and institutions" and "to think and operate in terms entirely new."

McNeil then moved on to ends and means, the ends being that Black people and communities "have an opportunity to develop their full potentiality," and the means being relevant "educational skills and resources" secured from the College. "We, now, are being realistic for 'to profess to have an aim and then neglect the means of its execution is self-delusion of the most dangerous sort,'" she argued, again citing Dewey.

She concluded by insisting on the College's moral responsibility to address their demands. "There is no innocence," McNeil flatly stated. "On the one hand this means that white Americans have the responsibility to recognize the worth of Black people regardless of custom," she asserted, foreshadowing the Black Lives Matter movement. "For you are responsible for continuing injustice unless you work against it. On the other hand it means that as long as Black people are dying horrible deaths and living deadly lives Blacks must take care of business."[88]

McNeil distributed her statement on campus and it was also printed in the May 23 issue of the *Index* as part of more than two full pages devoted to the BSO protests and the campus reaction. A more compelling call for action is hard to imagine, yet the impact of McNeil's statement on the faculty and administration, if there was one, evaporated amidst the frenetic activity of those weeks.

On May 24, the administration sent a second response to the BSO's demands that tried to strike a more conciliatory tone and emphasize the institution's commitment to change. "The Faculty is fully aware that the oppression of minorities has been a characteristic of American history and that our colleges have often reflected the prejudice and racism of the culture," the response began. "Recognizing that the Black experience has been inadequately presented at Kalamazoo, the Faculty is determined that courses pertinent to that experience will be added to the curriculum." The response recounted efforts made thus far, noting that "the President last summer obtained a grant for support of a Black urban sociologist, and from the date that grant was made, the College has been engaged in an intensive search. Offers have been made but refused, though the salary is well above the College average. The search goes on, and courses pertinent to minorities and the inner city will be available as soon as he is appointed. A search is also underway for a Black historian. Like the sociologist, he will be appointed as soon as he is found."[89] Ultimately, though, the administration's position remained the same, and after the BSO again found the response lacking, things came to a head on the eve of the board of trustees meeting.

"The Most Volatile Act That Can Be Taken"

Around noon on the day before the board meeting, the BSO sent Hicks a memo following up on their earlier demands. Hicks responded a few hours later and organized a meeting during which a small group of faculty and administrators discussed the demands with about twenty Black students for over an hour. Still feeling that their concerns had not been fully addressed, the BSO made the decision to take over the Mandelle administration building before the trustee meeting the next morning, June 6, to force the administration to act. The administration for its part had been worried about the potential for violence ever since the second set of demands had been issued in mid-May. By May 19, the administration had "made arrangements for an injunction and for calling the police," though Hicks recognized that this was "the most volatile act that can be taken."[90] Having failed to break the impasse with the BSO, the "administration had set up a secondary location for the Board meeting and was fully prepared for the takeover."

Arriving early the next morning at the Mandelle administration building, Business Manager Stuart Simpson found that both entrances had been chained shut. According to Hicks, Simpson "came at once to my home at 7:15. Within fifteen minutes we had gathered the Administrative

Committee at our home which was the headquarters in case of difficulty. We had communicated with our attorney and an injunction against the BSO was already on its way."

Hicks's patience had run out. For him, the take-over of Mandelle had crossed a line, and he dropped any semblance of acting in good faith and trying to understand the BSO's position. Hicks's account of what transpired next departs in tone from the many other memos and summaries he wrote about the BSO's demands and protests. A few things to keep in mind when considering this final confrontation between the BSO and the Hicks administration: first, Thom Seavers and Gerry Weaver, the BSO cochairs that quarter, were freshmen. Edwin Taliaferro continued to play a significant role in the BSO, but he was about to graduate. Perhaps that is why the leadership of the BSO had passed to its youngest members. Second, though the BSO had taken a militant stance, they had not indicated that they would act violently. And third, taking over a building was a commonly used tactic, and student protesters all over the country had taken similar actions.

Hicks had attempted conciliation and understanding in the administration's second response to the BSO demands, writing that the concerns expressed by the BSO, specifically "racism and internal colonialism," were "urgent, deep and pervasive." "They must be attended to," he affirmed, "and this attention can be productive of valuable changes in perspective, structures, and the academic curriculum." He concluded by saying, "to the BSO and to concerned White students the College owes a debt of gratitude for both vision and candor."[91] However, in his own mind he had also drawn a line in the sand, which he had hinted at in the cover memo to the first response to the demands, saying "those of us legally responsible for the administration of the College will insist that the rights and privileges of all in the community be respected, and will act strongly against any behavior not in accord with this principle."[92] For Hicks, the take-over of Mandelle was clearly "not in accord with this principle," hence the resort to "the most volatile act that can be taken."

The account of the final confrontation is unsigned and undated, but presumably written by Hicks. A handwritten note at the top of the page indicates that the document was drafted in 1971, two years after the fact:

> At daybreak on the morning of the 6th a few Black students took over Mandelle Hall, the administrative building in which the Board of Trustees was scheduled to meet . . . . Fortunately for the Blacks their coleader, Mr. Weaver, become [*sic*] frightened and came up to our house at 7:40. He was aghast to find how far we had gone and how ready the administration was for such a take-over. I told him then that our day began at 8 o'clock. He had twenty minutes to get his Blacks and any evidence of a take-over out of the building. I said I would be there at 8:00 and the College would go on as usual. I interpreted that if they were out before we arrived, then they had not violated a take-over and were not in danger. I said, too, we would call a faculty meeting on Saturday morning at which the Blacks could present their case still further. When I arrived at 8 a. m. the building was entirely clear and the meeting of the Board of Trustees and all activities of the day proceeded on schedule.[93]

Hicks's recollection that Gerry Weaver came to his house because he was "frightened" is at odds with Chokwe Lumumba's account as related to Eduard Avis in 1989, which indicated that Weaver had been tasked with informing Hicks that the BSO had taken over the administration building until such time as their demands were met. While it is not hard to imagine that Weaver felt trepidation in confronting Hicks, it was not fear that had motivated the visit. Unaware that Stuart Simpson had alerted Hicks to the take-over, Gerry Weaver ascended the College's fair arcadian hill, the quaint red-brick Academy Street on one side and an oak grove on the other as he made his way to the Hicks home perched at the top. We do not know how Weaver, probably all of nineteen at the time, experienced the encounter after he arrived, whether he was actually "aghast" as Hicks described, or whether he was feeling extreme discomfort as he stood in Hicks's home surrounded by the College's White power structure threatening not the College's disciplinary action but escalating to the involvement of civil authorities. The word "betrayed" comes to mind.

Why had Hicks leapt from handling the conflict internally to involving the police? Perhaps he felt that some covenant had been broken when the doors to Mandelle were chained, but he surely also broke a covenant by threatening to call the police on his own students, suddenly transforming

Gerry Weaver and "his Blacks" from student activists into perpetrators. The BSO had not vandalized the building, nor had they put anyone in danger. Was he simply tired of dealing with the BSO and their demands and so summoned higher authorities to finally put an end to the episode? Marilyn Hinkle, who worked with Hicks for many years, implies as much when she writes, "The prospect of an injunction had shifted the responsibility from the College to the court and carried the certainty of arrest."[94] In threatening arrest, did Hicks realize the historical weight of his actions, that he was resorting to the long-established practice of policing Black people to protect "respectable White people" like himself? Whether or not he understood the implications, it was probably not lost on members of the BSO. It was also a possibility they had anticipated.

As Avis wrote based on his interview with Chokwe Lumumba, the BSO "decided to occupy Mandelle only when they saw that their protests . . . were ineffective. And they decided before the occupation that under no circumstances would they risk arrest. Thus, it was not a lack of courage or commitment that caused them to give up the building so quickly, it was a premeditated plan that sought to protect the members of the group even if it meant the occupation failed. A red flag went up when Hicks indicated that he had an injunction for their arrest; that flag was their sign to give up the building."[95]

This bitter denouement to the BSO's Herculean efforts to bring about institutional change left Edwin Taliaferro in no frame of mind for conciliatory gestures. As he crossed the stage at Commencement nine days later, the last Black student of the 1960s to do so, Weimer Hicks extended his hand in congratulations. Edwin Taliaferro declined to shake it.

Though Kalamazoo College missed the opportunity to make many meaningful changes in response to the activism of the BSO, failing for example to establish a Black studies program as other institutions did, the BSO demands and protests were nevertheless not an end but a beginning. It was the first time students of color had openly voiced their concerns about the mismatch between a White-dominated campus culture and a racially and ethnically diverse society. Kalamazoo College did indeed seem to value "only one side of the cultural coin," as the BSO had asserted in their first set of demands. Student calls to address this problem have continued, and generations of faculty and administrators have grappled with issues of race, equity, and inclusion ever since. Whether that grappling has manifested as embracing or sidelining, resisting or engaging, the issues themselves have been ever present.

Endnotes

1 Oral history interview with Walter Hall, '64, by Anne Dueweke, July 26, 2016.

2 Oral history interview with Walter Hall, '64, by Anne Dueweke, July 26, 2016.

3 Oral history interview with Walter Hall, '64, by Anne Dueweke, July 26, 2016.

4 Oral history interview with Donna (Coleman) Odom, '67, by Anne Dueweke, January 16, 2018.

5 Flyer scanned with the April 8, 1960, issue of the *Index*.

6 "American Goals to Be College Lecture Series," *Index*, September 28, 1960, 1.

7 James Baldwin, "In Search of a Majority," in *Nobody Knows My Name* (New York: The Dial Press, 1961), 127–137.

8 "Our Uneasy Silence," *Index*, December 7, 1960, 2.

9 Email communication between Anne Dueweke and Walter Hall, March 7–11, 2021.

10 Email communication between Anne Dueweke and Walter Hall, March 7–11, 2021.

11 Marilyn Hinkle, *On Such a Full Sea* (Kalamazoo, MI: Kalamazoo College, 1982), 19–20.

12 Hinkle, *On Such a Full Sea,* 9.

13 "Boiling-Water College," *Time*, December 8, 1961, 42.

14 Debbie Foote, "African Studies Program Set," *Index*, February 7, 1969, 3.

15 Ruth Archer, "French View of Uncle Tom Flashes to Today's South," *Index*, November 7, 1963, 1.

16 Bertha Doleman, "Reflections," *Kalamazoo College Alumnus* (Spring Quarter 1964): 5–6.

17 Hinkle, *On Such a Full Sea,* 30.

18 Hicks memo, August 31, 1962, Kalamazoo College Archives, Weimer K. Hicks Papers, Admission 1962, Box 12, Folder 3.

19 Gordon F. Kurtz letter to Weimer Hicks, August 17, 1962, Kalamazoo College Archives, Weimer K. Hicks Papers, Admission 1962, Box 12, Folder 3.

20 Hicks memo, August 31, 1962, Kalamazoo College Archives, Weimer K. Hicks Papers, Admission 1962, Box 12, Folder 3.

21 Kalamazoo College Archives, Faculty Meeting Minutes, May 1955.

22 Kalamazoo College Archives, Weimer K. Hicks Papers, Admissions 1960–61, Box 12, Folder 2.

23 Kalamazoo College Archives, Weimer K. Hicks Papers, Admissions 1962, Box 12, Folder 3.

24 Oral history interview with Rev. Ronald Spann, '65, by Allia Howard, '17, July 26, 2016.

25 "The Spirit of Grace," *LuxEsto* (Winter 2018): 32.

26 "Grace Hayes to Attend Brussels World Fair," *Index*, February 14, 1958, 2.

27 Oral history interview with Walter Hall, '64, by Anne Dueweke, July 26, 2016.

28 Oral history interview with Walter Hall, '64, by Anne Dueweke, July 26, 2016.

29 Oral history interview with Walter Hall, '64, by Anne Dueweke, July 26, 2016.

30 Oral history interview with Rev. Ronald Spann, '65, by Allia Howard, '17, July 26, 2016.

31 Oral history interview with Denise Strong, '67, by Anne Dueweke, October 20, 2017.

32 Oral history interview with Donna (Coleman) Odom, '67, by Anne Dueweke, January 16, 2018.

33 Oral history interview with Donna (Coleman) Odom, '67, by Anne Dueweke, January 16, 2018.

34 Oral history interview with Clyde Solomon, '71, by Anne Dueweke, August 31, 2016.

35 Oral history interview with Clyde Solomon, '71, by Anne Dueweke, August 31, 2016.

36 "Black Panther Party USA," Black Past, Jan. 28, 2008, https://www.blackpast.org/african-american-history/black-panther-party/.

37 Kim Ridenour, "Carmichael Sways Crowds' Emotions," *Index*, May 26, 1967, 1.

38 "Albert Cleage Is Dead at 88; Led Black Nationalist Church," *New York Times*, February 27, 2000, Section 1, 49.

39 "Rev. Cleage to Probe Black Destiny Monday," *Index*, March 1, 1968, 1.

40 "Black Power from White Perspectives . . . ," *Index*, March 8, 1968, 3.

41 Oral history interview with DeMonte Johnson, '71, by Allia Howard, '17, July 19, 2016.

42 Ibram (Rogers) Kendi, *The Black Campus Movement* (New York: Palgrave MacMillian 2012), 77. Ibram Rogers later changed his name to Ibram X. Kendi.

43 Oral history interview with Clyde Solomon, '71, by Anne Dueweke, August 31, 2016.

44 Oral history interview with Sharon (Greene) McWilliams, '72, by Allia Howard, '17, August 4, 2016.

45 Oral history interview with Demonte Johnson, '71, by Allia Howard, '17, July 19, 2016.

46 Clyde Solomon, "Freshman Describes Black Consciousness," *Index*, March 15, 1968, 6.

47 Oral history interview with Clyde Solomon, '71, by Anne Dueweke, August 31, 2016.

48 BSO Constitution, ratified April 16, 1968, https://cache.kzoo.edu/handle/10920/19453.

49 Hicks, Weimer K. "Today's Youth in a Chaotic World," *Kalamazoo College Bulletin*, February, 1968. Reprinted in the April 16, 1968, issue of the *Index*, 1, 4.

50 Kendi, *The Black Campus Movement*, 117.

51 Statement from Kalamazoo College's Black Student Organization (BSO) about the creation of the Higher Education Committee within their organization, May 6, 1968, https://cache.kzoo.edu/handle/10920/19573.

52 Elvin Caldwell, based on an interview with Chokwe Lumumba, Senior Individualized Project, 2011, p. 37, http://hdl.handle.net/10920/23997.

53 Eduard Avis, interview with Chokwe Lumumba, Senior Individualized Project, 1989, p. 24, http://hdl.handle.net/10920/18856.

54 Eduard Avis, interview with Chokwe Lumumba, 23–24.

55 Douglas Martin, "Chokwe Lumumba, 66, Dies; Activist Who Became Mayor," *New York Times*, February 27, 2014, B17.

56 Elvin Caldwell, "Black Power and the Black Student Organization at Kalamazoo College," Senior Individualized Project, 2011, 38, http://hdl.handle.net/10920/23997.

57 Caldwell, "Black Power and the Black Student Organization at Kalamazoo College," 39.

58 Kendi, *The Black Campus Movement*, 5.

59 Kendi, *The Black Campus Movement*, 5.

60 Caldwell, "Black Power and the Black Student Organization at Kalamazoo College," 50.

61 Hicks's response to BSO demands, May 9, 1968, Kalamazoo College digital archive, https://cache.kzoo.edu/bitstream/handle/10920/19445/1968_05_09_Exhibit_D.pdf?sequence=1&isAllowed=y.

62 Memo from the BSO Regarding their Demands; https://cache.kzoo.edu/handle/10920/19444.

63 Memo from Weimer Hicks to the Executive Committee and other local trustees, May 13, 1968, https://cache.kzoo.edu/handle/10920/19442.

64 Hicks memo to BSO, May 13, 1968, https://cache.kzoo.edu/handle/10920/19570.

65 Senate White Paper, https://cache.kzoo.edu/handle/10920/19446.

66 Tim Lindstrom and Gail Stillwell, letter to the editor, *Index*, May 22, 1968 1.

67 Terry Brown, "Harmony a Myth," *Index*, May 17, 1968, 2.

68 Oral history interview with Dr. Romeo Phillips by Anne Dueweke, July 12, 2016.

69 Details on the Black Student Demands (Summary of '68 Confrontation), https://cache.kzoo.edu/handle/10920/19451.

70 BSO memo to Weimer Hicks, January 31, 1969, https://cache.kzoo.edu/handle/10920/19523.

71 BSO memo to Weimer Hicks, March 3, 1969, https://cache.kzoo.edu/handle/10920/19539.

72 Memo from Weimer Hicks to the BSO, March 13, 1969, http://hdl.handle.net/10920/19540.

73 Memo from BSO to Weimer Hicks with the second set of demands, May 12, 1969, https://cache.kzoo.edu/handle/10920/19554.

74 Weimer Hicks, Response to Demands Made Upon the College by the Black Student Organization, May 15, 1969, https://cache.kzoo.edu/handle/10920/19560.

75 Chokwe Lumumba, quoted in "Black on White: The Story of the Black Student Organization at Kalamazoo College in the Late 1960s," a Senior Individualized Project by Eduard Avis, '89, 32, https://cache.kzoo.edu/handle/10920/18856.

76 Minutes of the expanded Administrative Committee meeting, May 12, 1969, https://cache.kzoo.edu/handle/10920/19574.

77 Paul E. Wisdom and Kenneth A. Shaw, quoted by Ibram Kendi in *The Black Campus Movement,* 152.

78 A letter from Kalamazoo College's Acting Dean of Academic Affairs Laurence Barrett regarding the marking system for the 193 course taught by Edwin

Taliaferro, https://cache.kzoo.edu/handle/10920/19581.

79 Response to BSO demands, May 15, 1969, https://cache.kzoo.edu/handle/10920/19560.

80 Response to BSO demands, May 15, 1969, https://cache.kzoo.edu/handle/10920/19560.

81 Kendi, *The Black Campus Movement*, 138.

82 Kendi, *The Black Campus Movement*, 138.

83 Student Commission position paper, May 16, 1969, https://cache.kzoo.edu/handle/10920/19457.

84 Hicks Summary of the May 1969 Confrontation, May 19, 1969, https://cache.kzoo.edu/handle/10920/19448.

85 BSO memo to Weimer Hick, May 17, 1969, https://cache.kzoo.edu/handle/10920/19558.

86 Hicks Summary of the May 1969 Confrontation, May 19, 1969, https://cache.kzoo.edu/handle/10920/19448.

87 "Achievement Day Honors Senior Women," *Index*, May 9, 1969, 3.

88 Genna Rae McNeil, statement distributed to the Kalamazoo College faculty and administration, May 19, 1969, https://cache.kzoo.edu/handle/10920/19559.

89 Official reply from the Kalamazoo College Administration to the demands of the BSO, May 24, 1969, http://hdl.handle.net/10920/19576.

90 Weimer Hicks, "Sequence of the BSO Incident," May 19, 1969; https://cache.kzoo.edu/handle/10920/19448.

91 Weimer Hicks, "Reply of the Faculty and Administration to Demands," May 24, 1969, https://cache.kzoo.edu/handle/10920/19576.

92 Weimer Hicks, "Response to Demands Made Upon the College by the Black Students' Organization," May 15, 1969, https://cache.kzoo.edu/handle/10920/19560.

93 "Description of Second Confrontation, 1971, https://cache.kzoo.edu/handle/10920/19580.

94 Hinkle, *On Such a Full Sea*, 99.

95 Avis, "Black on White," 92.

Chapter Six

The Brick Wall

In the months following the spring of 1969, President Weimer Hicks attempted to make good on the promises he and his administration had made to the Black Student Organization (BSO). He was, after all, a man of his word. Two Black trustees were added to the board, and the search continued for the elusive Black sociologist and other faculty and staff positions. "Some black appointments lasted; most did not," wrote Marilyn Hinkle in 1980. "Dr. Romeo Phillips, hired in 1968, became head of the education department. Others—including some personnel that Western Michigan University had given approval to share—served part-time and eventually left the campus. Among them were an admissions counsellor, a coach, a personal counsellor, and [a] few teachers." "The College worked diligently on appointments, but difficulty lay in finding qualified candidates in the marketplace of the times,"[1] she concluded, citing an oft-used excuse for the failure of colleges and universities to diversify their faculties and staffs.

In 1970, one of those part-time appointments, an admissions counselor named Don Lester, wrote a ten-page report to Hicks detailing steps the College needed to take in order to create a welcoming environment for Black students. Among his suggestions was to drop the insistence on hiring faculty who had attended elite institutions and not to rely too heavily on credentialing. As he explained to Hicks, "since higher educational opportunities for black people have just recently been increased . . . we do not have a surplus of black PhD's to send to white universities." "This does not mean we don't have qualified black personnel to fill those positions," he went on. "We have numerous black educators and administrators who have earned their PhD's in the field and not in the sterile halls of ivy."[2]

He also argued that SAT scores did not reflect the potential of Black students due to cultural biases in the test and provided data showing that the SAT scores of Black students at Kalamazoo did not correlate with their academic achievement. "It is not enough for Admissions Departments to lower the numerical score upon which admission is considered," Lester wrote, urging Hicks to "take a progressive step forward" by eliminating test scores altogether, a step the College would eventually take forty-five years later.[3]

Lester also advocated for more Black personnel on the Admissions Committee, noting that "many times final decisions on applications are made more by sensitivity and emotion." Because of this, Lester noted "a definite need for a larger number of black faculty on this committee whose sensitivity to the potential of black students would be much keener."

Hicks read the report with care, making notes in the margins. In a reply to Lester, he thanked him for the report, noting the many good suggestions that they would try to implement, and admitted to "ineptitude and human frailty" impeding efforts thus far.[4] We will never know, however, whether Hicks would have undertaken Lester's suggestions in earnest because soon afterward he suffered a heart attack. In January of 1971, Hicks announced that he was cutting back on his duties and would retire within a year.[5]

Backsliding

In contrast to Weimer Hicks, his successor George Rainsford, who served from 1972–1983, did not make diversifying the faculty and student body a priority. As a result, enrollments of Black students dwindled during the 1970s and efforts to diversify the faculty stagnated. In fact, as if exhausted by the BSO's activism, the College largely turned away from issues of race in the 1970s. "The people are naïve and quite American," a Black student told the *Index* in November of 1970, "and the college just seems to be the ideal for white America."[6]

In 1972, a writer for the *Index* noted that since the 1969 BSO protests "discussion of the racial situation at Kalamazoo has been a clandestine affair. No more demands, no more college policy statements, and eventually, no more race relations at Kalamazoo College."[7] In looking into what had become of promises made to the BSO, he found a lack of follow-through and myriad excuses. Promises to alter the curriculum to include Black culture, arts, and history had been reduced to a tutoring program for Black students "designed to help them establish an equal academic footing with white students." Not only did this response fail to address the curricular issues raised by the BSO, it transferred the source of the problem from the curriculum to the students. According to the *Index*, "Dr. Chen noted that the tutoring programs had the effect of marking black students as inferior, thus creating an unavoidable resentment."[8]

In the area of admissions, the writer pointed out that "despite Dr. Hicks' earlier promises to bolster black enrollment at Kalamazoo, the black population is currently only 3.5% (approximately 50 black students in a total student population of 1400)." The explanations for a lack of progress included, according to President Rainsford, that "the college never had nor ever intends to have a quota system . . . Dr. Rainsford was particularly vehement on this point."[9] This reaction was a common one. Talk of increasing Black student enrollment often led to impassioned rejections of "quota systems," as if trying to achieve a goal for greater enrollment was the same as establishing quotas to keep the number of Black students to a minimum. Other types of enrollment initiatives, for example increasing geographic diversity or recruiting more full-pay students, never elicited such indignation.

In paraphrasing Rainsford's remarks, the author of the article said that since "admissions are now geared to white middle-class students (e.g. SAT scores) the college needs to become more sophisticated in its selection policy. In terms of admissions this means that the college must find more suitable methods of measuring motivation; it must look for other kinds of information. Again, 'none of this has to do with numbers,'" Rainsford insisted.

With regard to improving the racial climate on campus, the writer of the article reported that "administration officials are hopeful for change, but cognizant of its gradual nature." Herb Lindsay and Thom Seavers, Black students who had been active in the BSO protests, expressed pessimism about the College's ability to change, saying "that black seniors are in a state of despair at Kalamazoo, waiting only to get out."[10]

It was not just Kalamazoo College that turned away from issues of race in the 1970s. The nation was in the early stages of backlash to the Civil Rights and Black Power movements. Because the explicit racism of the pre-Civil Rights era had become socially unacceptable, politicians hoping to win the votes of White people uncomfortable with Black progress turned to "dog-whistles," appealing to voters' racist instincts without using racial language.

This approach was at the core of Richard Nixon's "Southern Strategy," as Republican political strategist Lee Atwater famously explained in a 1981 interview, thinking he was speaking off the record: "You start out in 1954 by saying, '[N-word], [N-word], [N-word].' By 1968 you can't say '[N-word]'—that hurts you, backfires. So you say stuff like, uh, forced busing, states' rights, and all that stuff, and you're getting so abstract. Now, you're talking about cutting taxes, and all these things you're talking about are totally economic things and a byproduct of them is, blacks get hurt worse than whites . . . "[11]

The backlash, with its goal of "blacks get hurt worse than whites," would lead in the coming decades to the mass incarceration of Black and Brown people through the "War on Crime" and the "War on Drugs," strategies that ramped up the over-policing of Black people and other people of color and won votes for Democratic and Republican politicians alike. During these years, implicit racism bloomed, allowing White people to harbor their biases—sometimes consciously, sometimes not—with plausible deniability. Many White people became convinced that racism was no longer an issue, especially with the rise of affirmative action policies, which some saw as "reverse discrimination." The solution to racial tension became, for many White people, not to talk about it, and Black people and other people of color who pointed out instances of racism were often accused of "playing the race card," as if naming racism was the problem, not the existence of racism itself.

In April of 1974, a student wrote what was intended to be a humorous piece for the *Index* about a made-up pool hustler who cheated unwitting students out of their hard-earned work/study paychecks in the Hicks Student Center game room. The hustler was described as "a dirty dude, man, a really filthy cat . . . When he walks into the game room, the whole place takes on a smell that is most definitely all his own." The writer muses about what should be done with the "hustler," noting that "one rotten apple can spoil a whole barrel" and concludes that "if we could only work together, like the vigilantes did a hundred years ago, I know that we could rid our school of its scavenging verminous scum. I know that we could trust ourselves again . . . I know that together, we could be a barrel of good red apples." To represent the "hustler," the writer of the article chose one of the very few Black students on campus and included a photo of him playing pool alongside the story.[12]

The following week a letter to the editor, presumably written by a Black student, called out the racism in the article. "I think the article was written to make a statement to both Blacks and Whites under the guise of humor: that Black people are 'undesirables' and are not wanted in the K-College community," the writer of the letter asserted. "They 'stink', they 'smell', they are 'hustlers.' They are 'rotten apples spoiling the barrel of good apples.' The age-old question raised by the white community was again raised in this article: what to do with THEM." She made clear who "the vigilantes of a hundred ago" were: "white racists who attempted to, and succeeded in, preventing Black people from asserting themselves."

"If the article was written with no intended harm," she continued, "why was a Black student singled out to represent the hustler when White students so greatly outnumber Black students? Why was this Black student not informed of the content of the article but instead, when asked to see the article before publication, told that it was (conveniently) 'locked up'?"

The letter writer then addressed the racial climate on campus, stating that "the article certainly couldn't have been written in 1968, 1970, or even 1973. What conditions in 1974 allow such blatant use of stereotypes which retard any positive image of the Black man? . . . Now, in this post-1960 period, we seem to have returned to a lack of respect, again blatant. Must this country always be crisis-oriented and only exhibit respect when it is forcibly demanded?"

Knowing her audience well, she then predicted "being told that my reaction to this article is one of paranoia, that the article didn't have reference to a Black hustler but a hustler that happened to be Black."[13] Disappointingly, but predictably, the *Index* editors' reply invoked plausible deniability rather than taking the letter writer's criticisms to heart: "The article was not meant to be read along racial lines. It was not about a BLACK hustler, but about a hustler who happened to be black . . . We won't go so far to say that a reading such as your own is paranoiac, but it does have the earmarks, and after all, the word is your own."[14] Not only did the "hustler" article make use of dog whistles, the editors then gaslighted the Black student who pointed out the racism.

As racial tensions continued to simmer, other social movements advocating for the rights of women, gay and lesbian people, and American Indians gained force in the 1970s. While the women's and gay rights movements were experienced personally on campus and stirred up controversy, students tended to approach the American Indian Movement (AIM) from a less personal and more intellectual perspective, probably because there were few if any American Indian students on campus. In 1972, as Indigenous activist Mike Chosa was leading protests in nearby Chicago over discrimination against American Indians living in the city, a group of students invited Chosa to campus to deliver a lecture on "The Indian, Old and New."[15]

The following week the *Index* published an interview with Chosa. The student interviewer was earnest in his intent and sincerely trying to understand, but his biases and ignorance came through in some of his questions. "What is your preference," he asked, "total assimilation into white American culture with loss of Indian identity or separate but equal subculture maintaining absolute identity," setting up a dichotomy that need not exist. "I don't see any difference in what we're aiming towards, in terms of goals, and any other ethnic community," Chosa replied.

"Is the reason behind the Indian's apparent stagnate socio-economic status in this country today due primarily to apathy or bigotry," the interviewer then asked.

"Neither, generally," explained Chosa. "It's a result of federal intervention in what we call self-reliance efforts by Indian people . . . It's the result of efforts by Christian communities to intervene in the internal affairs of our various tribes, in as much as trying to convert whole tribes to Christianity. This results in, if they are partially successful, you might say eradicating the culture of our people and leaves them without a root."

The *Index* interviewer then, astonishingly, asked: "Have you considered imigration [*sic*] to another country where you might not be subjected to these occurences [*sic*]?"

"We'll say no comment to that one," Chosa responded with admirable restraint.[16]

The students who brought Chosa to campus soon formed a campus organization called "Hozhoni," which had "risen out of the growing awareness that this type of thing has been happening for more than a century, and is still happening to the American Indian," according to the *Index*. The article explained that "'Hozhoni' is a Navajo concept concerning the achievement of harmony with life in all respects. It is to this idea, in the hope that national and cultural harmony might evolve, that the Hozhoni Organization is committed."[17]

The Hozhoni organization remained active for five years, holding an annual "Indian Awareness Week" and sponsoring films, lectures, and fundraisers for American Indian causes. During its brief existence, the group hosted prominent American Indian activists such as Chosa, who visited campus twice. They also brought Vernon Bellecourt,[18] one of the founders of AIM, and Madonna Gilbert,[19] a national leader in AIM who had participated in the occupations of Alcatraz Island in 1970–1971 and Wounded Knee in 1973.

Hozhoni and its programs caused little if any controversy on campus because they did not threaten the status quo. No one was calling for policy or curriculum changes or asking people to alter their personal behavior. American Indians continued to be seen as a people apart. This was not the case, however, for students concerned with women's rights, gay rights, and racial equity, who felt a personal stake in these movements and advocated for change on campus. In this new climate, straight White men would sometimes bristle at the need to watch their words and would express annoyance that the people they offended could not "take a joke." Indeed, all this activism felt tiresome to many White and straight people, especially to many straight White men. An article written in 1978 by a self-proclaimed WASP expressed this fatigue in a way meant to poke fun at WASPs but which got the point across anyway.

"Look. I admit it, I'm a WASP. So get off of my back," he began. "Manifest destiny isn't easy to live with. Bringing white man's medicine to the Dark Continent. Introducing Uncle Ben's Converted Rice to the Vietnamese. Packing Puerto Ricans into New York City tenements. Oh, the weight on my shoulders."

He goes on to describe how he tried to become progressive: "Once, in a really low point—I think it was when my GM stock fell to 49%—I slipped.

I renounced it all: the Buick, the private tennis lessons, even the family condo in Miami Beach. I became a Socialist."

"But always, while I wandered, something was nagging me," he went on. "Somewhere, deep inside, a little voice was crying out, 'Exploit the masses, exploit the masses.' I had this uncontrollable thirst for power, these urges to ruthlessly oppress and dominate my inferiors, to crush any and all opposition to my bid for total authority . . . . I learned the futility of progress and reform, the rewards of submission to the System, and I'm better for it."

"So, look," he concluded, "if you're part of some minority, or if you even think you might be down-troddened [*sic*], stay away from me. I don't want to go through all that again. Those country club re-admit fees are murder."[20]

The piece was satirical, but the sentiments it described, whether actually felt by the writer or not, were real for many in positions of racial and economic privilege who were loath to give up "the rewards of submission to the System" and take seriously issues stemming from systemic inequality.

"Where Are Your Cultural Differences?"

By the late 1970s, the Hozhoni organization had disappeared, enrollment of Black students had fallen precipitously, and the College coffers had been depleted. Facing a difficult financial outlook, Director of Admissions Paul Lane wrote to President Rainsford in 1978 suggesting three options for reducing the admissions budget, the third of which was "to reduce the quest for diversity, in out of state, in athletes, in minorities." "All forms of diversity are particularly expensive," he wrote.[21] Rainsford chose the third option, reduction of diversity, thereby making explicit his lack of interest in pursuing a diverse student body, a disposition that had been implied for years. Lane wrote to confirm Rainsford's decision shortly thereafter. "It is my understanding that you have selected Option #3—the reduction of diversity. I will, therefore, proceed to prepare a slightly different set of objectives and a detailed budget based on this plan of operation." "It is with great regret that I do this," Lane gently admonished, "believing that the College should push its Admissions Office efforts in diversity, quality, and numbers as far as it can during these last couple years when students are available."[22]

Shortly after Rainsford made that decision, the *Index* ran a series of articles calling attention to the lack of diversity on campus. An April 1978 article titled "K College Black Students a Vanishing Group?" noted that the College's Black student population had shrunk to 1.4 percent.[23] In a subsequent article, Lane admitted that recruitment of Black students remained "an issue on the back burner."[24]

Meanwhile, the few Black students who did enroll felt disillusioned and alienated, many finding that White students were "prevented from interacting with them on more than a shallow basis due to preconceptions about blacks which carryover from white, suburban, and often upper middle class backgrounds." According to one senior who had grown bitter toward White people during her time at Kalamazoo, "I expected people to be uncomfortable but I imagined that once the ice was broken I would make friends."[25]

Rainsford soon found that his decision to "back burner" efforts towards greater diversity was out of step with the wishes of the board of trustees, who in July of 1978 "directed that the 1979–80 budget assign resources specifically for the recruitment of minority students, faculty and administrative personnel." Though the board expected Rainsford "to submit a minority recruitment proposal in October . . . , Rainsford stated that the process of forming such a proposal would be a slow one." "I would like to think of this as a positive move forward rather than a dramatic one," he explained, adding that January of 1979 was "a much more realistic date" for submitting the proposal.[26]

The board's call for greater diversity on campus came amid mounting pressure on the College to divest from South Africa as the anti-apartheid movement intensified. "The increased concern on campus with the issue of race relations in South Africa appears to have influenced the timing of the Board's decision," a student reported in the *Index*. "Although Rainsford believed the Board was providing leadership," the writer went on, "he admitted that the South African issue had 'accelerated' the move. He stated that many of the Trustees believed the issue of racism on campus should be addressed before considering the College's involvement in South Africa." Rainsford added, "there is significantly more racism on this campus than many of us are willing to admit."[27]

It is not clear what measures were taken in response to the board's directive, but no discernible change resulted. By the time Rainsford left the College five years later, Black students still comprised less than 2 percent of the student body and faced the same alienating climate.[28] Some members of the BSO interviewed by the *Index* in February 1984 "expressed regret that they ever stayed at K. Other students voiced frustrations over racism in K's academics and athletics, claiming that it has lowered their GPAs and kept them on the bench when they should have played. All saw a need for a greater black enrollment at K."

"This is a liberal arts college," Randy Lewis, a senior BSO member, was quoted as saying. "What liberalism do you see here? Where are your cultural differences?" According to the *Index* article, "Lewis and the other students present said they felt slighted by the course offerings at K, claiming that blacks were portrayed negatively or given little coverage at all in almost every class they have ever had here."

"When we are busy protesting, when we're always constantly active, then they'll do something," said Lewis. "But if we're quiet for a minute, they forget about us."

"They talk to pacify us," Ken Sanders added. "Once a school has established its values and ideas and who it is going to cater to I don't think you're ever going to change that."[29]

Shortly after the inauguration of David Breneman, Rainsford's successor, the *Index* interviewed several faculty and administrators, including the new president, on the issue of diversity. Dr. Romeo Phillips, who continued to be the College's sole African American professor sixteen years after he was hired, commented that "if the college is truly concerned about enlarging black faculty with hard money, then they will adopt a program that the University of Michigan did, whereby . . . no department could hire an individual unless they showed the affirmative action officer step by step what was done to recruit a black faculty."

When presented with this idea, Provost Warren Board stated, "the truth is that that kind of systematic, affirmative action hiring position has not been our chief priority." Board gave a similar response when asked whether there were any plans to assess course offerings "for minority representation." "To integrate (the study of) black americans [*sic*] into our classes has not been the first priority for curriculum development," he said, noting that the current focus was on international studies and computer science.

President Breneman expressed concern about the low enrollment of Black students and proclaimed an increase in minority enrollment as one of his goals, but he nevertheless sought to lower expectations. "I guess I feel that before we can make a very realistic and aggressive effort to increase the number of black students here—because I figure there are some unique problems we face—the overriding priority is to get the total enrollment picture turned around."[30]

The Quest for Multiculturalism

A year and a half later, in response to a recommendation by the Campus Life Committee, Dr. Sandra Greene became the College's first assistant dean of minority affairs. Greene, an African American graduate from the class of 1974, had recently joined the faculty as an assistant professor of history and director of the African Studies program. Her responsibilities in the part-time minority affairs position were to include "advising minority students and recommending to Student Services ways in which K can better serve minority students." "Breneman also said that Greene might be able to do some recruiting for K at College Nights for high school seniors," the *Index* reported.[31]

This new position would mark the beginning of a period of sustained attention to issues of diversity that gained momentum in the late 1980s under Breneman and continued through the mid-1990s under Breneman's successor, Lawrence (Larry) Bryan. Those years spurred campus-wide efforts toward "multiculturalism," in the language of the times, which included initiatives to diversify the student body and take advantage of a wave of faculty retirements to hire more "minority" faculty, including women and people of color. "With less than two full-time American born minority faculty members, and many faculty vacancies opening up in the near future due to retirements," the *Index* reported in fall 1986, "K's Provost Dr. Timothy Light said . . . that the college will be striving for a much greater diversity."[32]

Efforts were also underway to broaden the cultures and cultural perspectives covered in the curriculum, a process that would prove to be slow and divisive. In the winter of 1987, the curriculum subcommittee of the Community Committee on Racism and Diversity surveyed the faculty to gain a sense of their views on the matter. On the whole, their responses did not communicate enthusiasm. More than half of the faculty did not respond to the survey at all. Of those who did, only 18 percent agreed that "a liberal arts curriculum should have minority studies," while 38 percent allowed that "a liberal arts curriculum should make effort to include minority issues where can."[33]

Given this inauspicious starting point, it is not surprising that the following year the minutes of the Educational Policies Committee (EPC) noted that "the EPC has not been able to reach consensus about how non-Western studies are to become part of every student's curriculum." As a result, a motion calling for "successful completion of at least one course which deals primarily with the non-Western world" had been tabled. Questions raised about the motion included the following: "Although . . . presumably all [seniors] have had some courses about Europe and the U.S., we have no specific requirement in Western culture. Should this be done first?"[34]

These arguments over the curriculum were part of a larger battle in academia about the canon that came to be known as the "culture wars." At Kalamazoo, the first sustained challenge to the longstanding Western, male-dominated curriculum after the BSO's protests in the late 1960s was the push for women's studies in the 1980s. That effort had been spearheaded by Dr. Gail Griffin, at the time an assistant professor, and a few other women faculty who were far outnumbered by their male colleagues. Now, a portion of the faculty was calling for multiculturalism in the curriculum, bringing in scholars of color and cultural perspectives and traditions that had long been marginalized. As a professor of comparative literature wrote in the *Chronicle of Higher Education* in 1992, "the truth is changing . . . We should not pretend that scholarly developments in feminism, multiculturalism, and gay and lesbian studies, for example, can be integrated into college curricula without threatening the truth as it previously has been taught."[35]

In February of 1989, the board of trustees again passed a resolution on diversity, stating "we are concerned that the pace of diversification of the population of the College remains too slow . . . We question whether any student can be fully liberally educated in a context that is at such variance from the society for which she or he is being prepared . . . In light of these considerations, we direct the President and Faculty to prepare actions that will lead within an early time period to noticeable increases in diversity at the College."[36]

The following month, the College announced a grant of $250,000 from the Knight Foundation "to promote ethnic diversity." The grant would greatly deepen and expand the work of multiculturalism over the next few years. To augment the funding, the board of trustees pledged to raise

$672,000 "for minority student scholarships during the 1990–96 period." The Knight grant led to the creation of a new full-time associate provost position dedicated to "minority recruitment."[37] Sandra Greene was chosen to fill this position and was also tasked with administering the grant. Dr. Jeanne Baraka-Love was hired to take over the part-time assistant dean for minority affairs position that Greene had vacated in accepting her new responsibilities.[38]

The work funded by the Knight grant was not just "a question of equity in society," Greene stated in an interview with the *Index*. "By the year 2000, one third of all young people will be minorities and by the year 2040, one half. For the college to survive it has to create a more diverse environment. It's a matter of demographic realities."[39]

Her point was driven home that summer in the final report from the Committee on Goals for Ethnic Diversity, which had been formed to address the board's diversity directive. "Only 2.8 percent of our students, 4.3 percent of the faculty, 3.5 percent of the administrators and 4.5 percent of the support staff are drawn from the historically disadvantaged group consisting of blacks, Hispanics and American Indians," the report pointed out. "It is difficult to imagine how the College can retain either its educational integrity or financial viability if these gross disparities persist over the coming decades." The report went on to warn that "continued remoteness from increasingly important sources of student, faculty, funding, intellectual ferment, and the American mainstream is simply not possible if we wish to remain a premiere liberal arts institution."[40]

In addition to the new associate provost position, the Knight grant supported a "Minority Faculty Fellows Program" in which graduate students of color would teach at the College while completing their doctoral degrees. It was hoped that some of these fellows would then be hired to fill faculty positions being vacated over the coming decade. "We are convinced that, to remain true to the heritage of the College, we must develop strategies that will successfully make the reach of the College more inclusive, both in its population and in its educational content," Provost Timothy Light asserted. "No student can be fully educated for the next century without being educated among students who represent a complete diversity of America, and without being educated about that cultural diversity."[41]

In 1991, Dr. John Dobbs, an African American with a background in educational leadership, was hired to serve as associate provost for minority recruitment while Greene was on sabbatical, and he continued in the position for two years after she returned. Greene, too, remained very involved in the work, as did the assistant dean for minority affairs, Jeanne Baraka-Love. Under Dobbs's leadership, five committees were established to create proposals for improving the racial climate on campus, expanding multiculturalism in the curriculum, and diversifying the student body, faculty, and administration.[42] He also worked closely with departments conducting faculty searches to ensure a diverse pool of candidates, helped recruit students of color, and developed programs called "Faculty Advances" (as opposed to faculty "retreats"[43]) to educate the faculty on intercultural issues.[44]

The work was not easy. In April of 1992, Provost Richard Cook sent a memo to Dobbs saying that "the Faculty Executive Committee has made it very clear that they do not want a faculty advance this coming fall. They indicate an interest in a dinner in conjunction with departmental fairs . . . but emphasize that it should be fun and community-building rather than issue-oriented." "Considering the degree of their feelings on this, I concur," Cook went on. "It would be counter-productive to attempt to force upon them any agenda we might like to advance."[45]

Later that month, as if to emphasize the importance of the diversity work, racial tension again erupted on campus and throughout the country after the acquittal of the Los Angeles police officers charged with brutally beating Rodney King. In the aftermath, there were racist incidents at nearby Hope College and Olivet College, and the president of the BSO, Quran Freeman, received a hate letter "claiming Aryan superiority."[46]

At a campus gathering on the quadrangle the following week, Quran Freeman "pleaded for more multicultural education, minority faculty and financial aid for minority students to improve racial understanding on-campus," the *Index* reported. Freeman also questioned the commitment of the board of trustees to these issues, saying "we don't trust you in all honesty."[47]

The following year, Dobbs expressed frustration at the lack of progress in hiring faculty of color. "Currently six departments are searching for new faculty members and no minority candidates have been named so far," the *Index* reported in January 1993. Though he had sent names of potential candidates to department chairs, Dobbs felt there was a lack of follow-through. "It's important to some that [all professors] 'fit in',"

Dobbs was quoted as saying. "People who say that are giving their own interpretation [of 'fitting in']. Maybe [there is] some deep-seated racism in the faculty. . . . You have to wonder."[48]

In a campus forum on multiculturalism sponsored by the Coalition on Race and Diversity that April, Dobbs stressed the importance of changing policy and noted that the committees would soon be finalizing their reports. Baraka-Love insisted that multiculturalism is part of life and "cannot be debated." She went on to say that "we need to exist in cocultures rather than subcultures." Director of African Studies Dr. Cynthia Schmidt pointed out that "the 'K' community needs to recognize its own isolation." "How much of the world are we bringing on campus?" she asked. Gail Griffin noted that the faculty had been trained in institutions where they were led "to believe that a truth that had been essentially shaped by white Western males was the truth," and called multiculturalism a "potential revolution in learning."[49]

As the committees focusing on various aspects of cultural diversity began finalizing their reports in the late summer of 1993, Dobbs told the *Index* that the purpose of the work was "to include the concerns and histories of groups 'left out of the mainstream'—African Americans, Hispanics and women." "The purpose goes back to the need for all institutions in this country to begin to restructure, reconsider their whole approach to how they provide learning," Dobbs continued, "so that learning can be more inclusive of all people who contribute to this country." When asked what he hoped the campus would be like in the year 2000 if the committees' recommendations were approved, Dobbs responded, "I think Kalamazoo College would be a more enlightened place than it is now. It would not be as insulated." He worried, however, that "they will come up with something that says we will have more diversity and leave it at that. If we came out with nothing but that sort of a plan then it would be a wasted effort."[50]

In March of 1994, the Cultural Diversity Coordinating Committee submitted its final report, "Achieving a Culturally Diverse Population and Curriculum," to President Bryan after combining the various reports drafted by the subcommittees and vetting the document with the campus community. The report set forth three goals:

1. Develop programs and policies that reflect the multi-dimensional interests and viewpoints of our pluralistic society
2. Establish clear definitions of the terms used to discuss issues of cultural diversity
3. Enroll an African American and Hispanic student population of ten percent in each entering class.[51]

The report went on to detail a host of recommendations under the headings of "Working with Students of Under-represented Ethnic Groups," "Working with Students of the Majority Population," "Recruitment and Retention of Faculty of Underrepresented Ethnic Groups," and "Addressing Cultural Diversity through the Curriculum."[52]

"The responsibility to execute the plans is going to be ultimately in my hands," President Bryan said. He planned to meet with administrative groups to discuss implementing the recommendations, begin procedures for faculty review of proposed curriculum changes, prepare a statement for the board of trustees, and form a monitoring committee to oversee the work.[53]

One of the more immediate and tangible outcomes was the Umoja House, a new campus living space for Black students announced in 1994. "First brought to the attention of Bryan by several African-American students, the house will serve as a place for students to be within their own cultural surroundings," the *Index* reported.[54] While the recently completed report by the Cultural Diversity Coordinating Committee elicited comments from just five faculty members and one student, the announcement of the Umoja House caused a flood of letters to the *Index*, including one by an anonymous writer expressing racial hatred. Because the policy of the *Index* was not to print unsigned letters, the *Index* editor, a Black woman, instead posted the letter in the Hicks Student Center.[55]

Soon afterward, the *Index* editor began receiving harassing phone calls, and a threatening letter was sent directly to her personal address. Dean of Students Dr. Marilyn LaPlante appealed to the campus community for information about the identity of the letter writer. "Please help us identify the person who is harassing and threatening this student," she wrote. "Kalamazoo College was not developed by 'white people for white people,'" LaPlante went on, quoting a phrase in the letter. "We must all work together to keep our College open to diversity in ideas, cultures, backgrounds, and life styles. Let's make this a place where every person can feel safe and valued."[56]

Though LaPlante refuted the claim that Kalamazoo College was developed "by white people for white people," the statement was not untrue. Certainly, the College had never excluded people of color, but it was not designed with people of color in mind. The College was, in fact, designed with White people in mind, which is why multicultural initiatives were proving so challenging. It was also why so many White people were disturbed by the Umoja House, an initiative that did not include them. Accustomed as they were to always being included, it felt wrong, even scary.

The *Index* editorial staff was divided over whether the Umoja House was a good idea or not, as was the rest of the campus. "In this rare occurrence, the editorial board could not reach a consensus regarding the Umoja House," read the lead-in to their opinion piece titled "Umoja House: Separatist Or Not?" "Instead, two editorials were written to present each side." Those opposed to the Umoja House expressed some of the same kinds of anxieties as students had in the late 1960s in response to the Black Power Movement. "The Umoja House will not send out a positive message, but rather a negative one," read the editorial in opposition. "We are saying that we could not find any solutions in which everyone could live together, so we had to separate. This idea scares us."[57]

Writing in response, Dafina M. L. Stewart, a Black junior, asked, "Why is it that whenever African-Americans achieve something for themselves, whites feel left out and excluded? Why do you feel the need to be a part of anything we do for ourselves, for our encouragement, for our upliftment?"

Stewart went on, "The editors point to the fact that the prerequisite for living in the House is being 'in good standing with the BSO.' They charge, 'The current number of non-black students in good standing with the BSO is zero.' The editors conveniently have only chosen to publicize one side of the issue. Left unsaid is the important fact that a non-black student has not in the past two years even come to a BSO meeting out of interest in joining the organization."

"The editors then ask," Stewart continued, "'What will the college do when Hispanic students, Asian students, or Polish students say that they too feel uncomfortable and need a separate place to live?' I say, if such a movement arises among the Hispanic or Asian students on this campus, that they should have the right to live in such a house as well. As far as Polish students go . . . come on, let's be real."[58]

Bryan and other administrators defended the Umoja House, with Bryan noting that the College for many generations had been predominantly White and pointing to the lack of progress since the Civil Rights Movement. There is "indeed a very clear need for a place of empowerment," he insisted.[59]

Baraka-Love said that the students who criticized the Umoja House as "separatist" were the same students who asked why all the Black students sat together in the cafeteria. "Baraka-Love . . . believes the Umoja House will provide these students with the unity and confidence necessary to live on 'K's' predominantly white campus," the *Index* reported.[60]

The controversy over the Umoja House continued, and the following year a group of faculty, clearly fed up with the anti-Umoja House sentiment, published a letter in the *Index* saying, "We believe that it is time for white students on this campus to understand a few important truths." Among these truths was that "separateness is not the same as segregation. Segregation is separation imposed on a subordinate group by a dominant group." "Unity among people of African descent does not interfere with other kinds of unity among people of various ethnic backgrounds," they went on. "Many forms and levels of unity are possible in the world . . . We suggest that before the next broadside against the Umoja House, white students try to imagine what it would be like for them on this campus if the relative numbers of white and black faculty and students were reversed."[61]

"The Sun Setting in the West"

Though actions such as establishing the Umoja House and recommendations coming out of the "Achieving a Culturally Diverse Population and Curriculum" report seemed to offer hope for meaningful change, things at the College were about to fall apart. During his eleven-year tenure, George Rainsford had done little in the way of fundraising, and David Breneman had resigned in part because of a lack of success in soliciting major gifts from donors.[62] Fundraising had continued to lag under Larry Bryan, causing a severe financial crisis by 1995 and leading to the elimination of faculty and staff positions and Bryan's departure from the College the following year.[63]

Perhaps because of the financial situation, Bryan did not sustain the associate provost position for minority recruitment after grant funding ran out, and he eliminated the Office of Multicultural Affairs in Student Services, causing the dismissal of Baraka-Love. As often happens during hard times, institutional priorities came sharply into focus, and multicultural work was seen as expendable. "We have to look at systems that always keep one group in prominence and always keep another group suppressed," Baraka-Love said in an interview with the *Index*. "At some point we have to look at, what are the mechanisms that keep these things happening? And one of the mechanisms is to say, 'We don't have enough money to take care of everything that's here, so let's cut this out.'"[64]

It was also around this time that Sandra Greene left the College for a faculty position at Cornell University. Though her reasons were varied, she later recalled feeling "alone at Kalamazoo, waging this battle to get more respect for things black, and in the curriculum." "By the time I left Kalamazoo, I had had it," Greene explained, "I felt like I was . . . banging my head against a brick wall." "I'm not a shouter or a screamer or anything," she went on, "but I remember getting into some conflicts . . . and there was a meeting when I said, 'I quit. I resign.'" When asked about the nature of the resistance, Greene replied, "Polite, liberal talk. No action."[65]

More resignations of Black faculty and staff followed. In 1996, Dr. Benson Prigg, one of the faculty fellows hired under the Knight grant, also resigned, feeling betrayed by the elimination of the Office of Multicultural Affairs, Baraka-Love's dismissal, and the College's failure to implement many of the recommendations for increasing cultural diversity on campus. As he wrote in a letter to the *Index*, "the inability of the institution to move ahead in its multicultural initiatives made it clear that unless there is a mandate from the Board of Trustees to institutionalize multicultural education as a top priority, every effort will come to naught."

"Throughout the 1995/96 academic year," he continued, "I have come to realize that in 1994/95 the sun I saw rising in the east was actually the sun setting in the west." He also made clear that the spate of Black faculty and staff resignations was not a coincidence. "We have declared the institution as an unsafe place for cultural diversity in general and people of African descent who know and believe in who they are in particular."

Prigg closed his letter with the following advice: "Listen, consider, perceive, understand. Listen to the marginalized voices and bring them to the center. De-center the voices which prevent substantial progress towards a multicultural climate and curriculum. Or decide to stop selling the college as a diverse campus where there is a place for all cultures and ethnicities to thrive because it is not."[66]

Adding to the turmoil was the decision to fundamentally alter the K-Plan by eliminating the summer quarter and moving to a more conventional trimester calendar. The change was controversial among the faculty and elicited outrage from many students and alumni. The work of transitioning the elements of the K-Plan to the new calendar also coincided with an overhaul of the general education program, both of which consumed the faculty for the next few years.

While the collapse of many multicultural efforts set the College back substantially in its goal of diversifying the faculty and staff and kept the student body overwhelmingly White, some important inroads were made in the curriculum. As Gail Griffin later recalled, "The Opposition really slowed things down, but a lot of us who were pushing things forward kept the momentum inside us, transformed our courses, spoke up more often, changed our pedagogy in anti-racist directions."[67] In addition to changes in individual courses, the faculty finally approved the controversial Cultures Requirement, which became part of the curriculum beginning in the 1996–97 academic year. This graduation requirement stipulated "study in the cultural complexity of two of the following regions: Asia, Middle East, Africa, Latin America, Europe" and one course involving "study in the cultural complexity of the United States."[68]

During this time, "intercultural understanding" also became a feature of the first-year seminar program,[69] another requirement of all students, and the faculty articulated "intercultural understanding" as one of the outcomes of a Kalamazoo College education. Intercultural understanding was defined as "an awareness that there are many ways to experience and organize the world and that no single cultural frame of reference is necessarily privileged or superior. Developing intercultural understanding involves moving from considering events, ideas, and beliefs through the filter of one's own culture, to learning about and experiencing other cultures on their own terms, to affirming the contributions of all cultures to the collective human wisdom."[70]

Born of the culture wars, these changes represented a paradigm shift at Kalamazoo College that broke down centuries-old structures upholding a predominantly Western White male truth as a universal truth and opened the way for the many curricular changes that have occurred since.

Bad Apples

When Dr. James F. Jones assumed the presidency in 1996, he had a clear mandate to raise money. Though he formed yet another committee to study diversity, resulting in yet another report, the Diversity Keystone, he did not take the lead on cultural diversity initiatives in the way that Larry Bryan had. During the presidential search process, Benson Prigg had felt that cultural diversity was being sidelined, a factor that contributed to his decision to leave. As he explained in his letter to the *Index*, "I have no bias against Dr. James F. Jones. I believe he has what the Board desires, and he will be successful for them. I do not believe the President knew the issues facing this institution in terms of multicultural initiatives, for his input focused on globalization. I do not believe the domestic aspect of multicultural initiatives was his top priority."[71]

Even though President Jones did not make "the domestic aspect of multicultural initiatives" his top priority, the lack of diversity, especially in the student body, continued to be a near constant topic of conversation, although usually surrounded by an air of impotence, and issues of race continued to rise up on campus.

In the spring of 1998, thirty years after the first BSO protests, the Black Student Organization held a demonstration and wrote a letter to President Jones and Provost Gregory Mahler calling for more diversity. "When students arrive at Kalamazoo College, they are told 'The World is our campus' and 'K College is committed to diversity,'" they began. "The students of this campus believed that those phrases not only signified a world of different experiences and opportunities, but also a world where both students and faculty of various cultural backgrounds could interact and share experiences with one another . . . Once upon a time, we believed that Kalamazoo College shared and valued this same vision of intercultural exchange. However, this ideal has proven to be a myth."

"Diversity at this institution seems to be defined only on an international level," they continued, pointing to the fact that the Kalamazoo College community had always been more comfortable with international diversity than with domestic diversity.[72] "We have held forums, sat on committees, and met with numerous administrators resulting in one report after another . . . The time for discussion has ended and we are entering a new era of fruition. In 1968, the Black Student Organization took a stand to bring about change regarding **THE SAME PROBLEM!!!!** Thirty years later, we are again forced to take a stand."[73]

Around this time the College lost yet another Black employee with the resignation of Associate Director of Admissions Kyle Malone. Malone was a talented recruiter, and during the five years he worked at the College, Black student enrollment more than doubled from 2.3 percent in 1993 to 4.8 percent in 1998. After Malone's departure, the number of Black students would decline as dramatically as it had risen during his tenure.

More challenges related to race were in store. As the 1998–99 academic year opened, a Black first-year student from Chicago took part in an open-mic night. One of fourteen African Americans in an entering class of 442,[74] the student read a poem asking to be seen not only as a Black man but as a scholar, a friend, and "most importantly," he concluded, "I hope you see a man."[75] The audience cheered and applauded in support, but about ten days later he found a hate-filled note on his dorm room door. It read:

> WE HAVE A NO [N-WORD] POLICY AT K-COLLEGE. IT IS DESIGNED TO INSURE THE FAILURE OF ALL NON WHITE PEOPLE HERE. The policy is meant to be a non-violent one, but whatever measures have to be taken, we will take. Once you people realize that we can not live together, the country will be a better fucking place. All of this peaceful talk around campus is sickening. YOUR POEM SUCKED. WE ALMOST HURLED WHEN WE HEARD IT. YOU FUCKING SUCK. WE WOULD ADVISE YOU TO KEEP THIS TO YOURSELF. THIS WILL BE YOUR ONLY WARNING.
>
> [signed] OPERATION ELIMINATE[76]

The following morning, a fire broke out in the student's room. No one was hurt, but the student and his roommate lost more than $2,000 worth of property.[77] The incident shocked the campus community and drew swift condemnation from the College's leadership. In a letter to the campus, Jones wrote, "this weekend a most vicious hate crime was committed against a new member of our community and therefore against all of us . . . This particular action is a violation against everything for which we stand. It is an act of cowardice intended to intimidate. As a community dedicated to learning and its values of curiosity, tolerance and justice, we cannot and will not abide such behavior."[78]

Students responded by covering the campus with hundreds of chalk messages denouncing racism and held a candlelight vigil "to advocate ethnic diversity and harmony on the campus."[79] To encourage anyone with knowledge of the incident to come forward, the administration announced a $2,000 reward for information leading to an arrest. The reward was later increased to $4,000 with the addition of $1,000 from the Silent Observer Program and $1,000 from an anonymous donor.[80]

The student who received the racist note went home to be with his family for a few days but soon returned to campus to finish the term. In an interview with the *Chicago Tribune,* he said he was scared, but "if I start running now, maybe I'll run the rest of my life."[81]

The Kalamazoo Department of Public Safety and the fire marshal opened investigations, but almost immediately they raised the possibility of self-involvement, a conjecture that angered the student and his parents. "What is bothering me is that the college is doing everything they can, but the police and fire marshal are not," the student told the *Chicago Sun-Times.*[82]

After months of little progress in the investigation, the Kalamazoo Department of Public Safety finally issued a press release in February of 1999 stating that they were closing the case after detectives had been "unable to determine the cause of the fire" and had also been "unable to develop any suspects possibly involved in the distribution of the 'hate letter.'"[83] Despite finding no evidence of self-involvement, a police officer told the *Kalamazoo Gazette* that he believed the student himself had set the fire and "written the letter in an attempt to find a graceful way to leave K-College and go home."[84]

Faculty and administrators who knew the student pushed back on any notion of self-involvement. "I'm completely convinced that he didn't write that hate note. It would be totally out of character," said Dr. Zaide Pixely, the student's first-year seminar professor and academic advisor, adding, "I think that saying he wrote it is taking the easy way out."[85] Dean of Students Marilyn LaPlante chided the police officer for his public conjecture given the lack of evidence. "If you close a case because you have no suspects and no direction to go," she remarked, "it seems to me that is all you should say."[86]

Indeed, the idea that the student would write himself a racist note and set fire to his room "to find a graceful way to leave K-College" seems to defy logic. He had attended Chicago's Latin School, a predominantly White institution located on the city's predominantly White north side, so he was accustomed to being among White people.[87] He was also engaged in campus life, displaying confidence and poise in publicly reading a poem about his identity during his first week on campus. That he would then write a hate letter highlighting his race after asking to be seen simply "as a man" makes no sense. And, if he had done these things as an excuse to leave, why would he then stay for the entire fall term? Not surprisingly, given the suspicion he faced from the police, the student decided not to return after the fall. According to his mother, he had transferred to "an excellent, prestigious school."[88]

The College's response to the incident drew praise from the editors of the *Kalamazoo Gazette*, who wrote that "students made it clear that racism and violence were unwelcome at K-College," referring to the chalk messages and candlelight vigil. "Faculty devoted class time to discuss the incidents," the editors continued, and "students, faculty, the Board of Trustees and the alumni association all drafted resolutions condemning the racist letter."[89]

While these actions were laudable and appropriate, they were also easy and seemed to imply that the incident was due to a few "bad apples" instead of a symptom of a more systemic problem. It was the inverse of the "bad apple" analogy in the 1974 "hustler" article, but the basic premise was the same: "If we can just rid ourselves of these few bad apples, our problems will be solved." Not addressed, however, was the thornier and more pervasive problem that many more people harbored unexamined biases against Black people and other people of color and that the institution continued to center White culture in its policies, programs, and practices.

In reference to this "bad apple" approach to racist acts on college campuses, the scholar Sara Ahmed suggests that even "eliminating the racist individual would preserve the racism of the institution in part by creating an illusion that we are eliminating racism."[90] Though Kalamazoo College was not able to eliminate the racist individual or individuals responsible for the hate letter and fire, it did succeed in creating the illusion of eliminating racism by voicing outrage, renouncing the acts, and extolling diversity. The candlelight vigil held in the days after the incidents had called for "harmony on the campus." But not only can racial harmony—an ideal embraced mainly by White people—exist without justice, it can perpetuate structural inequities by hiding them behind a façade of good intentions.

The other main response, spearheaded by the president of the Student Commission, was to establish a safe walk program "to assure a safe campus at night by having qualified students patrol the campus in teams of two."[91] That effort, though again laudable, seemed to miss the point by casting the problem as a campus safety issue that affected everyone instead of a racially motivated hate crime that specifically targeted Black people on campus.

Less than two weeks after the case was closed and a few months after the student who received the hate letter had left the College, someone wrote the N-word in large letters in the snow on the deck behind Hoben residence hall, sending a message that the events of the fall had not been an isolated incident. "We cannot tolerate this cowardly and blatant racism within our community, and we must take action against the perpetrators of this racist message," Jones wrote in an email to the campus community. "The honor of our institution has been called into question by some coward, presumably one in our midst."[92] The incident again elicited a "bad apple" response rather than inspiring a comprehensive effort to address all forms of racism on campus, blatant and otherwise.

When he departed in 2004, President Jones left the College much better off financially, thereby fulfilling his mandate and bringing needed stabilization. As a result of his fundraising, the faculty grew from a low of 83 in 1997 in the wake of the financial crisis to 102 by 2004.[93] Yet, the racial climate on campus changed little, and the student body remained overwhelmingly White. In the fall of 2004, just 9 percent of the student body identified as people of color,[94] down from 11 percent[95] when Jones arrived in 1996. And thirty-five years after the BSO protests, the population of Black students on campus had again fallen below 3 percent.

This is not to say that no efforts were made. Under the leadership of Provost Gregory Mahler, the percentage of faculty of color more than doubled from a low of 6 percent[96] in 1997, due largely to resignations of Black faculty, to 15 percent by 2005.[97]

In 2001, the Mary Jane Underwood Stryker Center for Civic Engagement was established with an endowed gift from local philanthropist Rhonda Stryker in honor of her grandmother. The Center's work "engages students, faculty, and community members in sustained partnerships that foster collaborative learning and civic participation in a diverse, democratic society."[98] Though there had been students and faculty who worked in the community for many years, the Center for Civic Engagement developed long-term, mutually beneficial partnerships with many community organizations, including organizations striving for racial equity.

The Office of Student Services, later renamed Student Development, also continued to address issues of diversity under the leadership of Marilyn LaPlante, and in 1996, the College hired Danny Sledge, an African American, to serve as associate dean of students. According to the *Index*, Sledge's responsibilities were to include, among other duties, "serving as a resource to students of color," "developing programs to address racism and multicultural education," "initiating programs in intercultural communication," "directing retention efforts for students of color," and "directing new student orientation activities for students of color as part of the overall orientation program."[99] Sledge would go on to become dean of students after LaPlante retired in 2000 and patiently worked to make the College a more welcoming place for students of color. Ultimately, though, he left the College suddenly and without explanation in 2004.[100] His departure came as a blow to many students, faculty, and staff, especially those dedicated to improving the racial climate.

Even under presidents who championed diversity work, such as David Breneman and Larry Bryan, meaningful progress required substantial effort that was difficult to sustain, especially for those individuals, usually people of color, specifically tasked with improving the racial climate. The brick wall of institutional culture that Sandra Greene, John Dobbs, Jeanne Baraka-Love, Danny Sledge, and others had bumped up against had proven mighty indeed. It had been built up over many decades by White institutional leaders using materials from White culture and laid with the needs of White people in mind. Dismantling that wall was going to take more than committees, reports, and a few dedicated individuals. "The official desire to institutionalize diversity does not mean the institution is opened up," writes Sara Ahmed, "indeed, the wall might become all the more apparent."[101] Though inroads had been made with regard to the curriculum, cocurricular programs, and faculty diversity, the brick wall's formidable presence would continue to make itself known to those working toward racial equity, and it would continue to marginalize students, faculty, and staff of color even as their numbers would begin to grow.

Endnotes

1 Marilyn Hinkle, *On Such a Full Sea,* (Kalamazoo, MI: Kalamazoo College 1982), 99.

2 Don Lester, admissions counselor, to Weimer Hicks, "Summary Report: Black Student Recruitment," Kalamazoo College, January 5 through June 15, 1970. Weimer K. Hicks Papers, Inter-office Correspondence, Hayden Ambrose - Admissions, 1970–71, Box 28, File 2.

3 "Test Optional Admission Approved," *Lux Esto* (Spring 2015): 9, http://hdl.handle.net/10920/30308.

4 Weimer Hicks memo to Don Lester, June 11, 1970. Weimer K. Hicks Papers, Inter-office Correspondence, Hayden Ambrose - Admissions, 1970–71, Box 28, File 2.

5 Hinkle, *On Such a Full Sea*, 105.

6 "Tokenism?" Index, November 3, 1970, 1, 3.

7 Daniel Silver, "RACE RELATIONS AT KALAMAZOO—THREE YEARS LATER," *Index*, May 18, 1972, 1–4.

8 Silver, "RACE RELATIONS AT KALAMAZOO."

9 Silver, "RACE RELATIONS AT KALAMAZOO."

10 Silver, "RACE RELATIONS AT KALAMAZOO."

11 Lee Atwater quoted in "Exclusive: Lee Atwater's Infamous 1981 Interview on the Southern Strategy," *Nation*, November 13, 2012, https://www.thenation.com/article/archive/exclusive-lee-atwaters-infamous-1981-interview-southern-strategy/.

12 S. S. Lydan, "Reporter Outfoxes Phony Hustler," *Index*, April 12, 1974, 4.

13 Beverly Jones, "About the Index Hustler," *Index*, April 22, 1974, 3.

14 Editors' note to the letter titled "About the Index Hustler," *Index*, April 22, 1974, 3.

15 "Vocal Forums," *Index*, January 20, 1972, 8.

16 Thomas C. Feige, "An Interview with Chief Chosa," *Index*, January 27, 1972, 1–3.

17 Constance Bostwick, "The Odyssey Continues: Mike Chosa and the Chicago Indian Village," *Index*, April 13, 1972, 11–12.

18 Sally Noble, "About Indian Awareness Week," *Index*, May 17, 1974, 2.

19 Paul Little, "AIM Leader To Discuss Indian Struggle In U.S.," *Index*, May 16, 1975, 1.

20 R.A. Bitzinger, "The Impotence of Being Earnest," *Index*, January 26, 1978, 8.

21 Paul Lane memo to George Rainsford, March 3, 1978, Kalamazoo College Archives, 3/13 Rainsford, George N., President, 1972–1983; Admissions.

22 Paul Lane memo to George Rainsford, March 15, 1978, Kalamazoo College Archives, 3/13 Rainsford, George N., President, 1972–1983; Admissions.

23 Andy Angelo, "K College Black Students A Vanishing Group?" *Index*, April 20, 1978, 1, 5.

24 Andy Angelo, "Black recruits: 'on the back burner,'" *Index*, April 27, 1978, 1, 4.

25 Andy Angelo, "Black students are quietly disillusioned," *Index*, May 11, 1978, 1, 5.

26 Steve Baker, "Trustees call for minority recruitment budget proposal," *Index*, July 6, 1978, 2.

27 Baker, "Trustees call."

28 Peter G. Schmidt, "Why *aren't* there more Blacks at K College?" *Index*, February 16, 1984, 4.

29 Schmidt, "Why *aren't* there more Blacks."

30 Peter G. Schmidt, "K administration discusses black enrollment," *Index*, February 24, 1984, 4.

31 J. Rubin, "Breneman specifies K's goals," *Index*, June 6, 1985, 1.

32 Paul Regelbrugge, "Light Seeks Increased Faculty Diversity," *Index*, October 31, 1986, 1.

33 CORD survey of faculty about diversifying the curriculum, Winter 1987, Kalamazoo College Archives, RG 4/8, Dobbs Collection, Box 8, Folder 6.

34 Note attached to the May 2, 1988, faculty meeting minutes, Kalamazoo College Archives, RG 4/8, Dobbs Collection, Box 8, Folder 8.

35 Gregory Jay, "The First Round of the Culture Wars," *Chronicle of Higher Education* (February 26, 1992), https://www.chronicle.com/article/the-first-round-of-the-culture-wars/?cid2=gen_login_refresh&cid=gen_sign_in.

36 Kathy Layden, "'K' Board of Trustees passes minority enrollment resolution," *Index*, February 22, 1989, 2.

37 Susan W. Allen, "Foundation awards grant," *Index*, April 6, 1989, 2.

38 Mika Osaki, "Director of Minority Affairs appointed," *Index*, October 19,1989, 2.

39 Maggie Catchick, "Greene oversees Knight Foundation grant," *Index*, August 18, 1989, 1.

40 Final Report from the Committee on Goals for Ethnic Diversity, July 21, 1989, Kalamazoo College Archives, RG 4/8. John Dobbs Collection, Box 4, Folder 8.

41 Allen, "Foundation awards grant."

42 Brian Enneking, "Dobbs advocates interculturalism," *Index*, November 13, 1991, 2.

43 Conversation with Gail Griffin, February 6, 2021.

44 Memo to the faculty from John Dobbs and Jeanne Baraka-Love, December 10, 1991, Kalamazoo College Archives, RG 4/8, John Dobbs Collection, Box 1, Folder 4, and Progress Report to the Knight Foundation for July 1991 to July 1992, Kalamazoo College Archives, RG 4/8, John Dobbs Collection, Box 1, Folder 4.

45 Cook Memo from Provost Richard Cook to President Bryan and John Dobbs, April 16, 1992, Kalamazoo College Archives, RG 4/8, John Dobbs Collection, Box 7, Folder 3.

46 Maria Carlson and Al Hannah, "Racial Tension Erupts Into Discussion," *Index*, May 6, 1992, 1.

47 Carlson and Hannah, "Racial Tension Erupts."

48 Tracee Washington, "Diversity Lacking in K's Faculty," *Index*, January 27, 1993, 1.

49 Kezia Pearlman, "CORD Forum Raises Concern," *Index*, April 7, 1993, 2.

50 Matt Sikora, "Committees study campus diversity," *Index*, August 25, 1993, 1, 2.

51 Memo from the Cultural Diversity Coordinating Committee to the campus community with the draft report, "Kalamazoo College Plan: Achieving a Culturally Diverse Population and Curriculum." February 10, 1994, Kalamazoo College Archives, RG 30/26/file.

52 Memo from the Cultural Diversity Coordinating Committee to the campus community with the draft report, "Kalamazoo College Plan: Achieving a Culturally Diverse Population and Curriculum." February 10, 1994, Kalamazoo College Archives, RG 30/26/file.

53 Matt Sikora, "Diversity Project Completed," *Index*, March 9, 1994, 1, 2.

54 Stacey Younger and Steve Allison, "New Cultural House on Campus," *Index*, July 21, 1994, 1.

55 Memo to the campus community from Dean of Students Marilyn LaPlante, August 10, 1994, Kalamazoo College Archives, 14/20.6.1994, Living Learning Houses - Umoja House (1994–2001).

56 Memo to the campus community from Dean of Students Marilyn LaPlante, August 10, 1994, Kalamazoo College Archives, 14/20.6.1994, Living Learning Houses - Umoja House (1994–2001).

57 "Umoja House: Separatist or Not?" *Index*, July 21, 1994, 6.

58 Dafina M. L. Stewart, letter to the editor, *Index*, August 4, 1994, 4. 6. [Note: "Dafina" is now a deadname.]

59 Stacey Younger and Steve Allison, "New Cultural House on Campus," *Index*, July 21, 1994, 1.

60 Younger and Allison, "New Cultural House."

61 Carol Anderson, Marigene Arnold, Amy Elman, John Fink, Pete Gathje, Gail Griffin, Bob Grossman, Beth Jordan, Ed Menta, Bruce Mills, Zaide Pixley, "Faculty supports Umoja," *Index*, November 8, 1995.

62 Anne Schwartz, "Brenemans will leave "K" College next spring," *Index*, May 18, 1989, 1.

63 Ryan Harbrage, "President Bryan concludes his stewardship," *Index*, October 4, 1995, 1.

64 Jennifer Getting, "Multiculturalism: And what a story it is, too," *Index*, October 4, 1995, 1.

65 Oral history interview with Sandra Greene by Anne Dueweke and Allia Howard, August 21, 2016.

66 Benson W. Prigg, "Placement of the sun," *Index*, October 16, 1996, 4.

67 Gail Griffin, email correspondence, February 3, 2021.

68 Kalamazoo College Academic Catalogue, 1996–97, 34.

69 Kalamazoo College Academic Catalogue, 1996–97, 39.

70 Kalamazoo College Academic Catalogue, 1996–97, 32.

71 Kalamazoo College Academic Catalogue, 1996–97, 32.

72 For example, though unable or unwilling to establish a Black Studies program, the College has had for many years an African Studies program as well as an Asian Studies program. In discussions with faculty and staff in 2014 about diversity on campus, remarks almost always veered away from

domestic students of color to international students. ("We Too Are K'zoo" Report, 2014, 3).

73 BSO letter to President James Jones and Provost Gregory Mahler, June 4, 1998, https://cache.kzoo.edu/handle/10920/19595.

74 Newspaper clipping, "Threat, fire won't keep black teen from college," *Chicago Tribune*, October 1, 1998, RG 76/33, Racial Incidents, 1998–1999 folder, Kalamazoo College Archives, Kalamazoo College, Kalamazoo, Michigan.

75 Newspaper clipping, "Threat, fire won't keep black teen from college," *Chicago Tribune*, October 1, 1998, RG 76/33, Racial Incidents, 1998–1999 folder, Kalamazoo College Archives, Kalamazoo College, Kalamazoo, Michigan.

76 Correspondence from James F. Jones, Jr. to the campus community, September 28, 1998, RG 76/33, Racial Incidents, 1998–1999 folder, Kalamazoo College Archives, Kalamazoo College, Kalamazoo, Michigan.

77 Newspaper clipping, "Dorm fire, hate note probed," *Chicago Sun-Times*, October 1, 1998, RG 76/33, Racial Incidents, 1998–1999 folder, Kalamazoo College Archives, Kalamazoo College, Kalamazoo, Michigan.

78 Correspondence from James F. Jones, Jr. to the campus community, September 28, 1998, RG 76/33, Racial Incidents, 1998–1999 folder, Kalamazoo College Archives, Kalamazoo College, Kalamazoo, Michigan.

79 Andrew Farkas, "Administration, Commission respond to incident," *Index*, October 7, 1998, 1.

80 Nancy El-Shamaa, "Police say they now believe the fire was arson," *Index*, November 11, 1998, 1.

81 Newspaper clipping, "Threat, fire won't keep black teen from college," *Chicago Tribune*, October 1, 1998, RG 76/33, Racial Incidents, 1998–1999 folder, Kalamazoo College Archives, Kalamazoo College, Kalamazoo, Michigan.

82 Newspaper clipping, "Bid for understanding met with racist threats," *Chicago Sun-Times*, October 5, 1998, RG 76/33, Racial Incidents, 1998–1999 folder, Kalamazoo College Archives, Kalamazoo College, Kalamazoo, Michigan.

83 Press release included in correspondence from President Jones to the campus community, February 2, 1999, RG 76/33, Racial Incidents, 1998–1999 folder, Kalamazoo College Archives, Kalamazoo College, Kalamazoo, Michigan.

84 Mike Collins, "Campus responds to closing of case," *Index*. February 10, 1999, 1.

85 Collins, "Campus responds," 2.

86 Collins, "Campus responds," 2.

87 Newspaper clipping, "Threat, fire won't keep black teen from college," *Chicago Tribune*, October 1, 1998, RG 76/33, Racial Incidents, 1998–1999 folder, Kalamazoo College Archives, Kalamazoo College, Kalamazoo, Michigan.

88 Newspaper clipping, "No arrest coming in racial incident at K-College," 1999, 76/33, Racial Incidents, 1998–1999 folder, Kalamazoo College Archives, Kalamazoo College, Kalamazoo, Michigan.

89 Newspaper clipping, "K-College Sends Strong Message," *Kalamazoo Gazette*, February 10, 1999, 76/33, Racial Incidents, 1998–1999 folder, Kalamazoo College Archives, Kalamazoo College, Kalamazoo, Michigan.

90 Sara Ahmed, *On Being Included* (Durham, NC: Duke University Press, 2012), 44.

91 Andrew Farkas, "Administration, Commission respond to incident," *Index*, October 7, 1998, 1.

92 Correspondence from James F. Jones, Jr. to the campus community, February 19, 1999, 76/33, Racial Incidents, 1998–1999 folder, Kalamazoo College Archives, Kalamazoo College, Kalamazoo, Michigan.

93 National Center for Education Statistics, Employees by Assigned Position, 2004, https://nces.ed.gov/ipeds/datacenter/Facsimile.aspx?unitid=170532.

94 National Center for Education Statistics, Fall Enrollment Survey, 2004, https://nces.ed.gov/ipeds/datacenter/Facsimile.aspx?unitid=170532.

95 AICUM Survey of Fall 1996 Enrollment, Kalamazoo College Archives, RG75-23, Box 2, Folder 5.

96 National Center for Education Statistics, Fall Staff Survey, 1997, https://nces.ed.gov/ipeds/datacenter/DataFiles.aspx?goToReportId=7.

97 National Center for Education Statistics, Human Resources Survey, 2005, https://nces.ed.gov/ipeds/datacenter/Facsimile.aspx?unitid=170532.

98 Kalamazoo College Center for Civic Engagement website: https://cce.kzoo.edu/about/.

99 Denna Evoe, "Sledge appointed new Dean of Students," *Index*, August 21, 1996, 1.

100 "What do you think about Danny Sledge leaving 'K'?" *Index*, April 8, 2004, 2.

101 Ahmed, *On Being Included*, 26.

Conclusion

Bending the Arc

Presidential leadership on issues of diversity returned under James Jones's successor, Dr. Eileen B. Wilson-Oyelaran, the College's first woman and first African American president. During her eleven-year tenure from 2005 to 2016, she established the Arcus Center for Social Justice Leadership with a mission to "develop and sustain leaders in human rights and social justice through education and capacity-building." To fund the Arcus Center and its work, the College received an endowed gift of $23 million from the Arcus Foundation, the largest gift in the College's history. Arcus's mission includes building capacity on campus as well as regionally, nationally, and globally. The Center often focuses on racism and colonialism and how these systems function on systemic, institutional, and personal levels. Students, faculty, and staff who have availed themselves of this programming have been challenged in ways that, for many, have brought about fundamental shifts in their understanding of these issues and of themselves.

Through Arcus, the College also began building relationships with Indigenous people in the area—the first sustained, meaningful connections to the people on whose land the College had been built. In 2017, Julie Dye, a citizen of the Pokagon Band of Potawatomi and direct descendant of Leopold Pokagon, and Linda Cypret-Kilbourne, an Anishinaabe woman who does not identify with one tribe, were awarded an Arcus regional fellowship.[1] Their project sought to raise awareness about the appropriation and misuse of Native names, images, and spiritual symbols in sports and media. A main focus was ending the use of American Indian mascots in primary and secondary schools throughout Michigan.

"We're teaching our kids wrong," Julie Dye said during a 2018 gathering in the city of Kalamazoo. "The schools are teaching our kids hands-on racism when they tell our story for us with stereotypes." "They just consider us, and still to this day consider us, a vanishing race," she continued, "a piece of the past bygone history, which is not the case. We survived, we're still here, and we're making a statement."[2]

Later that year, the Arcus Center held its biennial With/Out – ¿Borders? conference. The theme was "Toward a Futureland" and drew land activists from around the world to discuss "land as essential to Indigenous sovereignty movements," "land as contested through the forced dislocation of people within and outside the U.S.," and "land as strength and nurturance."[3] In the opening ceremony, citizens of the Potawatomi bands in the region—descendants of the Potawatomi who avoided forced removal in 1840—joined the Arcus Center in welcoming the conference participants to this land, to their land.

In addition to establishing the Arcus Center, Wilson-Oyelaran also made diversifying the student body a priority. In 2009, the College began partnering with the Posse Foundation, which helped bring more students of color to campus and also functioned as a faculty development program for the professors serving as Posse mentors. As a result of the Posse program and other admissions initiatives, the percentage of domestic students of color almost tripled from 10 percent in 2005 to 28 percent by 2016. The percentage of faculty of color also grew from 15 to 26 percent during that same time period.[4] These trends have continued under the current president, Jorge G. Gonzalez, with domestic students of color now comprising over a third of the student body.[5]

While "diversity" and "minority recruitment" had usually meant bringing more Black students to campus, growth in diversity in the 2010s was mainly due to greater enrollment of Latinx students. This change reflected the choice of Los Angeles as the College's partner city in the Posse program and efforts to recruit Latinx students from South Texas and other parts of the country with the Hispanic population growing faster than any other racial or ethnic group. Though the percentage of African American students more than doubled from 2.8 percent in 2005 to 5.8 percent in 2016, during that same period enrollment of Latinx students increased more than five-fold from 1.9 to 10.2 percent. The percentage of degree-seeking international students also increased dramatically from less than 1.0 percent to 5.6 percent, while the American Indian and Asian American student populations remained more or less the same at around 1.0 percent and 5.0 percent, respectively.

Yet greater representational diversity did not bring an attendant improvement in the racial climate. "The White people here are so different from the White people at home from L.A.," a Latinx student said in 2013. "White people who live there have encountered and been exposed to different cultures and races and class. And here, I didn't know what felt different, but I sensed it."

That comment was made during a focus group project in which many students of color shared their experiences with race on campus. What they said was consistent with what students of color had been saying ever since Black students first raised these issues in 1968.

"When you constantly think about your race, the way people look at me and treat me . . . all of these experiences make me feel so bad inside," another Latinx student explained. "Every time something ignorant is said my blood boils. I think it's almost a love-hate relationship with the college."

"It's hard to sort of feel like you're just a token on campus," a Black student said, echoing a sentiment many students had expressed. "You're just sort of there to make sure that rich White parents are sending their kids to this college and they can be sure that they're getting to be cultured by interacting with people who are Black or poor or Brown."

"They're really good about bringing diversity here," a Latinx student noted, "but they don't know what to do with us when we get here."[6]

These ongoing challenges with the racial climate are why I found myself on yet another committee in 2015 addressing, this time, "sense of belonging" on campus. It was also why the Arcus Center was sponsoring anti-racism workshops for students, faculty, and staff, and why racial tension was about to erupt again that winter.

The 2014–15 academic year had begun in the wake of the police killing of Michael Brown, a Black teenager, in Ferguson, Missouri, and in the midst of an ongoing student Intercultural Movement on campus protesting a lack of support for students of color and a Eurocentric curriculum. With outrage at Brown's death reverberating through Kalamazoo College and campuses across the country, a group of Kalamazoo students traveled to Ferguson that fall to take part in protests against police killings of Black people. After their experiences in Ferguson, which for a few students included arrest, the transition back to the College's cloistered halls was difficult. "It was so intense, and so much emotion," Justin Danzy '16, later recalled about being in Ferguson. "It was a really human environment where people are feeling their feelings, and people are caring for each other, and there was in that moment—and it's messed up that a dude had to get killed for it to happen—there was community. There really was community down there and that's probably the only time I've ever experienced real community like that." "And, coming back [to Kalamazoo], obviously, all that is gone," he went on. "I feel like you probably need some time to just reflect and to process all that, and there was no time . . . So I just coasted, coasted through class and was pretty just like dead the whole fall quarter . . . like a zombie, just sleepwalking through everything."[7]

That winter a series of incidents further stoked racial tensions on campus. In February 2015, an anti-Semitic post appeared in an online student forum called "Konfessions."[8] Because the post was anonymous and anyone could access the page, it was not clear whether it had come from inside or outside the campus community. A few days later, a student advocating for "campus carry" attended a Student Commission meeting requesting support for "his effort to allow him and others to carry a concealed weapon on campus, part of a national campaign for concealed carry on college campuses," according to a College news release.[9] The student had made the same request previously at multiple meetings and had been repeatedly turned down. When commissioners yet again denied his request, he reportedly flashed an empty holster, a symbol of the campus carry movement, and gestured in a threatening way towards the commissioners, especially the three women of color on the Commission.

The next day, one of the commissioners who had felt threatened started a Twitter campaign called "UnsafeatK." The campaign quickly took off, drawing media attention.[10] The student Intercultural Movement, reignited by these events, wrote a letter to the *Index* calling for "immediate administrative action on [their] demands, including the establishment of a permanent and physical Intercultural Center and the development of institutional accountability to anti-racist policies in both action and speech."[11]

Then, the following week, an anonymous person filled a Student Commission Google document with racist, anti-Semitic, sexist, and homophobic images and language. The violent and explicit content was accompanied by the following threat: "At 900AM 3/5/15 I am going to start systematically executing faculty at Kalamazoo U, that will teach them the value of campus carry."[12] Threats were also made to individual students, faculty, and staff. The campus community, already on edge, reacted emotionally with outrage, anger, fear, and frustration.

"Don't let them win," President Wilson-Oyelaran told students, faculty, and staff gathered in Stetson Chapel the following day. "Love is hard work. Struggle is hard work. Building community is hard work and we all have to work hard at it."[13]

"We have a powerful community here," Wilson-Oyelaran said later in an interview with the local media, adding, "we have a lot of work to do to make sure it's a community where everyone feels a sense of belonging."[14]

Shaken by these events and following a statement at a faculty meeting by Dr. Lisa Brock, academic director of the Arcus Center, that placed the events within a larger context, Wilson-Oyelaran formed four intercultural working groups made up of students, faculty, and staff. The purpose of the working groups was to accelerate diversity and inclusion initiatives already underway and to lay the groundwork for finally establishing the intercultural center many students had been calling for since 2012. The following academic year, the Intercultural Center opened and a director was hired to run the Center and oversee intercultural student life.

The Intercultural Center, while serving as a place of respite, support, and empowerment for students of color, did not, of course, solve the campus's racial climate problem. Indeed, the fact that the Center was needed at all reflected the marginalizing nature of the prevailing campus culture. As the director of the Intercultural Center, Natalia Carvalho-Pinto, had pointed out during her campus interview, the Center was really just a "band-aid," a measure that would be necessary until the entire campus had been transformed into an intercultural community. Many students were also disappointed that the space designated for the Intercultural Center was a room in the Hicks Student Center across from the Campus Safety Department rather than one of the campus houses. So although the Intercultural Movement had achieved one of its primary aims, there was still much work left to do.

Yet again serving as a touchstone, on the fiftieth anniversary of the 1968 BSO protests, a coalition of student organizations held an action in May 2018 that "reiterated previous demands and set forth new ones." Protesters re-created a 1968 photo of BSO students standing in a line across from the Mandelle administration building. They also marched through campus, ending with a sit-in in Mandelle that "involved 50 minutes of silence, to represent the 50 years since the BSO demands of 1968." Trevor Loduem-Jackson, '21, was quoted as saying, "They have seen 50 years of action, gone through multiple presidents. They just don't care. And it's now up to us students to make them care."[15]

Administrative responses to student demands and protests, at Kalamazoo College and elsewhere, have usually been to treat them as a crisis of the moment rather than as a recurring symptom of deep-seated racial inequity embedded in the very DNA of American higher education. The strategy has often been to invoke policy, to appease, to diffuse, to explain that change takes time, and to make promises for the future. Sometimes, the strategy is simply to wait the students out, a tactic that at Kalamazoo College is facilitated by ten-week trimesters.

On rare occasions, Kalamazoo College has acted quickly and meaningfully, as with the remarkable growth in student diversity during Wilson-Oyerlaran's tenure and the creation of a Critical Ethnic Studies major in 2014 in response to student demands first issued in 2012, lightning speed in academic time. Usually, though, change has come as a result of trauma, such as the assassination of Martin Luther King in 1968, after which the College hired its first Black professor, and the hack of the Student Commission Google document and subsequent death threats in 2015, which led to the establishment of the Intercultural Center.

The arc of the moral universe has indeed proven to be long, but must it be that way? On the occasion of the death of Congressman and civil rights activist John Lewis, Ibram Kendi wrote an article for *The Atlantic* warning of the dangers of "gradualism." He recalled John Lewis's speech during the 1963 March on Washington for Jobs and Freedom when Lewis declared, "to those who have said, 'Be patient and wait,' we have long said that we cannot be patient. We do not want our freedom gradually, but we want to be free now!" Kendi then pointed to the United States' long tradition of gradualism in response to racial injustice, noting that "the gradualists of today admonish the gradualism of yesterday, condemning all those who opposed immediate emancipation, all those who told Lewis to tone down his speech in 1963. Reformists don't age as well as revolutionaries." "A century from now," he concluded, "when almost all of us are dead, if we don't act with urgency and boldness, I can only imagine what our descendants will be saying about us. *How could we allow the evil of racial inequity to live another hour?*"[16]

At the onset of the 2020s, the United States again finds itself in the crucible, as it did in the years leading up to the Civil War and later during the Civil Rights Movement. The fuel firing the crucible is, as it has always been, racial injustice. Such times of turmoil are unsettling and dangerous, but they also offer an opportunity to change the shape of things. Decrying the racist Chinese Exclusion Act in 1885, Sam Song Bo, one of the first Asian students to attend Kalamazoo College, had written, "whether this statute against the Chinese or the statue to Liberty will be the more lasting monument to tell future ages of the liberty and greatness of this country, will be known only to future generations."[17] More than 135 years later, we are still waiting to know whether the United States will live up to the ideals in its founding documents.

Those of us alive today will all play our part in the crucible to determine the direction in which the arc will bend, whether it will bend toward justice or solidify existing racial and colonial hierarchies. Likewise, current students, faculty, staff, and administrators are writing the next chapter in Kalamazoo College's story. They are developing the plot line in their everyday words and actions and in their many decisions large and small. In the shape-shifting times of the 1850s and early 1860s, James and Lucinda Stone were able to mold the College around progressive ideals, but the institution sprang back to its more provincial form after their departure. A little more than a hundred years later, Black students tried mightily to bring about structural changes amid the social and racial turmoil of the late 1960s. While they succeeded in riveting the campus's attention for a time, the institutional culture ultimately moved little with regard to race. Over fifty years on now, in a time of profound national division stemming largely from unresolved issues of racism and colonialism, there are those at Kalamazoo College who are working hard to change the shape of things again. Whether they succeed in bending the arc toward justice will be known only to future generations.

Endnotes

1 "2017–2018 Cohort," Arcus Center for Social Justice Leadership, Kalamazoo College, https://arcuscenter.kzoo.edu/fellowships/regional/previous/2017-2018-cohort/.

2 "Group: Racial Healing Requires an End to Stereotypes as School Mascots, History Lessons" January, 16, 2018, https://wwmt.com/news/local/group-racial-healing-requires-and-end-to-stereotypes-as-school-mascots-history-lessons.

3 "With/Out—¿Borders?"Arcus Center for Social Justice Leadership, Kalamazoo College, https://arcuscenter.kzoo.edu/global-convenings/wob2018/.

4 National Center for Education Statistics, Human Resources Survey, 2005, https://nces.ed.gov/ipeds/datacenter/Facsimile.aspx?unitid=170532.; Kalamazoo College 2016–17 Common Data Set, http://www.kzoo.edu/ir/KCommonDataSet2016-2017.pdf.

5 Kalamazoo College 2020-21 Common Data Set, https://www.kzoo.edu/about/files/2021/06/CDS_2020-2021-Kalamazoo-College.pdf.

6 Anne Dueweke, "In Their Own Words: Students' Experiences with Diversity and Inclusion at K," Report on Focus Groups and Survey, Kalamazoo College Office of Institutional Research, May 2013.

7 Oral history interview with Justin Danzy '16, by Anne Dueweke, May 19, 2016.

8 "Miles to Go: Toward an Equitable, Inclusive Campus Learning Experience," Kalamazoo College News and Events, March 12, 2015, http://www.kzoo.edu/news/miles-to-go-toward-an-equitable-inclusive-campus-learning-experience/.

9 "Miles to Go."

10 Mlive.com, "Kalamazoo College Students Start #UnsafeAtK Social Media Campaign, Say They Feel Threatened," posted Feb 25, 2015, updated Jan 20, 2019; posted Feb 25, 2015, https://www.mlive.com/news/kalamazoo/2015/02/unsafeatk.html.

11 "Intercultural Center Movement Declares State of Emergency," *Index*, March 4, 2015, http://www.thekzooindex.com/intercultural-center-movement-declares-state-of-emergency/.

12 Mlive, "'Don't Let Them Win': Solidarity Sought at Kalamazoo College in Aftermath of Online Shooting Threat," posted March 4, 2015, updated January 20, 2019, https://www.mlive.com/news/kalamazoo/2015/03/dont_let_them_win_solidarity_s.html.

13 Mlive, "'Don't Let Them Win.'"

14 Mlive, "'Don't Let Them Win.'"

15 Cavan Bonner, "Demands Unmet, 50 Years Later," *Index*, May 16, 2018, 1.

16 Ibram Kendi, "Patience Is a Dirty Word," *The Atlantic*, July 23, 2020, https://www.theatlantic.com/ideas/archive/2020/07/john-lewis-and-danger-gradualism/614512/.

17 Sam Song Bo, "A Chinese View of the Statue of Liberty," *The Sun*, New York, NY, June 30, 1885, 2, https://www.newspapers.com/clip/16261363/letter-from-saum-song-bo-re-statue-of/.

About the Author

Anne Dueweke worked at Kalamazoo College, her alma mater, for over twenty years. During most of that time she served as director of faculty grants and institutional research. Other roles included director of the Academic Resource Center and director of student fellowships. Throughout her time at Kalamazoo, she served as an academic advisor to many students and was very involved in outcomes assessment and reaccreditation work. Dueweke led a number of equity and inclusion initiatives, including student focus groups on race, campus climate studies, and the effort to draft Kalamazoo College's first land acknowledgement statement. In 2016, she received the Outstanding First-Year Student Advocate Award, and from 2015–2021 she held a fellowship from Kalamazoo College's Arcus Center for Social Justice Leadership. Dueweke currently works as a resource developer for the Pokagon Band of Potawatomi Indians. She lives in Kalamazoo, Michigan.

Index